Japan and Africa

Since the early 1990s, Japan has played an increasingly important and influential role in Africa. A primary mechanism that has furthered its influence has been its foreign aid policies. Japan's primacy, however, has been challenged by changing global conditions related to aid to Africa, including the consolidation of the poverty reduction agenda and China's growing presence in Africa.

This book analyzes contemporary political and economic relations in foreign aid policy between Japan and Africa. Primary questions focus on Japan's influence in the African continent, reasons for spending its limited resources to further African development, and the way Japan's foreign aid is invested in Africa. The context of examining Japan's foreign aid policies highlights the fluctuation between its commitments in contributing to international development and its more narrow-minded pursuit of its national interests.

The contributors examine Japan's foreign aid policy within the globalized economy in which Japan and Africa are inextricably connected. Japan and many African countries have come to realize that both sides can obtain benefits through closely coordinated aid policies. Moreover, Japan sees itself to represent a distinct voice in the international donor community, while Africa needs foreign aid from all sources.

Howard P. Lehman received his PhD in political science from the University of Minnesota in 1987 and has been teaching at the University of Utah since 1986. His publications include a book on economic development and many articles on South Africa, foreign debt negotiations, and African interest groups.

Routledge Contemporary Asia Series

1 **Taiwan and Post-Communist Europe**
Shopping for allies
Czeslaw Tubilewicz

2 **The Asia–Europe Meeting**
The theory and practice of interregionalism
Alfredo C. Robles, Jr

3 **Islamic Legitimacy in a Plural Asia**
Edited by Anthony Reid and Michael Gilsenan

4 **Asian–European Relations**
Building blocks for global governance?
Edited by Jürgen Rüland, Gunter Schubert, Günter Schucher and Cornelia Storz

5 **Taiwan's Environmental Struggle**
Toward a green Silicon Island
Jack F. Williams and Ch'ang-yi David Chang

6 **Taiwan's Relations with Mainland China**
A tail wagging two dogs
Su Chi

7 **The Politics of Civic Space in Asia**
Building urban communities
Edited by Amrita Daniere and Mike Douglass

8 **Trade and Contemporary Society Along the Silk Road**
An ethno-history of Ladakh
Jacqueline Fewkes

9 **Lessons from the Asian Financial Crisis**
Edited by Richard Carney

10 **Kim Jong Il's Leadership of North Korea**
Jae-Cheon Lim

11 **Education as a Political Tool in Asia**
Edited by Marie Lall and Edward Vickers

12 **Human Genetic Biobanks in Asia**
Politics of trust and scientific advancement
Edited by Margaret Sleeboom-Faulkner

13 **East Asian Regionalism from a Legal Perspective**
Current features and a vision for the future
Edited by Tamio Nakamura

14 **Dissent and Cultural Resistance in Asia's Cities**
Edited by Melissa Butcher and Selvaraj Velayutham

15 **Preventing Corruption in Asia**
Institutional design and policy capacity
Edited by Ting Gong and Stephen Ma

16 **Expansion of Trade and FDI in Asia**
Strategic and policy challenges
Edited by Julien Chaisse and Philippe Gugler

17 **Business Innovation in Asia**
Knowledge and technology networks from Japan
Dennis McNamara

18 **Regional Minorities and Development in Asia**
Edited by Huhua Cao and Elizabeth Morrell

19 **Regionalism in China–Vietnam Relations**
Institution-building in the Greater Mekong subregion
Oliver Hensengerth

20 **From Orientalism to Postcolonialism**
Asia–Europe and the lineages of difference
Edited by Sucheta Mazumdar, Kaiwar Vasant and Thierry Labica

21 **Politics and Change in Singapore and Hong Kong**
Containing contention
Stephan Ortmann

22 **Inter-Ethnic Dynamics in Asia**
Considering the Other through ethnonyms, territories and rituals
Edited by Christian Culas and François Robinne

23 **Asia and Latin America**
Political, economic and multilateral relations
Edited by Jörn Dosch and Olaf Jacob

24 **Japan and Africa**
Globalization and foreign aid in the 21st century
Edited by Howard P. Lehman

Japan and Africa
Globalization and foreign aid in the 21st century

Edited by Howard P. Lehman

Routledge
Taylor & Francis Group
LONDON AND NEW YORK

First published 2010 by Routledge
2 Park Square, Milton Park, Abingdon, Oxon OX14 4RN

Simultaneously published in the USA and Canada
by Routledge
270 Madison Ave, New York, NY 10016

Routledge is an imprint of the Taylor & Francis Group, an informa business

© 2010 Editorial selection and matter, Howard P. Lehman. Individual chapters, the contributor.

Typeset in Times New Roman by Bookcraft Ltd, Stroud, GL5 1AA
Printed and bound in Great Britain by

All rights reserved. No part of this book may be reprinted or reproduced or utilised in any form or by any electronic, mechanical, or other means, now known or hereafter invented, including photocopying and recording, or in any information storage or retrieval system, without permission in writing from the publishers.

British Library Cataloguing in Publication Data
A catalogue record for this book is available from the British Library

Library of Congress Cataloging-in-Publication Data
Japan and Africa : globalization and foreign aid in the 21st century / edited by Howard P. Lehman.
  p. cm.
  1. Japan--Foreign economic relations--Africa.
  2. Africa--Foreign economic relations--Japan.
  3. Economic assistance, Japanese--Africa. I. Lehman, Howard P.
HF1062.15.A4J37 2010
338.91'5206--dc22
                              2009052679

ISBN: 978-0-415-56217-1 (hbk)
ISBN: 978-0-203-84887-6 (ebk)

Contents

List of figures	ix
List of tables	xi
List of contributors	xiii
List of abbreviations	xv
Acknowledgements	xvii

1 Introduction: the global politics of Japanese–African relations 1
HOWARD P. LEHMAN

2 An historical analysis of Japan's aid policy in Africa 8
MAKOTO SATO

3 The Asian economic model in Africa: Japanese developmental lessons for Africa 25
HOWARD P. LEHMAN

4 The ambiguous Japan: aid experience and the notion of self-help 38
MOTOKI TAKAHASHI

5 International debt management: Japan's policy towards Africa 71
JUNICHI HASEGAWA

6 Policy coordination among aid donors: Japan's position
   from a European perspective   93
   NOBUYUKI HASHIMOTO

7 Japan and the Poverty Reduction Aid Regime:
   challenges and opportunities in assistance for Africa   117
   MOTOKI TAKAHASHI

   Index   149

Figures

4.1a	Regional distribution of Japan's ODA, net (1973)	43
4.1b	Regional distribution of Japan's ODA, net (2000)	43
4.2	Changes in Japan's ODA net (constant prices 2004)	47
5.1	Growth rate of African HIPC and non-HIPC countries	85
6.1	The Paris Framework on partnership for greater aid	100
6.2	The donor relationships, with a particular focus on the Like-Minded Group (LMG) and Japan	103
6.3	Aid proportion to Africa (2004–5 average)	105
6.4	Aid amount to Africa (2004–5 average)	105
6.5	Attitudes toward an international aid and development agenda: a contrast between the UK (a member of the LMG) and Japan	109

Tables

4.1	Top five aid recipient countries of Japan and the UK	57
4.2	Aid dependency ratio in main recipient countries of Japan and the UK	63
5.1	Major events surrounding the debt issue	77
5.2	Status of HIPC countries as of the end of July 2007	79
5.3	Safe water, health, school enrollment, and Human Development Index indicators	81
5.4	World Bank and bilateral aid for African debt cancelled countries	83
5.5	African debt cancelled countries' lawsuits at the end of 2006	84
5.6	Waivers of completion point conditions: African countries	87
5.7	Change in governance indicators from 2000 to 2006	88
5.8	Health, school enrollment, and safe water indicators of pre-decision point countries	89
6.1	The MDGs' relationship with past UN goals	96
7.1	Various effects of additional development aid	143

Contributors

Junichi Hasegawa is Research Professor and Head, Development Strategy Research Section, International Centre for the Study of East Asian Development, Kitakyushu, Japan. <hasegawa@icsead.or.jp>

Nobuyuki Hashimoto is Project Formulation Adviser, International Cooperation Agency, JICA Ghana Office. <Hashimoto.Nobuyuki@jica.go.jp>

Howard P. Lehman is Professor of Political Science, University of Utah Salt Lake City, UT, USA. <Lehman@poli-sci.utah.edu>

Makoto Sato is Professor, Faculty of International Relations, Ritsumeikan University, Kyoto, Japan. <satomako@ir.ritsumei.ac.jp>

Motoki Takahashi is Dean and Professor, Graduate School of International Cooperation Studies, Kobe University, Kobe, Japan. <tmotoki@kobe-u.ac.jp>

Abbreviations

ADB	Asian Development Bank
AU	African Union
BHN	Basic Human Needs
BoP	Balance of Payments
CDF	Comprehensive Development Framework
CFAA	Country Financial Accountability Assessment
CPA	Country Procurement Assessment
DAC	Development Assistance Committee
DfID	Department for International Development
FIL	Fiscal Investment and Loan system
GBS	General Budgetary Supports
HIPC	Heavily Indebted Poor Countries
IBRD	International Bank for Reconstruction and Development
IDA	International Development Association
IDT	International Development Targets
IMF	International Monetary Fund
JBIC	Japan Bank for International Cooperation
JICA	Japan International Cooperation Agency
LMG	Like-Minded Group
MDBS	Multi-Donor Budget Support
MDG	Millennium Development Goals
MITI	Ministry of International Trade and Industry
MOF	Ministry of Finance
MOFA	Ministry of Foreign Affairs
MTEF	Medium-Term Expenditure Framework
NEPAD	New Partnership for Africa's Development
NGO	Non-Governmental Organizations
ODA	Official Development Assistance
OECD	Organisation for Economic Co-operation and Development
PAF	Progress Assessment Framework

PER	Public Expenditure Review
PRBS	Poverty Reduction Budget Support
PRS	Poverty Reduction Strategy
PRSC	Poverty Reduction Support Credit
PRSPs	Poverty Reduction Strategy Papers
SAP	Structural Adjustment Program
SIP	Sector Investment Programs
SWAPs	Sector-Wide Approaches
TICAD	Tokyo International Conference on Aid and Development
UN	United Nations
USAID	US Agency for International Development
WB	World Bank

Acknowledgements

An edited book is, by definition, a collaborative product involving many individuals. The original idea for a book on Japanese foreign aid to Africa emerged from my year as a Fulbright Scholar in Japan where I first discussed this idea with Professor Motoki Takahashi, Dean of the Graduate School of International Cooperation Studies (GSICS) at Kobe University. The Fulbright program provided essential support for my research. I would like to thank the Japan–US Educational Commission that oversees the Fulbright program in Japan. In particular, I greatly appreciate my hosts at Kyushu University, Professor Yuzo Yabuno and Professor Machiko Hachiya, for their support and assistance while I was a Fulbrighter. As a Fulbright Scholar, I also taught at Fukuoka Jo Gakuin University.

I am indebted to Professor Takahashi for inviting me to return to Japan in 2006 as a research scholar associated with Kobe University. During my time at Kobe, I was able to discuss the topic of Japanese–African foreign relations with the faculty at GSICS, interviewed scholars and government officials, and presented my research to various institutes. In particular, I would like to thank Professor Yasuyuki Sawada of Tokyo University and the Research Institute of Economy, Trade and Industry for facilitating my presentation. Moreover, Professor Takahashi was kind enough to submit two chapters to this project and he also helped me to contact the remaining scholars and policy-makers who contributed to this edited book. I would like to thank all the contributors to this volume for patiently putting up with all the correspondence that led to this book.

Finally, I would like to thank the hard-working research assistants who helped me with the multitude of complex international editorial responsibilities: Carrie Humphreys, Masaki Kakizaki, Todd Bailey and Cameron Nelson.

1 Introduction
The global politics of Japanese–African relations

Howard P. Lehman

Japan's foreign policy relationship to the African continent may appear at first glance to be paradoxical. After all, Japan never established a colonial relationship with Africa. Unlike most of Europe, Japan never sought to colonize or settle its citizens in Africa. Indeed, its historical connection to the region only began in the 1950s. Additionally, until the recent activity of China, Japan had been the main non-Western country extensively involved in Africa. Yet, since 1993, Japan has emerged as a major and forceful actor in Africa, especially in the area of foreign aid. While this important relationship has been extensively studied in Japan, non-Japanese have rarely considered or examined the scope and implications of Japanese foreign aid in African countries. This book seeks to fill this gap by bringing together Japanese scholars and policy-makers who have considerable experience in the field and in scholarly analysis of this neglected topic.

The book's analysis of Japanese foreign aid relations to Africa is framed by two issues: globalization and Japan's domestic experiences. First, the forces of globalization combined with Japan's own interests and unique historical perspective have brought these two disparate regions of the world together. Globalization since the early 1990s incorporates economic pressures to expand Japanese economic influence to non-Asian regions. While the bulk of its foreign aid targets its Asian neighbors, a considerable amount since the 1990s focuses on African countries. Moreover, globalization also refers to the extended network of the global donor community and rising pressure on Japan to conform to the consensus on the general goals and specific policies of foreign aid. Finally, in recent years, globalization has forcefully elevated China's role in Africa to serve as a direct challenge to Japan's unique status as the primary non-Asian country in providing foreign aid.

Second, Japan's foreign aid policy has been shaped by powerful domestic and historical experiences. Its unique contribution to the foreign policy debate stems from its experiences of profound failures and great successes. In particular, its past resonates in its foreign aid policy by advocating a self-help policy, focusing on loans instead of grants, reluctance to embrace comprehensive debt cancellation, and strongly arguing for African ownership of foreign aid.

History of Japanese official development assistance to Africa

Japan has had a lengthy foreign aid relationship with the African continent. Although its relationship has deepened and widened since the early 1990s, Japan began its foreign aid policy to the region in the decade following the end of World War II. Chapter 2, by Makato Sato, highlights the important historical markers in this lengthy relationship to African countries. Sato sets the historical record in the context of the debate between the 'reactive state' approach formulated by Calder's argument on a cultural understanding of Japan's foreign policy. Sato is critical of these views since they rely heavily on a model of foreign aid used with regard to US relations to Japan. Instead, Sato suggests that a more appropriate model should focus on third countries which are engaged with both African countries and Japan. While other observers have focused on the domestic context of Japan's foreign aid policy, Sato emphasizes the international dimensions of policy relationships among Japan, Africa and other countries, especially China.

Sato divides the historical account of Japan's foreign aid relationship to Africa into five sections. He points out that the initial reason for involvement was linked to trade interests, but Japan's policy diversified as it came to reflect more complex economic and political goals. Japan developed the enduring and unique principles of 'self-help' and 'on-request basis' during this early stage. These principles remain important markers for the evolution and development of foreign aid. The second stage was a crucial moment when a substantial increase in aid to African countries was implemented by Japan. While the Asian region has always been significant with regard to Japan's foreign policy, at this time in the 1970s Africa began to emerge as a region with natural resources and diplomatic weight in the United Nations (UN) General Assembly. The third stage, in the 1980s, witnessed the growth of Japanese relationships with other donor countries and the beginning of a more coordinated strategy among donors. By the fourth stage, in the 1990s, Japan became the largest donor of foreign aid in the world. Japan formulated its first Official Development Assistance (ODA) Charter in 1992 and demonstrated its commitment to aid to Africa with the creation of the Tokyo International Conference on African Development (TICAD) in 1993. The economic objectives of earlier phases were now outweighed by political goals, especially in terms of gathering support among African countries in the UN. Finally, Japan experienced severe financial challenges in the most recent period of foreign aid policy to the continent, and this resulted in significant reductions in foreign aid. Additionally, Japan began to reform the domestic institutions of foreign aid and, finally, Japan's policy could no longer ignore the rise of China's active foreign policy in the continent. As Sato observes: 'it is essential to investigate the third parties which have had decisive impacts on decisions about Japanese–African relations in each case, and to evaluate each policy in the context of a Japan–Africa–third party triangle.'

The Asian economic model in Africa: Japanese development lessons for Africa

The establishment of the TICAD in 1993 and its successive conferences through 2008 demonstrate for many the distinctive approach contained in Japan's foreign aid policy to Africa. In Chapter 3, Lehman asserts that this policy suggests important differences from the international donor community. A primary question concerns to what extent the so-called East Asian development model can be relevant to development goals in Africa. To a great extent, Japan's view of this model serves the purpose of solidifying its position as the dominant Asian leader in the African foreign aid arena. The actual and perceived success of the Asian model demonstrates that Japan has a useful vision of development that could be applied to other regions of the world.

Another component of this development model consists of a self-help-based ideology. To many in Japan, this reflects its own struggle and success with developing during the Meiji period and once again following World War II. In its current relationship to African countries, self-help allows poor countries to identify their own development priorities and to request from Japan funds to invest in those priority areas.

Japan's non-Western identity as a major global donor and its constitutionally mandated pacificism demarcate its strategy from that of other international aid donors. These differences have been played out in Japan's willingness to depart from the Washington Consensus. Some have argued that this break from the dominant neoliberal strategy has resulted in the so-called post-Washington Consensus framework, with a renewed emphasis on poverty reduction.

Yet Japan's determination to maintain a distinctive foreign aid policy is under pressure from several directions. The donor community places pressure on Japan to direct its aid back to the confines of the Washington Consensus. Moreover, China's expansion into Africa clearly worries the Japanese government since China clearly challenges Japan's previous dominance as the Asian model.

Ambiguous Japan: aid experience and the notion of self-help

For many observers, Japan historically has struggled with reconciling aspects of its national identity with the norms and demands of a global player. For centuries, Japan pursued an inward-looking and outward-isolationist policy, yet quickly opened up economically and socially to the world by the late 19th century. More recently, the country struggled with the consequences of its major role in World War II and the subsequent domestic transformation towards a more democratic, capitalist and peaceful society. Equally relevant are Japan's historical experiences, which provide the foundation for a distinct 'Asian' model for its foreign aid strategy. Chapter 4, by Motoki Takahashi, draws from the historical development of Japan's awkward and ambiguous relationship with the rest of the world. Japan's emergence as a foreign aid provider since 1990 can best be understood as a result of these struggles.

This chapter highlights four factors that have shaped Japan's current foreign aid philosophy. First, the painful history with militarism, imperialistic invasions and ultra-nationalism deeply affected the consciousness of Japanese society. Japan's aggressive policies substantially damaged its neighbors and undermined any moral strength it may have developed. An important outcome of this devastating history has been a government-initiated focus on its moral obligations to its Asian neighbors and to the rest of the world. This shift was highlighted by Japan's commitment to war reparations and to its constitutionally mandated national pacifism.

Second, as a consequence of Japan's destructive policies towards the Asian region, the most significant component of Japan's foreign aid budget has gone to those countries. Yet, since 1993, Japan has sought to diversify its foreign aid commitments away from relatively developed Asian countries to poorer African societies.

Third, Takahashi refers to Japan's foreign aid bureaucracy as organized according to vertical sectionalism in that traditionally decisions were made within separate ministries (Ministry of Finance, Japan International Cooperation Agency [JICA], Ministry of Foreign Affairs, etc.). In recent years, administrative reforms have modified the decision-making approach through the creation of what is called 'super JICA'. It is unclear whether this administrative change will alter the traditional seat of influence in the Japanese government.

Fourth, Japan's ODA approach has been influenced by the country's early reliance on foreign loans in order to rebuild its economy. Japan basically adheres to this focus in its willingness to extend loans to African countries.

Japan's more recent emergence as a major donor to African countries has been predicated on significant changes in its ODA philosophy. As other chapters discuss, Japan has sought to follow a policy that was less strategic with a greater consideration of humanitarian needs, and a unique stance labeled 'self-help'. The combination of these concepts was solidified and demonstrated with the creation of the TICAD in 1993. Takahashi then describes the important differences that make Japanese foreign aid policy distinct from that of other donors. Although he portrays important limitations on Japan's ODA approach, he also outlines significant policy changes meant to better coordinate Japan with the donor community. The ambiguity of Japan's historical identity still exists, yet this may be an advantage since Japan could serve as a bridge between the different cultures of foreign aid strategies.

International debt management: Japan's policy towards Africa

In Chapter 5, Hasegawa examines Japan's policy towards debt cancellation and the management of Africa's debt. Clearly, foreign loans and assistance are an important source of economic growth in poor African countries. However, excessive debt becomes a burden for the indebted country and a warning for the lender. This chapter analyzes the issue of debt overhang and Japan's policy response to excessive borrowing.

Japan's approach to debt overhang focuses on the weak credibility of indebted countries. If the overhang is only a short-term problem, Japan has favored rescheduling. However, long-term indebtedness has often resulted in debt cancellation, which Japan has often opposed. Japan's policy, often termed the 'New Money Approach,' stands in contrast to the policy of other major donor countries. Japan's response to severe indebtedness focuses on a decline in credibility of the debtors and the moral hazard which places rising risk on Japan's investments. From Japan's perspective, this risk generates a downward cycle of rising costs of borrowing which, in the long run, will exacerbate the levels of poverty and place debtor countries further behind in economic development.

Hasegawa argues that Japan's 'New Money Approach' is based on three factors. First, Japan is motivated by the impact of debt overhang on external credibility. Foreign debtors in particular are cautious about the effect of credibility on the valuation of their investments. Second, Hasegawa makes clear that Japan's policy is dependent in part of its own history of economic growth. For Japan, external credibility became a valuable commodity as it emerged from isolation. Third, Japan also is restricted in seeking to cancel debt by its national financial laws.

This chapter also examines the evolution of the idea of debt cancellation among the donor community. Japan, as a member of the Paris Club, had to conform to a certain extent to this new policy. Yet Japan had to be confident that debt cancellation would lead to positive results for the indebted African country and not adversely affect its external credibility. To that end, Hasegawa examines data on the impact of debt cancellation on poverty reduction. Hasegawa concludes that the saved funds from the Heavily Indebted Poor Countries (HIPCs) Initiative led to improvements in meeting the basic needs of African countries. He also analyzes changes resulting from declining credibility and the creation of a moral hazard. His analysis suggests that debt cancellation, under specific conditions, allowed governments to increase expenditures aimed at poverty reduction. He writes that 'in terms of poverty reduction, the HIPC Initiative succeeded'. Yet many other indicators point to lingering adverse effects of debt cancellation and a remaining moral hazard problem that needs to be resolved.

Policy coordination among aid donors: Japan's position from a European perspective

Effective aid often correlates with donor country alignment and coordination of policies. As Japan's foreign aid policy to Africa deepened and became institutionalized in the early 1990s, pressure mounted on Japan to better coordinate its policies and goals with the other major donor countries. The dilemma that Japan faces is the concurrent requirement to coordinate development goals along with lending coordination. Japan has to work within the dominant development agenda set by the global aid regime as illustrated by the Millennium Development Goals (MDGs) and the International Development Targets. In Chapter 6, Hashimoto examines Japan's policies with regard to aid coordination.

Hashimoto discusses the differences and similarities among the donor community, including the Nordic countries and the United Kingdom. The initial differences have been set aside and the two groups reflect a more common aid policy. Debt cancellation once again became a focal point for coordinated aid policy. Coordinated policy led to the debt relief campaign of Jubilee 2000. Figure 6.3 in this chapter best illustrates the different relationships of countries in the Like-Minded Group 9 (LMG) and Japan.

This chapter then compares the aid policy towards Africa of the United Kingdom and of Japan. The UK has developed an integrated approach towards foreign aid and a common theme along with other European donors. Japan has long emphasized ownership and partnership with its recipient countries in Africa. The UK and other donors also adhere to these concepts, but for Japan they resonate deeply in its history and cultural development. Ownership is a reflection of its own aid philosophy and partnership derives from its request-based aid approach.

Introduction 7

Finally, in Chapter 6 Hashimoto examines in detail policy coordination issues in Ghana. The case study demonstrates the important common practices and goals between Japan and the donor community, but also important differences. Hashimoto shows that Japan has been less active in coordination practices.

Japan and the Poverty Reduction Aid Regime: challenges and opportunities in assistance for Africa

In Chapter 7, Takahashi highlights the importance of 'fungibility' in the Poverty Reduction Aid Regime. Fungibility refers to the ability of a debtor country to borrow money for one purpose while using it for another. Such fungibility could enable 'the recipient country to spend its own monies, freed by aid provision, for non-developmental purposes'. Takahashi provides an historical overview of fungibility from its introduction in the 1950s to renewed interest in fungibility beginning in the 1990s. As a means to counter the negative effects of fungibility, donor governments focused on specific aid modalities and effective intervention. Yet, Japan deviated from the stance of most donor countries as it pursued a different aid modality. Japan has demonstrated hesitation regarding the deep intervention required to stem adverse results from fungibility in foreign aid.

As other chapters demonstrate, Japan's foreign aid policy framework has been shaped by its history and Japan's own experiences with development. Moreover, Japan is sensitive to the misappropriation of borrowed funds, especially when directed towards military ends. As a means to regulate fungible aid, Japan has often incorporated loans or technical assistance as significant components in its foreign aid package to African governments. While there is no perfect prevention for negative fungibility, aid-in-kind is more effective than aid-in-cash.

Chapter 7 details Japan's approach to managing fungibility through its debt relief scheme and its stance on the General Budgetary Support program. Takahashi argues that Japan's position can be explained by the country's indifference to poor countries and relatively weak commitments to indebted African countries. Takahashi then examines the Poverty Reduction Aid Regime and the problematic issue of selectivity. In the final section, Takahashi turns to the rise of China as a major foreign aid player in Africa. An important question which needs to be examined in greater detail is how China's aggressive role will impact on the Poverty Reduction Aid Regime. Japan is currently faced with a choice of either diminishing its differences with the international donor community or following its specific self-interest which, in turn, would narrow its differences with China.

2 An historical analysis of Japan's aid policy in Africa

Makoto Sato

In May 2008 the Japanese government held the Fourth Tokyo International Conference on African Development (TICAD-IV), a summit-level policy forum on African development. It was a rare thing, for a single government to organize a summit-level conference solely on African development over a period of 15 years. TICAD-IV was attended by representatives of 51 African countries, 34 other countries, 75 international and regional organizations, and representatives of other institutions and non-governmental organizations (NGOs). Fukuda Yasuo, prime minister of Japan, boasted that they were commencing a century of African growth, and promised that Japan would double its official development assistance (ODA) to Africa over five years, including a US $4 billion credit mainly for building infrastructure (Fukuda 2008).

Although his promises were welcomed by African leaders, some of the participants began to question the role of the TICAD as a policy forum. Some have concluded that the historical role of the TICAD is over (Ochiai 2008). These reactions seem to suggest that Japan is now concerned with strengthening practical economic relations through trade and investment, rather than continuing foreign aid and development policies. In the background to this were the changing circumstances in Africa. When the TICAD was introduced in 1993, Japan was the top donor of overall ODA and the prime donor to many African countries. Fifteen years later, Japan is no longer the prime donor; other donors have increased their aid to Africa, and China's commitment there has become significant. Moreover, the African economy began to grow markedly at the beginning of the new century.

This chapter intends to sketch out the basic characteristics of Japanese African aid policy by surveying its historical development. I first divide the history of Japanese aid to Africa into five stages, describing the basic features of each period, and then I identify the fundamental characteristics common throughout this history. In addition to the bilateral relationships between Japan and the countries of Africa, I pay special attention to the relationships between Japan and third parties (nations and regions) outside of Africa, as well as the relationships between Africa and those third parties. The chapter argues that Japan's Africa policy has been formed and implemented in a web of triangular relationships between Japan, Africa and the third parties. I conclude that changes in international circumstances, which became marked in the new century, now require Japan to initiate a reformulation of Japan–Africa bilateral relations by increasing its economic and political commitment to Africa.

Debates over the characteristics of Japan's aid policy

In the study of Japanese foreign policy, the 'reactive state' thesis offered by Calder has had a seminal impact on Japanese scholars. In his analysis, the term 'reactive state' does not refer to a state which formulates and implements diplomatic policies by carefully observing other states' policies and reactions. Rather, Calder's 'reactive state' is a state which (1) cannot take initiatives for the sake of its own economic foreign policy in spite of the fact that it has sufficient power and incentives to do so; and (2) changes policies without systematic consistency simply by responding to foreign pressure. Calder concludes that every dimension of Japan's economic foreign policy, including development assistance, is reactive in nature.

In general, while several reasons may explain the condition of reactive states, such as net external debt and large-scale foreign investment, in the case of Japan Calder sees essentially two reasons to explain its reactivity: considerations of state strategy and the internal political structure. First, Japan's national strategy avoids a pro-active global role so as to devote maximum attention to its own economic growth. Second, weak political leadership and the fragmented character of state authority discourage a pro-active foreign policy. Japan's powerful ministries, such as the Ministry of International Trade and Industry (MITI) and the Ministry of Finance (MOF), deal with narrow technical issues within their individual areas, but are not capable of handling complex questions of global economic management (Calder 1988).

Inspired by Calder, there have been various debates over the reactive state model. Miyashita (2001) supports Calder's thesis based on his analysis of Japanese foreign aid issues – the resumption of aid to a post-Tiananmen Square China and economic assistance to Russia under Yeltsin. In both cases, Japan ultimately agreed to follow the decisions taken by Europe and the United States. Miyashita argues that although Japan has become more active in foreign policy, especially in the areas of finance and development assistance, such activism takes place in areas where it does not challenge American hegemony and interests. However, he questions Calder's reasoning that Japanese reactivity to *gaiatsu* (foreign pressure) works because the

Japanese government is divided and fragmented. He argues that 'Japan's sensitivity to *gaiatsu* stemmed from the desire to avoid major disruption in US–Japan relations', and that 'concern for a deterioration of the bilateral relations altered the cost–benefit calculations of Japan's policy options'. Miyashita thus concludes that 'the responsiveness is a result of choice rather than inability to act on the part of the Japanese government' (2001: 58).

Yasutomo (1995) provides an alternative to the reactive state model and emphasizes that Japan has recognized 'the inadequacy of its past diplomacy in a new world environment' where Japan has become a leading ODA donor. Additionally, Japan is now 'embarking on a more active, involved, and independent diplomacy' (1995: 45). Maswood (2001) points out the differences in understandings of the term 'leadership' because Japanese society does not value such leadership as it is understood in the West. Japanese-style leadership can be understood as leading from behind the scenes, rather than taking forceful, assertive action. While the reactive state model tries to find the reasons behind Japan's reactivity in state structural features, the consensual leadership model opts for a more cultural understanding of Japan (Maswood 2001). The Japanese leadership understood by Maswood is the leadership of the conciliator, broker, and behind-the-scenes mediator. This is close to the argument of Hook *et al.* (2001: 444), who see Japanese diplomacy as 'quietly proactive'.

When applying the reactive state thesis to the analysis of Japan's African aid policy, it should be noted that the existing arguments over this thesis are mostly based on an assumption: they implicitly, or explicitly in some cases, draw theoretical models by examining Japanese foreign policy in the context of Japanese–US relations. It is doubtful whether the models drawn from empirical analyses of Japanese–US bilateral relations could be automatically applied to analyses of Japanese–African relations. First, Japan and Africa have a shorter history of relations and also weaker political-economic ties compared to those between Japan and the US. Second, in the formation of Japan's Africa policy, third parties (nations and regions) outside of Africa have had decisive impacts. I will outline the characteristics of Japan's African aid policy, paying special attention to the triangular relationships between Japan, Africa and third parties.

History of Japanese aid in Africa

Initial stage

Overall, Japan's development aid has a half-century of history. The history of its aid to Africa can be divided into five developmental stages including: (1) from the beginning of Japanese aid diplomacy to the first oil crisis

(1954–73); (2) through the first and second oil crises, up to 1980 (1974–80); (3) the period of rapid expansion of Japanese aid (1981–8); (4) the period when Japan became the prime global donor and began examining the policy initiatives regarding aid in the international community (1989–2000); and (5) the period when the Japanese government faced a shift in aid diplomacy internationally and domestically (2001–present).

The first stage of Japanese aid diplomacy began in 1954 when Japan became a member of the Colombo Plan. This was initially a part of the war reparations to the Southeast Asian countries which suffered from Japanese occupation during the Second World War. This stage lasted for nearly 20 years until the outbreak of the Yom Kippur War (the fourth Middle East War) and the subsequent first oil crisis. During this period, Japanese aid was almost exclusively concentrated in the Asian region. Even as late as 1970, 98.2 percent of Japanese aid was directed to Asian countries (Ministry of Foreign Affairs [MOFA] 2002).

According to a major policy paper equivalent to a white paper on ODA produced by the MITI in the late 1950s, aid was rationalized as part of the goal to 'expand the export market and to secure the import market of important raw materials' (MITI 1958). It was based on a sense of fear within the MITI that Japan would be left behind in a rapidly changing international economic environment, particularly with trade liberalization and regional integration progressing as exemplified by the case of Europe. The immediate tasks for Japan, as recognized by the MITI, were to strengthen industry by shifting from light to heavy manufacturing in production as well as exports, and to intensify economic cooperation with Asia, which accounted for 40.9 percent of Japanese exports and 32.4 percent of its imports in 1956 (MITI International Trade Bureau, 1958). The Japanese export market was still led by textiles (35.1 percent of total Japanese exports in 1957), and the share of machinery exports was 23.8 percent, far behind that of Britain (40.2 percent of its total exports in the same year) or Germany (43.7 percent) (MITI 1959). Japan's Asian partners were predominantly Southeast Asian countries, as diplomatic normalization with South Korea and China was yet to be realized.

The MITI saw that expanding the percentage of machinery in Japanese exports would only be possible when Southeast Asian countries got on the right track of industrial development and their demand for Japanese machinery expanded. The industrial development of Southeast Asian countries was also necessary for expanding their exports to Japan, since their exports of raw materials such as iron ore, oil and coal to the Japanese market faced severe competition from commodities from other regions, with the exception of wood from the Philippines. Japanese ODA was expected to supply purchasing power to Asian countries through long-term credit, and give them opportunities to learn of Japanese technological advancements through technical cooperation.

The fact that the Japanese government justified development aid as a means of trade expansion during this initial period has given an overly strong impression to observers.[1] Yet, in the course of historical development, the objectives of Japanese aid became far more diversified, including economic benefits for the long and short term, humanitarian considerations, security concerns, cooperation and coordination with other donor countries, and the desire to undertake political initiatives on the international scene.

Most of the recipient Asian countries suffered to various degrees from their invasion and occupation by the Japanese military during the war. Also, immediately following their independence or liberation from foreign domination, the people in those countries experienced rising nationalism. Under such circumstances, the Japanese authorities had to implement aid projects with deliberation and caution in order to avoid attracting nationalistic criticism from the people of recipient countries. Globally, Japan had just been allowed to become a member of the United Nations (UN) in 1956, and put priority on being accepted by other countries as a good member of the international community. At this stage Japan consciously chose a low-key, behind-the-scenes position.

Some practical principles were gradually formulated by the Japanese authorities engaged in development assistance, such as the 'on-request basis' aid principle, and the emphasis on supporting the 'self-help efforts' of the recipient countries. The former meant that Japan would respond to requests for aid for development projects only in cases where the recipient countries initiated planning and proposed the projects themselves. The latter implied that, although Japan would give assistance financially and technically during the initial stage, once the project had begun, the recipient countries themselves would assume all the responsibilities, not only for economic management but also for social, political and other related issues which might appear thereafter. Although these principles were initially inspired by the specific historical conditions pertaining between Japan and Asian countries at the time, they came to be applied to the Japanese worldwide aid strategy.

Another important characteristic of this period was that, although Japan gave assistance to Asian countries, it concomitantly received an enormous amount of financial assistance from the World Bank and other international institutions. World Bank loans to Japan started in 1953, a year before the Japanese entrance into the Colombo Plan, and continued for 14 years (up to 1966). Japan was a major recipient, second only to India, for World Bank loans in the early 1960s. The Japanese debt to the World Bank was finally paid in full in 1990 (Akira and Yasutami 1997). By that time,

Japan had become the second-largest donor country in overall aid after the United States. In other words, for nearly 40 years Japan was concurrently a recipient and a donor of development assistance in the international community. Japan's experience in this regard was emphasized by the Japanese government who, over the time it has offered aid to East Asia and later to Africa, suggested that African countries should learn from the experiences of East Asia.

Japanese aid to Africa was negligible during this stage. Nevertheless, this period proved to be quite important, since it formulated the main characteristics of Japan's aid policy. These principles, the 'on-request basis' and supporting the 'self-help efforts' of the recipient countries, came to shape the Japanese aid policy in Africa in later stages by providing an Asian development model applicable to other regions. In other words, I can already see here a triangular relationship developing, one that affects Japan's aid policy in Africa: the relationship between Japan, Africa, and the Asian region as a third party.

The oil crisis and the change of aid strategy

The second stage was kicked off by the outbreak of the Yom Kippur War. The world economy was plunged into chaos following the oil embargo by Arab countries and the quadrupling of oil prices by the Organization of Petroleum Exporting Countries (OPEC). Faced with this disaster, Japan promptly tried to acquire Arab oil by approaching Arab nations and adopting a more pro-Arab diplomatic stance in the Middle East. The Middle East comprised 77.5 percent of Japanese oil imports in 1973 (Institute of Applied Energy [IAE] 2008). At the same time, however, it began searching for alternative oil sources in order to diversify the countries of origin for its oil imports. Africa became one such newly spotlighted region. In 1974 Kimura Toshio, the Minister of Foreign Affairs, visited Egypt and four sub-Saharan African countries (Ghana, Nigeria, Zaire, and Tanzania); he was the first sitting Japanese foreign minister to do so. Similarly, in 1979, immediately after the second oil crisis, Foreign Minister Sonoda Naoshi visited five sub-Saharan countries (Nigeria, Côte d'Ivoire, Senegal, Tanzania and Kenya), becoming the second such minister to visit Africa.

Kimura later explained the two major motives for his visit to Africa. First, shocked by the vulnerability of the Japanese economy in the face of scarce natural resources, he began to consider Africa, a place of rich natural resources but an almost virgin region for Japanese economic diplomacy. Second, he was concerned by the popular resentment of the economic activities conducted by Japanese corporations in several Southeast Asian countries at the time. In extreme cases, this resentment led to anti-Japanese riots. For example, when Prime Minister Tanaka Kakuei visited Indonesia in January 1974, he was welcomed by student demonstrations protesting against the flood of imports of Japanese goods and investment into the country. Amplified by popular resentment to the Suharto regime and power struggles within the regime, the demonstrations developed into riots, with demonstrators stoning the Japanese embassy and destroying hundreds of Japanese cars in Jakarta. Learning from these negative experiences, Kimura wished to build friendly relationships between Japanese and African countries (Afurika Kyokai [Africa Society] 1975, 1976). In other words, the major motives which compelled Kimura to visit Africa were less concerned with events in Africa than with events in the Middle East or Southeast Asia at the time.

In this period, Japanese aid to regions other than Asia significantly increased. Bilateral aid to African countries increased nominally from 1970 to 1980 by 27.5 times while the national general budget increased nominally 5.3 times (MITI 1984). Although Japan embarked on aid to Africa primarily motivated by long-term economic security considerations, diplomatic priority was given to countries possessing rich natural resources, economic growth potential or influential political power, as exemplified by the countries visited by the two ministers. Moreover, Japan's existing close trade relationship with South Africa was not shaken by its new efforts to develop cooperation with 'Black African' countries. Also Japan came to see African countries as possible allies on the international political scene, particularly at the UN. Such considerations were most salient when Japan became a candidate for election as a non-permanent member of the Security Council. The MOFA consciously worked for the votes of African countries.

The third stage: cooperation with other donors

In the next stage, Japanese aid to Africa continued to expand. As before, Japanese aid became more globalized and expanded in absolute terms. However, there is a key difference between the second and third stages. In the former, Japanese aid was motivated by economic security considerations, and its prime target was the resource-rich recipient countries. In the latter, Japan's prime diplomatic target was not so much the aid recipients as the other donor countries, which demanded that Japan increase its financial contributions to international development.

During the 1980s, Japan was more successful than other major industrialized countries in maintaining stable economic growth. Because of this, it faced growing pressure from other industrialized countries on trade and foreign exchange issues. In 1985, the United States, suffering from twin deficits in trade and the federal budget, propelled the decision by the finance ministers and central bank governors of five major industrialized nations to drive down the price of the dollar (the Plaza Accord). The price of the yen and of Japanese assets went sky-high, and, as a result, Japan entered a so-called 'bubble economy'. The United States also put stronger pressure on Japan to increase its aid to areas other than Asia. In the same year as the Plaza Accord, US Under-Secretary of State Armacost visited Japan and requested that Japan increase its aid to other regions as well as Asia, and to include a higher proportion of grants in its aid. At another 1985 meeting in Paris between the Administrator of US Agency for International Development and the Director-General of the Economic Cooperation Bureau of MOFA, the Americans requested that Japan increase aid specifically in Africa (Orr 1990). This US pressure partly reflected the aid guidelines of the National Security Council (NSC) under the Reagan administration. The NSC emphasized aid coordination between donor countries, and argued that Japan should share more of the burden internationally by increasing aid in areas other than Asia, such as Latin America, the Pacific region and Africa (Browne 1990). It also reflected a UN policy which called for an increase in aid to Africa, which had been hit by successive famine disasters in the 1980s (Orr 1990).

Under such international pressures, Japan came to make ODA one of the three pillars of its policy for counterbalancing the trade surplus and addressing domestic demands for expansion and promotion of imports. The proportion going to Africa out of the total Japanese ODA continuously increased, reaching a record 15.3 percent in 1989. Subsequently it dropped slightly, but maintained a proportion of some 10 percent thereafter. In short, the increase in Japanese aid to Africa during this period was a response to the pressure not from Africa but from the major industrialized nations.

In the mid 1980s Africa experienced a historic drought, which swept over the Sahel and much of the eastern and southern regions. In addition, several other factors, including civil wars exacerbated the situations, causing millions of deaths on the continent. A famine relief campaign was organized worldwide in 1984–5. In the case of Japan, the first report on the famine in Mozambique appeared as headline news in the *Asahi Shimbun* on 2 April 1984. This report was followed by other media coverage of famines all over Africa. These reports triggered a massive response from Japan's civil society, and spontaneous famine relief campaigns were organized. In the case of Europe, and subsequently the United States, it was a report on BBC television on 23 October 1984 covering the famine in Ethiopia which shocked viewers and triggered a massive famine relief campaign. Until that time the media had paid little attention to the famine in Ethiopia, although the Ethiopian government had issued statements calling for help as early as 1983. The relief campaigns worldwide culminated in the Live Aid event in

July 1985. Chronologically, the reaction of the civil society in Japan preceded that of Europeans and Americans. It was the first time that Japanese society was organized to take action on solely an African issue. Partly responding to such popular moves, the Japanese government embarked on famine relief operations, sending Foreign Minister Abe Shintaro to the famine-stricken areas in Zambia and Ethiopia in November 1984. The famine relief campaign marked the advent of a new period in Japanese–African relations, since the Japanese government now had to listen carefully to voices from Japanese civil society, and not simply respond to foreign pressure.

Top donor Japan and political commitment

In the fourth stage, Japan became a top donor of bilateral aid worldwide. In 1989, Japan surpassed the United States to become the prime donor country, maintaining this position for the next ten years from 1991 through 2000. Japan also became a major donor in Africa. As the amount of Japanese aid increased worldwide, the political implications of its foreign aid became a serious concern. The revolution in the Philippines in 1986 and the Gulf War in 1991 raised grave questions over the legitimacy and appropriateness of Japanese aid to the Philippines and Iraq respectively. The Japanese government had to justify political principles for its aid, breaking from the traditional 'on-request basis' policy. In 1992 the cabinet officially adopted the ODA Charter, which stipulated the coexistence of environmental conservation and development efforts, no aid to be used for military purposes, attention paid to recipients countries' military expenditures, and attention paid to democratization and human rights.

In fact, sanctions on the grounds of the ODA Charter violations were applied to countries in Africa on several occasions. Eyinla (1999) wrote of an episode when both the United States and Japan imposed sanctions on Nigeria due to the annulled 1993 presidential election. The US ambassador stated that the sanctions were dictated by official US policy, which prohibits aid to countries where the democratic process has been abused, while the Japanese ambassador 'attributed Japan's decision to impose sanctions on Nigeria as a fall-out from its membership of the G.7, which agreed to ban economic ties with Nigeria' (Eyinla 1999: 426). This episode seems to indicate not only 'a pusillanimous attitude towards Africa' (Eyinla 1999) by Japanese official circles, in that they attributed negative policies taken against any African country to Japan's membership in the West, but also Japanese reactivity to the Western powers in that Japan cooperated with and followed the action of these powers rather than taking a different initiative.

The Japanese political commitment in Africa deepened and broadened throughout this phase. The first major commitment came with the dispatch of the Self-Defense Forces (SDF) for peace-keeping operations and humanitarian relief activities. In 1993, Japan sent the SDF to Mozambique to participate in the UN peace-keeping operations after the ceasefire between the Frelimo government and the Resistência Nacional Moçambicana (RENAMO) forces backed up by apartheid South Africa. It was the second time the SDF participated in UN peace-keeping operations, and the first time in Africa. However, Japan could have intervened in the Mozambique peace process much earlier if it had utilized its strong trade ties with South Africa. Later, in 1994, the SDF was sent to refugee camps in Zaire for humanitarian relief operations aiding the Rwandan refugees. In the case of Rwanda, Japanese troops were dispatched when the missions of other countries began withdrawing from the region. In both cases, the priority of the Japanese government may be seen more as appealing for cooperation from the international community than exercising activities appropriate to the area. There was a strong resentment among the Japanese public towards overseas deployment of the SDF, which was believed by many to be unconstitutional. Also the Japanese government had to take into account the wariness of neighboring Asian countries regarding the overseas activities of the Japanese military. For the realization of the SDF deployment, the Japanese government required an international credential such as a UN decision.

The second political commitment by Japan was the organization of the Tokyo International Conference on African Development in 1993 in order to initiate a development strategy for Africa. The second TICAD was held five years later. Several new developmental initiatives were proposed, such as promoting South–South cooperation by utilizing Japanese aid for training African personnel in Asian countries. Mostly, however, what the TICAD did was to endorse the existing development strategies. Some argue that the TICAD was more a substantial diplomatic initiative with little in the way of development initiatives by Japan (Obayashi 2003). TICAD-III was held in 2003, and TICAD-IV followed in 2008.

The driving force for Japan to organize the TICAD at the initial stage seemed more political than economic. At this stage, Japan did not expect to drastically expand its trade or investment in Africa, except in South Africa. In contrast, Japanese political ambition was real. Japan wished to utilize the TICAD as an international stage to demonstrate its development initiative. At the same time, political support by African countries was seen as indispensable for Japan to gain a permanent seat on the UN Security Council.

The TICAD was born in the context of several historical conditions. Japan was the top donor of ODA overall, and the prime donor to many African countries, at a time when many other donors had scaled down their aid to Africa due to 'aid fatigue'. African countries welcomed the Japanese initiative as long as it would work to revive people's interest and concern about

Africa. The development approach proposed by Japan, that Africa should learn from Asia's experiences, appeared attractive since African countries were not able to find any alternative development plans. Conversely, when these historical conditions which induced the birth of the TICAD are lost or changed, the attitude of and evaluation by the African countries regarding the TICAD can be expected to change.

Another historical event of the period was the abolition of *Apartheid* and the establishment of a democratic South Africa in 1994 under the leadership of the African National Congress (ANC) and newly elected President Nelson Mandela. Japan had officially condemned apartheid at UN meetings, prohibited direct foreign investment by Japanese corporations, and strictly regulated cultural exchanges. Yet it had continued to trade with South Africa and, in 1987, Japan became South Africa's primary trade partner. Criticized by the international community, the Japanese government introduced measures to reduce trade with South Africa, including self-restraint by the corporations involved. Such measures were maintained until 1991 when Japan lifted sanctions. The amount of Japanese trade (imports and exports) with South Africa was reduced by 22 percent between 1987 and 1991 (MOF 2008). The factors which drove Japan to take these restrictive actions were its relationships with other governments and the criticism from civil societies in other industrialized countries. After the announcement of the abolition of apartheid, Japan finally resumed diplomatic relations with South Africa in 1992. Since the ANC came to power, Japan has supported South Africa as a core nation in Africa.

A new development policy for Africa in the 21st century

The fifth stage began as the new century arrived. The situations in and surrounding Africa substantially changed at the turn of the century. Signs of economic growth were seen mainly in countries with mineral and energy resources, while economic differences between nations broadened. The international community came to pay more serious attention to Africa from both economic and security perspectives. In striving to attain the UN Millennium Development Goals (MDGs), financial assistance from international organizations and donor countries to Africa increased. The G8 Kananaskis Summit in 2002 adopted the Africa Action Plan, responding to the New Partnership for Africa's Development (NEPAD), a major development plan formed by the newly organized African Union (AU). At the G8 Gleneagles Summit in 2005, African issues were one of the summit's main agenda items.

Along with these international developments, there was also a change of attitude within Japan domestically towards its aid policy. First, the aid

An historical analysis of Japan's aid policy in Africa 19

budget was rapidly reduced at the turn of the century due to the recession and financial deficit. The ODA budget for 2001 was reduced by 27 percent in US dollar terms, and the top donor position was retaken by the United States (MOFA 2002). The ODA to Africa too was substantially reduced. Yet, after the Kananaskis and Gleneagles summits the Japanese government introduced debt relief on a large scale. In 2006, the ODA to Africa reached $2.56 billion, 2.2 times that of the previous year. The share of ODA to Africa out of the total ODA (34.2 percent) surpassed that of Asia (26.8 percent) for the first time. However, of the $2.56 billion going to Africa, 79.8 percent was in fact applied to debt relief (MOFA 2006, 2007a).

Second, the ODA system was reformed following a series of scandals in and around the MOFA. In 2001 and 2002 some dozen scandals involving embezzlement, fraud and bribery were disclosed, involving trade company representatives and MOFA officials in both its head office in Tokyo and overseas diplomatic establishments. In one case a MOFA official was charged with fraud amounting to 500 million yen gained by inflating the budget with items such as hotel charges for the prime minister's overseas visits. In another case it was disclosed that a number of sections of the MOFA ran a dual bookkeeping scheme for the purpose of evading inspection (*Nihon Keizai Shimbun* 06 February 2002, 12 March 2002).

Third, in August 2003 the cabinet adopted a new ODA Charter. It tried to integrate ODA with concepts of human security and peace-building: humanitarian assistance, facilitating peace processes, assistance for disarmament, and the demobilization and reintegration of ex-combatants. The new charter seemed to mark the final departure from the traditional 'on-request basis' attitude towards aid.

At the same time, Chinese commitment to Africa surged. The ODA White Paper for 2007 mentioned emerging donor countries for the first time, and noted that China had embarked on active resource diplomacy in Africa, citing rare metals as an example. The White Paper argued that it is extremely important for Japan that 'Japanese corporations attain interests overseas related to major resources such as rare metal through direct investment', and 'it will become increasingly important for the future to support such corporate activities by utilizing official development assistance' (MOFA 2007a: 20). It can be seen here once again that reaction to a third party actor, China in this case, has again induced a new direction for Japanese foreign policy in Africa.

Chinese diplomacy in Africa became active in the late 1990s; President Jiang Zemin's visit to six Africa countries in 1996 served as a springboard for strengthening China–Africa bilateral relations. The introduction of the Forum on China–Africa Cooperation (FOCAC) in 2000 accelerated these trends. The amount of Chinese trade with Africa shot up by 3.8 times, from $9.6 billion in 2000 to $36.3 billion in 2005 (IMF 2001–7); China was most active in importing oil resources. Angola and four other African countries together made up 28.1 percent of China's oil imports in 2005 (MOFA 2007b). China does not hesitate to approach notorious human rights violating 'pariah regimes' (Alden 2007) such as oil exporting Sudan because of its policy of non-interference in internal affairs. Thus, it is certain that China's Africa policy is very motivated by economic issues, particularly securing natural resources. China, however, has also been politically motivated. Initially its major aim was to compete with and defeat Taiwan in establishing diplomatic relations with African states. China emphasized its special position as a regional hegemon as well as a large developing country, which could be used to represent the voices of other developing countries. By the time the first China–Africa Summit was held in 2006, China had diplomatic relations with 48 African countries, while Taiwan had only relations with only five. For China, the support of African counties has a global political meaning, while China's backing has become a necessary condition for African countries that want to send their representatives as permanent members of the UN Security Council.

China's economic and political successes in Africa have had an impact on Japan. First, Japan expects that the competition between countries over natural resources in Africa will become more severe. In particular, Japan is concerned with securing rare metals which can only be imported from a limited number of countries, China and South Africa being two major suppliers. Minister of Economy, Trade and Industry Amari Akira was sent to Botswana and South Africa in November 2007 to sign joint agreements to investigate prospective mines for rare metals. China's rapid expansion of trade and FDI (Foreign Direct Investment) in Africa also challenges the previous Japanese contention that Africa should follow the self-reliant East Asian development model with the assistance of Japanese yen credit.

Second, from a political viewpoint, the rapid development of friendly relationships between China and African states raises a concern that Japan can no longer expect the strong support of African countries that it used to enjoy in UN politics, especially concerning its goal to become a permanent member of the Security Council. At the TICAD-IV, Fukuda held successive separate meetings with 40 African heads of state and government who attended the conference in order to obtain their political support for Japan in UN politics. However, it was reported that only 17 heads of state and government expressed support for Japan to become a permanent member of the UN Security Council (*Nihon Keizai Shimbun* 31 May 2008). Such a response from the African countries was not totally unexpected, however. Japanese diplomacy on the issue of the expansion of the Security Council membership failed three years before. In July 2005, Germany, India, Brazil and Japan (G4) put forward a joint resolution at the UN General Assembly, which proposed the expansion of the Security Council to include these four countries plus two other countries as new permanent members. However, the AU member countries adhered to their own resolution to the end, which resulted in the rejection of the G4 resolution.

Triangular relationships in Japan's Africa policy

The examination of each stage of the historical development of Japan's Africa policy indicates that, in many cases, Japan has formulated its Africa policy by responding to events, pressure and activities of third parties outside of Africa itself. For example, in the first stage, the principles of 'on-request basis' aid and of supporting the 'self-help efforts' of recipient countries were formulated out of the Japanese government's consideration of the nationalistic sentiments of Asian nations when it first embarked on development aid in the 1950s, and then were subsequently applied to Africa during later stages. In the second stage, the first visit to Africa by a Japanese foreign minister was motivated by the events in the Middle East and Southeast Asia rather than Africa.

The expansion of aid in Africa in the third stage was induced mainly by concerns from other industrialized countries, which were pressuring Japan to accelerate its financial contributions to international development in areas other than Asia. In the fourth stage, the shift from the passive 'on-request basis' attitude to the adoption and application of the ODA Charter, as in the Nigerian case, was motivated by criticism from the international community over past Japanese aid to the Marcos regime in the Philippines or the Hussein regime in Iraq. Japan's sanctions against South Africa during the same period were motivated by international criticism of Japan's trade with the *Apartheid* regime rather than by actual events in South Africa. Even the new policy introduced in the fifth stage at the start of the 21st century, which emphasized the use of aid for securing essential raw materials from developing countries, was again motivated by the brisk aid diplomacy of China in Africa.

Overall, the historical experiences described above indicate that the Japanese 'reactivity' as seen in its Africa policy is quite different in nature from the 'reactivity' examined in past debates on the reactive state thesis, which were mainly demonstrated by case studies of Japan–US bilateral relations. In the case of Japan–US relations, the Japanese government tends to cautiously observe and follow the opinions of the US State Department, the Congress and the media, and reformulates its next policy in reaction to them. However, in the case of Africa, what the Japanese government is cautiously observing are the opinions of the governments and civil societies in other industrialized countries, and/or the international community as symbolized by institutions like the UN, rather than the opinions of African states and societies.

Thus, it is far from adequate to evaluate Japan's Africa policy simply by examining Japanese–African bilateral relations. It is essential to investigate the third parties which have had decisive impacts on decisions about Japanese–African relations in each case, and to evaluate each policy in the context of a Japan–Africa–third party triangle. In other words, the historical development of Japan's Africa policy can be properly understood only when located in the complex web of relationships between Japan, Africa and the third parties.

However, this does not mean that Japan–Africa relations will and should continue to be formed by simply reacting to the third parties. The changing international environment surrounding Africa seems to push Japan to reconstruct Japan–Africa bilateral relations. This was illustrated by the attitudes of African leaders at the TICAD-IV. In spite of Fukuda's promise that Japan would double its ODA to Africa over five years, some of the African leaders openly complained about the limited commitment by Japanese investors and private companies (*Nihon Sangyo Shimbun* 02 June 2008).

Gradually challenges regarding the reconstruction of Japan–Africa relations have been witnessed in several fields by various actors. Concerning trade and investment in Africa, private companies have recently strengthened their commitment on the continent, as exemplified by Mitsubishi's aluminum refinery project in Mozambique and Toyota's adult training project in South Africa. At the civil society level, there have been attempts to strengthen cooperation between Japanese and African NGOs, such as joint actions taken at the TICAD-IV.

Also in the field of peace-building, the Japanese government has tried to demonstrate its own initiative: promoting the human security ideals of peace-building and development assistance. However, in Japanese foreign policy the relationship between human security and state security, centering on the Japan–US security arrangements, has often been unclear and remains unexplained. On some occasions human security seems to be used as an excuse for, or a complement to, Japan–US security arrangements.[2] Should Japan wish to take a peace-building initiative in Africa, it may be necessary to reconsider the current state security arrangements which tend to involve Japanese reactivity to US foreign policy.

Notes

1. For example, Schraeder argued as late as 1999 that: 'Japan has traditionally pursued a neo-mercantilist foreign policy toward Africa' for economic self-interest. The recipients are either countries with important sources of raw material such as South Africa and Zambia, or countries capable of absorbing Japanese exports (Schraeder 1999: 232). However, statistics for 2000 indicate that Japanese aid to Africa was dispersed among 44 African counties, and that the amounts of aid to, for instance, Malawi ($38.50 million) and Burkina Faso ($21.30 million), both less attractive as suppliers of raw materials and export markets, were equivalent to those given to South Africa ($19.80 million) and Zambia ($31.90 million). The aid to the latter two countries was even surpassed by that to Tanzania ($217.10 million) and Zimbabwe ($62.40 million) (MOFA 2001).
2. In the Iraq War, Japan supported the preemptive attack by the United States on the grounds of weapons of mass destruction alleged to have been hidden by the Hussein regime, and Japan sent the SDF to Iraq to engage in humanitarian assistance in various fields such as health, water, electricity and transport for the Iraqi people's human security. Most of these activities would not have been necessary if the war had not been started (Sato 2007).

References

Afurika Kyokai (The Africa Society of Japan) (1975) *Gekkan Afurika*, February.
Afurika Kyokai (1976) *Gekkan Afurika* (Africa Monthly), August.
Akira, N. and Yasutami, S. (1997) *Kaihatsu Enjo no Keizaigaku*, Japan: Yuhikaku.
Alden, C. (2007) *China in Africa*, New York and London: Zed Books.
Browne, S. (1990) *Foreign Aid in Practice*, New York: New York University Press.
Calder, K.E. (1988) 'Japanese Foreign Economic Policy Formation: Explaining the Reactive State', *World Politics* 40(4): 517–41.
Eyinla, B. (1999) 'The ODA Charter and Changing Objectives of Japan's Aid Policy in Sub-Saharan Africa', *Journal of Modern African Studies* 37(3): 409–30.
Fukuda, Y. (2008) 'Address by H.E. Mr. Yasuo Fukuda, Prime Minister of Japan', given at the Opening Session of the Fourth Tokyo International Conference on African Development (TICAD-IV), MOFA, 28 May 2008, online (accessed February 2010): http://www.mofa.go.jp/region/africa/ticad/ticad4/pm/address.html
Hook, G.D., Gilson, J., Hughes, C. and Dobson, H. (2001) *Japan's International Relations: Politics, Economics and Security*, New York and London: Routledge.
Institute of Applied Energy (IAE) (2008) 'Nihon no Genyuyunyu no Chuto Izondo' (Japan's Dependence on the Middle East for Crude Oil Supply), online: http://www.jae.or.jp/energyinfo/energydata/data2004.html
International Monetary Fund (IMF) (2000–7) *Direction of Trade Statistics Yearbook*, Washington, DC: International Monetary Fund.
Maswood, S.J. (2001) 'Japanese Foreign Policy and Regionalism', in S.J. Maswood (ed.) *Japan and East Asian Regionalism*, New York and London: Routledge, 6–25.
Ministry of Finance Japan (MOF) (2008) 'Zaimusho Boeki Tokei: Yusyutsunyugaku no Suii' (Ministry of Finance Trade Statistics: Changes in Export and Import), Ministry of Finance, Japan, online: http://www.customs.go.jp/toukei/suii/html/time.htm

Ministry of Foreign Affairs Japan (MOFA) (2001) *Seifu Kaihatsu Enjo Hakusyo* (Whitepaper of Official Development Aid) *2001*, Tokyo: Ministry of Foreign Affairs Japan.

Ministry of Foreign Affairs Japan (MOFA) (2002) *Seifu Kaihatsu Enjo Hakusyo 2006*, Tokyo: Ministry of Foreign Affairs Japan.

Ministry of Foreign Affairs Japan (MOFA) (2006) *Seifu Kaihatsu Enjo Hakusyo 2006*, Tokyo: Ministry of Foreign Affairs Japan.

Ministry of Foreign Affairs Japan (MOFA) (2007a) *Seifu Kaihatsu Enjo Hakusyo 2007*, Tokyo: Ministry of Foreign Affairs Japan.

Ministry of Foreign Affairs Japan (MOFA) (2007b) 'Shuyo Kakkoku niokeru Kunibetsu Genyu Yunyuryo 2005' (Major Countries' Crude Oil Import Categorized by Exporters), online: http://www.mofa.go.jp/mofa/gaiko/energy/pdfs/b-5.pdf

Ministry of International Trade and Industry Japan (MITI) (1958) *Keizai Kyoryoku no Genjo to Mondaiten 1958*, (The Current Status and the Problems of Economic Cooperation 1958) Tokyo: Ministry of International Trade and Industry Japan.

Ministry of International Trade and Industry Japan (MITI) (1959) *Keizai Kyoryoku no Genjo to Mondaiten 1959*, Tokyo: Ministry of International Trade and Industry Japan.

Ministry of International Trade and Industry Japan (MITI) (1984) *Keizai Kyoryoku no Genjo to Mondaiten 1984*, Tokyo: Ministry of International Trade and Industry Japan.

Ministry of International Trade and Industry Japan International Trade Bureau (MITI ITB) (1958) *Boeki Tokei Geppo*, (Monthly Trade Statistics) Tokyo: Ministry of International Trade and Industry Japan, International Trade Bureau. January.

Miyashita, A. (2001) 'Consensus or Compliance? Gaiatsu, Interests, and Japan's Foreign Aid', in A. Miyashita and Y. Sato (eds) *Japanese Foreign Policy in Asia and the Pacific: Domestic Interests, American Pressure, and Regional Integration*, New York: Palgrave, 37–61.

Nihon Keizai Shimbun, 06 February 2002.

Nihon Keizai Shimbun, 12 March 2002.

Nihon Keizai Shimbun, 31 May 2008.

Nihon Sangyo Shimbun, 02 June 2008.

Obayashi, M. (2003) 'Afurika to Nihon no Atarashii Kankei ni mukete' (Toward New Relations between Japan and Africa), in M. Obayashi (ed.) *Afurika no Chosen*, (The Challenges Africa Faces) Japan: Showa-do, 280–306.

Ochiai, T. (2008) 'TICAD o koete,' 'Beyond TICAD' *Afurika Repoto* 46, IDE-JETRO, 17–20.

Orr, R.M. Jr (1990) *The Emergence of Japan's Foreign Aid Power*, New York: Columbia University Press.

Sato, M. (2007) 'Human Security and Japanese Diplomacy: Debates on the Role of Human Security in Japanese Policy', in G. Shani, M. Sato and M.K. Pasha (eds) *Protecting Human Security in a Post 9/11 World: Critical and Global Insights*, New York: Palgrave Macmillan, 83–96.

Schraeder, P. (1999) 'Japan's Quest for Influence in Africa', *Current History* 98(628): 232–4.

Yasutomo, D.T. (1995) *The New Multilateralism in Japan's Foreign Policy*, New York: Palgrave Macmillan.

3 The Asian economic model in Africa
Japanese developmental lessons for Africa

Howard P. Lehman

Japan has emerged in recent years as a major donor country to African countries. At one level, Japan's renewed assertiveness in providing foreign aid to Africa is on par with the more active approach by other donor countries. It might appear to some that Japan's motivations to lend capital and technical assistance to African countries are similar to those of other lending countries. However, I argue that Japan's official development assistance (ODA) policy makes important departures from the widely accepted ideology and policy objectives of the Washington Consensus. By taking a more distinctive path of foreign aid policy towards Africa, Japan seeks to demonstrate its own leadership position in the donor community. As one well-regarded Japanese economist claimed recently, Japan has been 'walking the splendid path of isolation' (Ishikawa 2005: 34).

Conventional explanations of Japan's motivation for giving aid typically stem mention its own commercial self-interests (Inukai 1995) or the particular configuration of domestic bureaucratic politics (Hook and Zhang 1998). But there have been few studies on Japanese foreign aid to Africa from the basis of developmental strategy. The focus on these traditional analyses is understandable given that Japan's foreign policy towards Africa is not widely known nor studied. Japan does not have a clear historical connection to Africa nor has it been a colonial power in that continent. Yet the Japanese government has organized a series of important conferences on Africa, held every five years. Along with representatives from the United Nations (UN), the World Bank and non-governmental organizations (NGOs), Japan hosts the Tokyo International Conference on African Development (TICAD; see Lehman 2005). Representatives of dozens of African governments and many NGOs attend these conferences, with the most recent taking place in May 2008. Despite the budgetary constraints and cutbacks in Japan's ODA in the last several years, Japan has remained consistent in scheduling these conferences. Rather than turn its attention away from Africa during this economic slump, Japan has moved forward with its aid policies toward Africa. Japan has sought to portray its own developmentalist model as a series of lessons by which African countries could adapt and modify according to their own constraints and development objectives. This chapter thus examines the complicated and revealing Japanese national economic development identity that can explain its aid policy to Africa. The chapter considers Japan's East Asian development model, the self-directed development approach, Japan's attempt to mold its own foreign aid strategy and finally some possible lessons for African development.

East Asian development model

A Japanese observer wrote that the distinctive Japanese approach towards pro-growth development rests on three features. First, the government places the highest priority on the supply side of the economy, namely on production and employment. Second, the government focus is on a long-term perspective based on economic growth. And, third, the market does not grow spontaneously without the help of the government (Kohama 1998: 58). This development model has been embedded in Japanese policy at least since the Meiji period and continued following the end of World War II. Vestal makes the argument that: 'perhaps the most valuable lessons concerning pro-growth industrial policy for developing economies today lie in Japan's utilization of competition as a tool to shape the direction of growth' (1993: 163). Competition for a developmental state does not mean the same as for a liberal state. In Japan's case at this time, the meaning of competition arose out of a complex relationship among the large holding companies, the bureaucratic state, and a defensive posture that focused on domestic development. In the aftermath of the war's destruction, the government felt it had no alternative but to utilize government regulations, including subsidies and trade barriers, to promote economic growth.

One underlying theme in Japanese foreign aid is its history in relation to economic development both within Japan and towards Asia. The historical importance of Japanese development patterns stems in part from the late 19th-century adaptation of the development state. Many of the elements of contemporary development policy can be found in earlier periods of Japanese history. But, as one scholar pointed out, the foundation for Japanese growth and development was in place at this earlier time. Adem writes that: 'the foundation which had been laid during the Edo period was thus solid when the country was fully opened to the outside world after the Meiji Restoration in 1868' (2005: 635). One of the key components from the Meiji period is the recognition of government engagement with the management of the national economy. Some observers point to the 1868 Meiji Restoration and the experiences of post-World War II development as lessons for successful economic strategies. In both cases, the push for growth derived from importation of foreign technology, high productivity, low consumption and a dualistic structure of the economy (Okita 1980: 116). The initial principle of Japanese economic growth at that time was production-oriented policies that led to rapid economic growth. As Okita describes the process, the government at that time focused on basic industries, then the modernization of those industries, followed by the establishment of new industries, which led eventually to export promotion policies (1980: 127).

Japan's status as a major donor in Africa relies heavily on the image it attempts to disseminate to countries. The Japanese government has sought for many years to portray its contemporary foreign aid policy to Africa as stemming from its post-World War II relationship with other Asian countries. Indeed, as another section will discuss, the Japanese effort to redefine its aid image has led to an alternative type of donor support. The creation of this image first started immediately after World War II in its relations with its neighbors. According to Inoguchi, Japan's post-World War II national identity was based on debt, disdain and detachment. By this he means a deep connection to its Asian neighbors that continues to shape how Japan thinks of itself as a major economic power and its relations with its neighboring countries. The debt that Japan owes to the surrounding countries, of course, is based on the history of colonialism, exploitation and expansion. Each generation in Japan has sought to internalize this debt by continuously focusing its foreign policy, in general, and foreign aid, in particular, on that region. As Ishikawa has written, Japan's model of foreign assistance started as reparations to its neighbors, but now has expanded to the African continent (2005: 2).

The second historical theme of Japan's relationship to East Asia centers on disdain. This emotive response derives from the historic isolation of Japan from the West, but, in more recent terms, the term refers to the economic success of a nation that was not highly dependent on the West. Japan was the only non-Western nation that developed into a rich and industrialized country in the 20th century. Given the success of Japan as a non-Western country, its leaders have looked towards its Asian heritage as a reason to continue to assert itself as an Asian leader in foreign policy.

The third theme, according to Inoguchi, is detachment. He writes that 'detachment derives from ambivalence' (2004: 35). Japan has tried, until recent years, to keep China at arm's length and to remain a strongly anti-militaristic country. By doing so, it sought to be economically active in Asia yet remain distant militarily from the rest of the world. That policy of relative isolationism and detachment has changed substantially in the last several years.

These three themes have evolved since 1993, since Japan's decision to mobilize its resources for more forceful and strategic foreign aid to the developing world. Japan's self-identification has evolved to be more based on its leadership role as a successful non-Western industrialized nation. Japan strongly believes that its economic development pattern offers profound lessons, not only for its neighbors but for other developing countries as well.

One of the more important aspects underlining Japan's ODA policy is its relationship to the 'Asian economic model'. Former Prime Minister Junicho Koizumi said in a speech at the 2005 G8 summit that 'Asia's post-war experiences in economic development are valuable assets for us in assisting African development' (2005a: 3). He went on to argue that 'in view of Asian experiences, the key to African economic development is to foster the private sector through the promotion of trade and investment' (2005a: 3).

The East Asian economic miracle has been a powerful force in linking African and Asian societies. According to Japanese economists: 'a key lesson from East Asia is that if aid is to be effective in the long run, it would have to lead to private capital formation, both domestic and foreign' (Hino and Iimi 2006: 16). Moreover, the East Asian experience has affected Japan's approach to development aid in Africa. In particular, the main characteristics of Japan's ODA facilitate self-help and partnership through industrialization and trade. Experience has shown that Japan puts a high priority on economic infrastructure development, with a heavy emphasis on loans.

As one Japanese economist noted with regard to Japanese policy to Ghana: 'based on its own and East Asian catch-up experiences, Japan considers it essential to address the structural problems of the Ghanaian economy and support its economic growth and attainment of self-reliant and sustainable economic development' (Ohno 2007: 18). Given its success in East Asia and its own economic history, Japan has increasingly shown assertiveness in the donor community. The organization of and commitment to the TICAD process has been one important and visible affirmation of Japan's self-identity as a leading donor country.

Compared with the neoclassical orthodoxy that stresses macroeconomic stability and free markets, the Japanese development view is distinct in many areas, including the pursuit of long-term real targets, emphasis on the active role of government as an initiator of change; and, though not explicit in official documents nonetheless real, the acceptance of authoritarian developmentalism in the early stages of development.

Japan's historical development during the Meiji period and since World War II has shaped its relationship with developing countries. Several themes have played a key role in Japan's foreign aid policy to the developing world in general, and to African countries in particular. First, following Japan's adaptive response to the destruction of the war, it adheres to a self-help focus in which the recipient country assumes ownership over the aid. As has often been said in Japan foreign aid circles, aid is neither charity nor a moral obligation. Second, government, at least in the early stages of development, should take an active role in creating an environment favorable to economic production and industrialization. One scholar strongly supports this view, maintaining that: 'perhaps the most profound impact of Japanese efforts in foreign aid is the emergence of Japan's own development philosophy, favoring a role for government in directing private sector growth versus what it terms the "excessive free-market reliance" of multilateral institutions' (Grant 1998: 59). Third, in congruence with Japan's emphasis on production and industrialization, the time-frame is equally long term. Foreign aid is not simply a quick fix, but an ingredient in a complicated recipe of long-term development.

Self-directed development

Richard Grant writes: 'an emphasis on "self-help" runs through Japan's aid planning and implementation, a focus that derives from Japan's experience of postwar economic development, which depended relatively little on foreign aid' (1998: 45). The idea of self-help, to a certain extent, also derived from the Meiji period. This period reflected the advantages of state-managed and state-directed development. The key trait was to modify existing institutions and values by incorporating more capitalist features. Meiji Japan borrowed foreign technology, imported Western models of development, and placed greater emphasis on education. But the overarching objective of this strategy was to maintain control over its national economy by emphasizing export expansion and import substitution (Nafziger 2005). Further reinforcing the image of 'self-help' was the Meiji government's effort to build upon Japan's cultural base as much as possible. In other words, according to Adem: 'Japan's culture did not change to fit the putative requirements of modernity; instead it was modernity which was made to serve the dictates of Japan's culture' (2005: 657). As Nafziger observes: 'the Japanese experience indicates the advantages of self-directed development to transform a country away from its peripheral position in the global economy' (1995: 166).

The basis of self-directed development hinges on the influential and accepted role of the government creating and regulating economic institutions. The historical roots of this focus clearly are set in the Meiji period. As Preston writes, the government was the only mechanism that could pursue long-term industrial development, engage in necessary social, political, and economic reforms, and develop a collaborate policy emphasizing growth and welfare (2000: 47–50).

Self-help refers to the ability of the recipient country to identify its priority development concerns and to marshal domestic and foreign resources towards those areas. In theory, this approach focuses on Japan's willingness to have a 'policy dialogue in which the two parties participate with independence and on equal footing' (Ishikawa 2005: 24). In other words, the recipient country identifies its own financing needs and approaches Japan with an informed request. By allowing the receiving countries to initiate the dialogue over aid, Japan is meant to share 'ownership' with those countries. Ownership implies accountability and responsibility over the use of foreign aid, and thus responsibility over the payment of that loan. Several reasons have been put forth to explain the use of self-help in Japan's foreign aid policy. Ishikawa suggests that it reflects: 'the Japanese sense of atonement inherited from reparations to East Asian countries' (2005: 22). The official statement in the ODA White Paper argues that: 'regarding the support it has provided to East Asia, Japan has provided support to the recipient countries on a request-basis, so as not to force Japan's views on them' (Ministry of Foreign Affairs [MOFA] 2006: 11). Akira and Yasutami write that the:

> aid donor should not impose its plans on aid recipients but rather do its best to search out and discover nascent independent projects in a developing countries and then lend a deft and experienced helping hand to ensure that these small seeds can grow to fruition. This is what self-help efforts is all about.
>
> (1999: 147)

They go on to write that self-help emphasizes that: 'aid means helping those who help themselves, i.e., supporting the people of developing countries in their own efforts to improve their present circumstances, efforts that are their responsibility to work out for themselves' (Akira and Yasutami 1999: 152–3).

Yet, Japan also recognizes that self-help itself is not sufficient for an effective aid policy. While ownership is crucial to the overall lending strategy, the content of that strategy needs to incorporate the mobilization of private capital. According to Hino and Iimi: 'an objective of aid should be to assist the private sector development, and its effectiveness should be judged to a large extent by its impact on private investment' (2006: 16). A leading Japanese foreign aid scholar writes that: 'what is clear from the lessons learned from the East Asia model is that mutual trust was established when Japan provided aid without conditionalities and by continuing serious policy dialogue based on equal partnership' (Ishikawa 2005: 28).

Japanese foreign aid models as distinct from other donors

Japan has tried to carve out its own separate path of ODA policy. Two historic factors make Japan's aid and development vision distinctive from those of other donors. Japan is the only non-Western country with a history of successful industrialization and Japan's postwar decision to abandon military forces implies that ODA plays a special role in Japanese diplomacy. Japanese officials, moreover, have at times distanced themselves from the dominant policy prescriptions embedded in the Washington Consensus. The Washington Consensus has been widely criticized in Japan as being ineffective and unfair in its application to African countries. The typical structural adjustment program may be most effective in middle-income economies, but it is less effective in low-income economies with underdeveloped markets. An influential Japanese economist has suggested that in such economies there is a need to build appropriate institutions. These country-specific institutions should be based on a 'proper understanding of cultural values and social norms' (Hayami 2003: 56).

The fundamental principles of the Washington Consensus are well known. Some of them include fiscal discipline, competitive exchange rates, trade liberalization, openness to foreign direct investment, privatization, and deregulation (Williamson 1989). Japanese foreign aid policy clearly differentiates itself from many of these principles. Indeed, the Asian approach has been referred to as the Third Way between neoliberalism and bureaucratic interventionism. Jayasuriya and Rosser (2001) commented that the Third Way is based on three elements: governance, civil society and expanded social safety nets. Whereas neoliberalism posits the importance of reduced state activism, this new policy paradigm emphasizes the appropriate mixture of government and market functions. Hayami, who refers to this new paradigm as the post-Washington Consensus (PWC), equally argues for the acceptance of the critical role of institutions in the developing countries (2003: 57).

In this departure from the Washington Consensus framework, government officials in Japan also advanced poverty reduction, not as an immediate objective of development assistance, but as a consequence of economic growth. What this entails for Japanese aid agencies is a justification of a 'new paradigm which emphasized strengthening the voice and power of poor people (empowerment) and maximizing the initiative of aid-recipient communities (ownership) in the design of development assistance' (Hayami 2003: 57). Japan's ODA White Paper for 2006 asserts that poverty reduction should be carried out through economic growth. It highlights the experience of East Asia, where development was based on economic growth which ultimately contributed to poverty reduction (MOFA 2006: 13). Koizumi took the lead in this discussion in 2005 when he declared in a speech that: 'the Japanese government has been leading international discussion on African development by advocating the importance of ownership of Africa and partnership with the international community' (2005a: 1). The PWC offers a new identification of poverty reduction. The dominant Washington Consensus views poverty reduction as a consequence of economic growth, while the PWC argues for poverty reduction as an immediate objective of foreign aid (Hayami 2003: 57). This is a crucial difference since: 'if poverty reduction is considered an overarching immediate objective, non-market instruments may have to be used to redistribute market-produced income in favor of the poor' (Hayami 2003: 57). Japan's aid policy fits directly into this updated version of the Washington Consensus. In the Medium-Term Policy on ODA, the government stated that poverty reduction should not longer be a tangent of growth, but an immediate consequence of a growth strategy (MOFA 2005).

Additionally, the Japanese emphasis on self-help and ownership resonates within the PWC. As Hayami stated, this understanding of good governance and the proper role of public institutions is suggestive of the Japanese focus on self-help. Hayami highlights this view by asserting the 'need to incorporate country-specific institutions based on proper understanding of cultural values and social norms' of the recipient countries (2003: 56).

Japan's foreign aid strategy has developed into a distinctive path that is considered to present an alternative to the dominant lending position of the other donor countries. Japan's strategy draws extensively from its ties to its own historical development and from its emergence as a non-Western economic power. Several observers suggested that Japan's rise as an industrial power came about from its own decisions, separate from the rest of the world and, moreover, its development became a uniquely Asian path. Japanese officials and observers frequently point to Japan's domestic economic progress and the success that Japan has obtained in assisting its Asian neighbors as examples of the Asian economic strategy.

An influential Japanese economist has explored the distinctive vision of Japan's ODA strategy. Ohno has presented several important fissures between Japanese and other donor perspectives. First, self-help efforts and ownership are important traits in foreign aid. Aid is neither charity nor a moral obligation; rather the results are what matters most and aid effectiveness is seen to be based on establishing a stake in the process by the recipient country. Second, the public–private sector tension should be resolved so that government intervention is permitted and encouraged during the early stages of development (Ohno 2007)

Japan also has tried to break away from the dominant Washington Consensus framework in order to examine what Japan believes to be the essential barriers to development, i.e. lack of economic productivity. The president of Japan International Cooperation Agency (JICA) said in a 2007 speech that her agency will pay more attention to African development. She said that until now:

> Japan's assistance to Africa has followed the international consensus to focus on poverty reduction through promoting projects, covering education, healthcare, water, and agriculture.... While remaining active in these fields we are, however, beginning to look more and more to accelerating overall economic growth.
>
> (Ogata 2007: 2)

Even with the adoption of the UN Millennium Development Goals (MDGs) in which poverty reduction took center stage, the Japanese government's belief only was reinforced that 'economic growth is a strong driving force for poverty reduction and betterment of people's lives' (Sunaga 2004: 18).

Japan has come under pressure from the donor community to abandon its somewhat isolationist donor strategy. A 2005 study reported that it remains apart in terms of its self-help focus and its emphasis on infrastructural development, instead of social sector investment, to fight poverty (Court 2005: 16). A Japanese development institute's examination of Japan's ODA strategy highlights this pressure to realign itself with the rest of the donor community. Donor countries are promoting aid harmonization, which is meant to rationalize and coordinate the use of aid resources 'through focusing on shared goals and strategies and avoiding redundancies and duplications' (Sunaga 2004: 17). Japan doesn't oppose this harmonization mode, yet it supports it only when the strategy 'supports ownership of the development process by recipient developing countries and ensures a diversity of aid modalities' (2004: 17).

Lessons for Africa?

The Japanese emphasis on self-help, ownership and the economic objectives of production has become a comprehensive policy embedded in TICAD. An earlier official statement co-sponsored by Japanese and African delegates offered these objectives. First, the representatives agreed to pursue poverty reduction through economic growth; that is, only through industrial development and production can there be sufficient growth to reduce the poverty rate. A high-level Japanese diplomat said in 2005 that:

while East Asia has made great strides over the last 25 years – particularly between 1990 and 2001 – when there was an improvement in the economic situation of about 200 million people – Africa has not had such progress. Japan has been trying to replicate the 'East Asian miracle' in Africa'

(*Japan Times*, 2005)

In recent years, Japan's ODA moved towards social development and the government has supported the Development Strategy of the Development Assistance Committee (DAC) and the MDGs. However, according to one analyst, the continued reliance on the economic infrastructure is a:

recognition that even if resources are put into social development in an effort to reduce poverty – by building schools to improve education, for example – it will not reduce poverty unless there are jobs for educated people, and in order to create jobs, economic infrastructure needs to improve so that it will be easier to attract foreign investment.

(Yamauchi 2003: 87)

The Japanese government underscores this view in the 2006 ODA White Paper. Drawing on the economic success in East Asia, where Japan's foreign aid assisted in reducing the number of those living in absolute poverty, the government has argued that 'an increase in direct investment received and trade resulting from economic stabilization' played a role in poverty reduction (MOFA 2006: 3).

The government's stance on poverty reduction was embedded in a 2005 document: Japan's Medium-Term Policy on Official Development Assistance. In it, the government catches up with the other donors' position on human security, yet it does so with a twist. Human security involves poverty reduction and sustainable growth, as well as more social development issues. The report states that: 'as the experience of development in East Asia demonstrates, sustained economic growth is a necessary condition for reducing poverty. Therefore, poverty reduction should be pursued comprehensively through actions that address both the economic and social dimensions' (MOFA 2005: 5). Moreover, as taken from the East Asian strategy, African ownership is crucial for promoting growth that will lead to sustainable development.

And, finally, development strategies need to utilize private capital resources within the context of appropriate government incentives (TICAD-NEPAD, 2004). TICAD's self-help initiative received widespread support, including from former Prime Minister Koizumi, who said in 2005 that 'to achieve nation-building, the most critical thing is each nation's determination to bring about development through its own will and its own effort'. Moreover, he went on to say that: 'Japan through public and private sectors will provide assistance in applying to Africa the knowledge garnered through Asia's movement towards higher productivity' (Koizumi 2005b).

Unlike Japan's relationship with its Asian neighbors, Japan's African relationship is relatively unknown even within Japan. However, a cornerstone of Japan's foreign aid policy in Africa is the recognition of clear and crucial interests in facilitating Africa's development. This view of strong connections has also been supported by former Prime Minister Koizumi, when he said in a speech that 'as we fortify the partnership between Asian and Africa, it will be critical to share our experiences and our knowledge through dialogues between civilizations, between cultures, and between individuals' (2005b). The acknowledgment of shared concerns is, by definition, expressed by African officials. According to one report: 'at the TICAD conference, a number of African participants pointed to the attraction of the Asian development model as one of the factors drawing them towards closer ties with that continent' (Harsch 2004: 1). At this conference, a Kenyan official said that 'given our two continents, Africa and Asia, are faced with globalization in an era when pressures for liberalization are pretty strong, we in Africa have a lot to learn from the Asian experience' (Harsch 2004: 1).

Japan's foreign aid experience in East Asia has led to another set of lessons for its aid relationship to African countries. The combination of ownership, capital mobilization and long-term development has initiated an innovative yet controversial foreign aid strategy towards Africa. First, aid needs to complement sound macroeconomic policies and good governance. This objective does not waver from the traditional International Monetary Fund (IMF) financing approach. Japan's ODA White Paper explores this point by asserting that:

> because one key to sustainable economic growth is the private sector taking on a leading role, it is important to promote and stimulate the activities of the private sector, including trade and investment. However, there are a vast number of policy measures that the governments of developing countries must carry out in order to develop investment climate to attract the private sector.
>
> (MOFA 2006: 1)

Second, the focus on immediate social needs is understandable and appropriate given the dire living circumstances of so many Africans. However, according to one analysis, 'the balance has shifted too far in that direction at the expense of long term development objectives, including economic infrastructure.' (Hino and Iimi 2006: 17). The government's Medium-Term Policy statement continues this stance:

> Infrastructure is of fundamental importance in promoting private sector activities. Japan has actively supported the provision of economic and social infrastructure underpinning economic growth through such means as yen loans, and has played a particularly major role in providing the basis for economic growth mainly in the Asia region.
> (MOFA 2005: 10)

Third, in consideration of the self-help philosophy still embedded in Japanese aid policy, additional support of ownership is necessary. Aid projects that develop the social sector should complement long-term production goals, but all within the framework of ownership and accountability. What is being called for is greater accountability and full ownership. Thus, these authors argue that program aid should be given to 'local communities to fund social projects they select and implement, instead of supporting the central government budget' (Hino and Iimi 2006: 18).

Conclusion

Japan currently is struggling to maintain its self-perception as a unique donor to African countries while being pressured by other foreign donors to coordinate its policy with the other governments and funding agencies. Given these pressures, Japan is faced with numerous challenges as it seeks to expand its foreign aid presence in Africa. First, Japan uneasily recognizes the growing and influential existence of China on the continent. As China emerges as a powerful economic force, the pressure builds on Japan to respond in kind. Yet, Japanese policy is constrained by domestic political constraints and by its image as a democratic nation seeking to promote humanitarian efforts. Second, the current debate with Japanese ministries is how to increase the quantity of aid without incurring the displeasure of its citizens. For many people, Africa is essentially marginal to Japan's economic and political interests. At TICAD-IV, MOFA made a major announcement, boosting its ODA to Africa, since 'Japan's influence in the international community has diminished due to ODA cuts' (*Daily Yomiuri Online* 2008). Third, Japan will continue to focus its aid on infrastructural development although this is at odds with other donors who emphasize social sector development. Japan has been committed to this form of development for a very long time. Court observes that 'this is a big opportunity: it is an area where Japan has a comparative advantage and an issue to which it can bring its experience from East Asia' (2005: 27). Fourth, the government is in the process of reorganizing its aid agencies, which is meant to align the structure with the new aid agenda. In part, there is an expectation that its policy will support governance issues in African countries. Yet, Japan has shown reluctance to work with societal groups in order to create a better governing environment. Traditionally, Japan has shown most interest in the technical aspect of foreign aid or in expanding capacity rather than in building political governance. Finally, Japan continually is faced with questions regarding its experience with East Asian countries and how that experience can be applied to African cases. There are many important lessons from the so-called East Asian experience, but it is important to note that Japanese aid in Asia was effective because those governments were more developed and able to absorb the capital. Such development components may not exist to that degree in many African countries.

References

Adem, S. (2005) 'Is Japan's Cultural Experience Relevant for Africa's Development?', *African and Asian Studies* 4(4): 629–64.

Akira, N. and Yasutami, S. (1999) *The Economics of Development Assistance: Japan's ODA in a Symbiotic World*, Tokyo: LTCB International Library Foundation.

Court, J. (2005) 'Aid to Africa and the UK's "2005 Agenda": Perspectives of European Donors and Implications for Japan', in J. Court (ed.) *Final Report, JICA*, London: Overseas Development Institute, December.

Daily Yomiuri Online (2008) 'Social Security Cuts in Crosshairs', 10 March.

Grant, R. (1998) 'Japan: A Foreign Superpower', in R. Grant and J. Nijman (eds) *The Global Crisis in Foreign Aid*, Syracuse, NY: Syracuse University Press, 44–60.

Harsch, E. (2004) 'Africa and Asia Forge Stronger Alliances', *Africa Recovery* 18(1) April.

Hayami, Y. (2003) 'From the Washington Consensus to the Post-Washington Consensus', *Asian Development Review* 20(2): 40–65.

Hino, H. and Iimi, A. (2006) 'Aid as Catalyst for Private Investment: A Lesson from Asia to Africa', unpublished paper, February.

Hook, S. and Zhang, G. (1998) 'Japan's Aid Policy Since the Cold War', *Asian Survey* 38(1): 1051–66.

Inoguchi, T. (2004) 'The Evolving Dynamics of Japan's National Identity and Foreign Policy Role', in S. Katada, H. Maull and T. Inoguchi (eds) *Global Governance: Germany and Japan in the International System*, London: Ashgate, 31–49.

Inukai, I. (1995) 'Why Aid and Why Not? Japan and Sub-Saharan Africa', in B. Koppel and R. Orr, Jr (eds) *Japan's Foreign Aid*, Boulder, CO: Westview Press, 252–74.

Ishikawa, S. (2005) 'Supporting Growth and Poverty Reduction: Toward Mutual Learning from the British Model in Africa and the Japanese Model in East Asia', discussion paper no. 8, JBIC Discussion Paper Series, March.

Japan Times (2005) 'Development Vital to International Security, Says Japanese Envoy to UN', 12 February.

Jayasuriya, K. and Rosser, A. (2001) 'Economic Orthodoxy and the East Asian Crisis', *Third World Quarterly* 22(3): 381–96.

Kohama, H. (1998) 'A Review of Systemic Transition', in K. Ohno and I. Ohno (eds) *Japanese Views on Economic Development*. London: Routledge, 53–60.

Koizumi, J. (2005a) 'Japan's Policy for African Development', Message to Africa Towards G8 Summit, 6 July.

Koizumi, J. (2005b) 'Speech', 22 April.

Lehman, H. (2005) 'Japan's Foreign Aid Policy to Africa: An Assessment of Ten Years of the Tokyo International Conference on African Development', *Pacific Affairs* 78(3): 423–42.

Ministry of Foreign Affairs (MOFA) (2005) Japan's Medium-Term Policy on Official Development Assistance, Tokyo: Ministry of Foreign Affairs.

Ministry of Foreign Affairs (MOFA) (2006) Japan's Official Development Assistance White Paper, Tokyo: Ministry of Foreign Affairs.

Nafziger, E.W. (1995) 'Learning from the Japanese', Armonk, NY: M.E. Sharpe.

Nafziger, E.W. (2005) 'Meiji Japan as a Model for Africa's Economic Development', *African and Asian Studies* 4(4): 443–64.

Ogata, S. (2007) 'Japan's Development Assistance is at a Crossroads', Japan International Cooperation Agency, 22 June.

Ohno, I. (2007) 'Country-Specific Growth Support in East Asia and Africa: Japan's ODA to Vietnam and Ghana', discussion paper 16, GRIPS Development Forum, National Graduate Institute for Policy Studies.

Okita, S. (1980) *The Developing Economies and Japan*, Tokyo: University of Tokyo Press.

Preston, P.W. (2000) *Understanding Modern Japan*, London: SAGE.

Sunaga, K. (2004) 'The Reshaping of Japan's Official Development Assistance Charter', discussion paper on Development Assistance No. 3, Foundation for Advanced Studies on International Development (FASID). November.

TICAD-NEPAD (2004) 'Joint Policy Framework for the Promotion of Trade and Investment between Africa and Asia', Bandung, 2 November, online: http://www.mofa.go.jp/region/Africa/ticad/aatic/joint0411.pdf

Vestal, J. (1993) *Planning for Change: Industrial Policy and Japanese Economic Development, 1945–1990*, Oxford: Clarendon Press.

Williamson, J. (1989) 'What Washington Means by Policy Reform', in J. Williamson (ed.) *Latin American Readjustment: How Much has Happened*, Washington, DC: Institute for International Economics.

Yamauchi, M. (2003) 'Trends in Development Aid in Major Developed Countries', in T. Akiyama and M. Kondo (eds) *Global ODA Since the Monterrey Conference*, Tokyo: Foundation for Advances Studies on International Development (FASID).

4 The ambiguous Japan
Aid experience and the notion of self-help[1]

Motoki Takahashi

Kawabata Yasunari and Oe Kenzaburo, Japan's two Nobel Laureates in literature, presented Nobel lectures bearing contrasting titles. Kawabata's lecture entitled 'Japan, the Beautiful, and Myself', embodies perspectives of a unique kind of mysticism often found in Japanese thought, but adverse to those held by Oe in his lecture 'Japan, the Ambiguous, and Myself'. When Kawabata was awarded the Nobel Prize in 1968, the ambiguous Japan of the 1960s displayed attractive aspects of exoticism sparking the interest of Westerners. However, this ambiguity could no longer be maintained as it had been by 1994 when Oe received the Nobel Prize. Japan had become a great economic power in the 1990s and was urged to express itself more clearly in the international community. Yet, as Oe deplored, present-day Japan perpetuates ambiguities that are still incomprehensible to foreigners, including Westerners and even its Asian neighbors.

By 'ambiguity', or 'the ambiguous', Oe intended to shed light upon the multifaceted agonies of Japan. First, Japan has held a very ambivalent status due to its unique history. In terms of its economy, Japan developed rapidly after the Meiji Restoration in 1868, and was the only non-Western member of the Organisation for Economic Co-operation and Development (OECD) until Mexico and the Republic of Korea (i.e. South Korea) became members in the mid 1990s. Japan is an Asian country nonetheless, and the Japanese sometimes feel mentally or culturally torn between the East and West. Such ambivalence is one aspect of the ambiguity previously mentioned.

Another aspect of Japan's ambiguity is enveloped in its experience of invading and devastating Asian countries during World War II. Thus, postwar Japan commenced with reflection about its crimes related to its invasion and colonial rule throughout East Asia. On the other hand, as Japan recovered economically and achieved its status as an industrialized country, it began to have aspirations of leading Asia. Again, Japan has been torn between reflections on the past and its ambition to lead the region. These factors are evident in the discussion of Japan's particularity and its difficulty formulating its official development assistance (ODA) approach, and must be considered when discussing the characteristics of Japan's ODA.

This chapter, by taking the historical background into account, will discuss Japan's awkward position in the recent international aid trends of emphasizing poverty reduction, and harmonization and alignment of aid which mainly focus upon assistance for Africa. The chapter will also discuss new moves towards change in Japanese aid.

On the one hand, these new policies could overcome Japan's awkward position in international aid. To do so, the Japanese have to face the country's ambiguity and make an attempt to change it into something comprehensible for colleagues in the international aid community.

On the other hand, Japan's new policies, combined with its distinct historical background, may have the potential to propose an alternative to the current dominant trend in aid for Africa, which has apparently not been completely effective. This point will be discussed in Chapter 7.

The historical background and philosophy of Japan's aid

Background of Japan's ODA

Even among ahistoric social scientists, path dependency is now commonly used. Certainly, historical backgrounds must be recognized to truly understand the characteristics of contemporary social phenomena. In this section, four historical developments germane to the current characteristics of Japan's ODA are briefly introduced, namely, ethical debt to recipient countries; concentration on Asian countries; vertical sectionalism; and reliance on loans.

Ethical debt to main recipient countries

After starting the process of modernization or Westernization in 1868 (the so-called Meiji Restoration), under the slogan of building 'a rich country with a strong army', Japan achieved well-known and remarkable economic and military expansions. Building a strong army was, at first, for the purpose of protecting the country from an invasion by Western powers. The Japanese military and diplomatic policies gradually mutated to incorporate more aggressive features.

From the 1890s, when Japan militarily defeated the Ching dynasty, another slogan emerged and was popular among elites and intellectuals: escaping 'out' of Asia and entering 'into' Europe. This implied that Japan should escape from the status of being ruled to become a ruler. After colonizing

Korea in 1910 and successfully joining the victors of World War I, Japan strengthened its engagement against China. In the 1920s, though Japan's economic size was still far smaller than that of the British Empire or the United States, it became one of the great military powers. This circumstance finally gave birth to ultra-nationalism, which inflamed the country's aspiration to challenge the West's rule over Asia. This ultra-nationalism and early, yet apparently successful, invasion into China, including the near colonization of Manchuria paralyzed Japan's national leaders' rational thinking. This led the country to the catastrophic Pacific War. In the end, Japan became the first and only victim of a nuclear attack with the bombing of Hiroshima and Nagasaki.

The militarism before and during World War II drove Japan and its Asian neighbors into a nightmarish situation. Eventually, Japan was left devastated socio-economically after World War II. Asian countries, notably Korea and China, were pushed into socio-political turmoil, which still affects the two nations. The whole of East Asia, especially Korea and China, long maintained suspicion and mistrust toward Japan.

The memories of imperialism and defeat made postwar Japan abandon its ambition to challenge Western hegemony in political, militaristic and philosophical dimensions, which existed before 1945. In addition, Japan has been, in many spheres, hesitant to speak loudly of its own philosophies. Thus, it could be said that Japan had few agenda issues to propose to aid recipient countries, especially in the early postwar days.

As one condition of peace, postwar Japan was obligated to pay war reparations to its victim countries. Historically, the origin of Japan's ODA can be found in war reparations to the Asian countries it had invaded and colonized, which has yielded many implications for its ensuing history. After the peace agreement with the allied forces in 1951, Japan started to pay war reparations or sub-reparations[2] to Southeast Asian countries. At first in 1965, the Republic of Korea (South Korea) and Japan, after a thorny negotiation, agreed that both sides had abandoned economic claims to each other.[3] Subsequently both countries agreed that Japan would provide a substantial amount of financial assistance including ODA. The China–Japan agreement in 1978 likewise stipulated that if China abandoned its claim for war reparations, it would be entitled to receive ODA and other assistance.

Whether or not Japanese national leaders, as a whole, sincerely regretted and reflected upon their prior agenda of warfare, invasion and colonization, Japan had no choice but to be apologetic to its neighbors and/or at least restrain from overtly intervening in their domestic affairs in the early days while formally initiating its ODA. For almost 20 years after Japan entered the Colombo Plan in 1954 to become an ODA donor, Japan endured animosity from Southeast Asians. Latent hostilities against Japan are still prevalent in China and South Korea today. Under these circumstances, where Japan owed ethical debts, it would be diplomatically impossible for Japan to intervene in the domestic politics or policy issues of Asian recipients of its ODA.

This historical origin and the vicissitudes of ODA are very different from those of Western donor countries. As discussed later in this chapter and in Chapter 7, in recent years, especially since the 1990s, the Western donor countries have tended to be engaged both economically and politically in the domestic affairs of recipient countries. Japan is somewhat hesitant to act in a similar way to the West, despite the countries no doubt sharing basic common political values.

Japan's national pacifism is a product of its postwar defeat and devastation. On the basis of the new Constitution created after World War II, Japan adopted peace-oriented national principles including a policy of non-nuclearization and opposition to the arms trade. The Japanese government still has maintained the consensus that peace is a prerequisite for socio-economic prosperity, which at least tacitly influences Japan's later approach to ODA.

Concentration on Asian developing countries

The distribution of Japan's ODA in terms of recipients is relevant in this discussion. Partly a result of the fact that Japan's ODA originated from war reparations, Japan always has given priority to its Asian neighbors, though recipient countries have varied and continue to change (see Figures 4.1a and 4.1b).[4] While European donors did not provide aid to other countries in Europe until the end of the Cold War, and North American donors have provided most of their aid to non-North American recipients, Japanese ODA has largely been disbursed in the East Asian region.

While a major part of Japanese ODA is concentrated on its Asian neighbors, Japan has been gradually diversifying the direction of its aid. Poor countries, including those in Africa, are targets of this re-direction and essential diversification of aid. Recently, Japan has been increasing and intensifying its ODA to Africa. This re-direction was clearly pronounced at the fourth Tokyo International Conference on African Development (TICAD-IV) in 2008.

A final unique factor characterizing the history of Japan's ODA is that, until recently, Japan had not experienced serious aid weariness. Major recipients of Japanese ODA were Asian states with good economic performance that achieved high levels of human and economic development – another major difference distinguishing Japan from its Western counterparts. Therefore Japan continues to maintain quite orthodox approaches to aid.

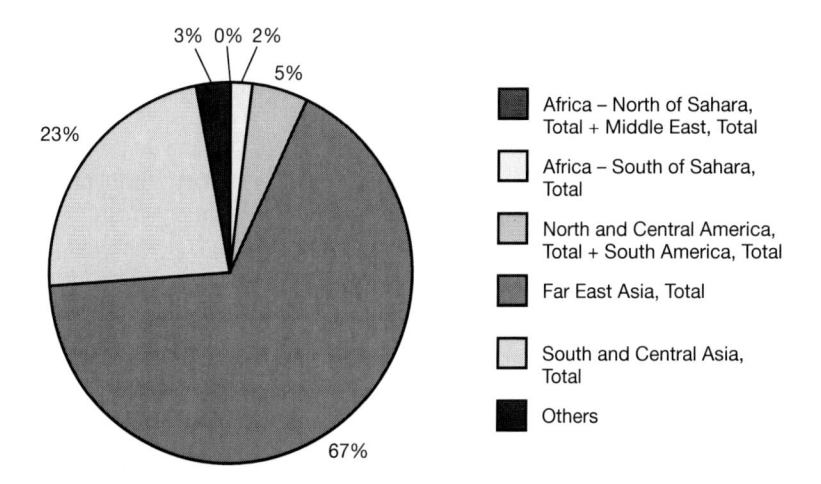

Figure 4.1a Regional distribution of Japan's ODA, net (1973)

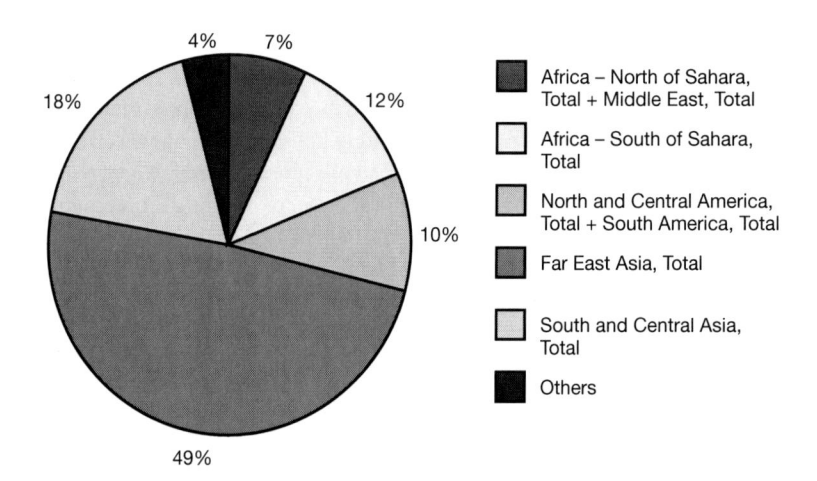

Figure 4.1b Regional distribution of Japan's ODA, net (2000)

For example, the modalities of Japanese ODA are still based upon the traditional idea of ODA as filling gaps in savings, foreign exchange and technology. Filling the fiscal or institutional gap has been largely outside Japan's scope until recently, and the country has been uncomfortable with Western donors' inclination to fill the latter two gaps. One of the reasons is that the fiscal and institutional gaps for Japan's main recipient countries might not be as serious as those for Western donors' recipients in Africa. Furthermore, a more important reason is that as fiscal and institutional gaps are closely related to the domestic affairs of a country, Japan and its recipients did not raise these issues. This point, however, has been changing slightly since Japan recently started engaging in institutional building in former-socialist Asian countries.

Vertical sectionalism

A third unique aspect of the origin of Japan's ODA is evident when examining the structure of its administration. The Japanese national government structure has been referred to as vertical sectionalism since the country initiated the modern cabinet system in 1885, as a pillar of the Japanese imperial administration. Under this system, each minister or ministry was directly responsible and accountable to the emperor, the supreme power, instead of the prime minister or the Diet (parliament). It is understood that this ministerial autonomy led to the rapid expansion of the military before World War II, and the uncontrollable invasion of the Asian continent by the army, as the Ministries of Army and Navy did not respect the leadership of civilian premiers. Today, the national administration is not yet free from the inertia of this initial framework, though the current constitution places the Diet, the legislature elected by the universal suffrage, as the supreme power instead of the emperor. While the strength of the prime minister's political leadership is evident, and the cabinet as a whole is legally responsible and accountable to the Diet, this does not necessarily imply that the national administration is unified as an entity.

Notably, decision-making and daily administrative exercises are conducted quite separately in different ministries. For example, while government officials are recruited through a merit-based, competitive examination, they are hired not by the whole government but by each ministry, and they formally belong to the latter from the beginning of their career to its end. Their loyalty, therefore, tends to be to each specific ministry rather than the government as a whole or the nation. Bills are mostly drafted separately by each ministry, prior to being proposed to the cabinet and then to the Diet. Before the latest administrative reform was undertaken in the 1990s, the description 'a country with ministries and without government' had been often cited, in a bit of caricature. Each individual ministry exerts strong controls over public agencies and specific projects separately. It means that vertical sectionalism, originating from the imperial government, still greatly influences the ODA decision-making and implementation process in Japan.

Financial sources and reliance on loans

A fourth aspect of Japanese ODA is that of financial sources. Due to the constraints on budgetary resources, Japan opted for reliance on the unique Fiscal Investment and Loan (FIL) system[5] to pay for a part of war reparations. This system was succeeded by ODA. It has largely relied on the yen-denominated development loan, financed partly by FIL. Reliance on FIL has enabled the country to provide a large amount of ODA in gross terms, and a major part of it has been directed to relatively economically profitable sectors such as infrastructure development. It has been well absorbed well by countries in Asia that have performed well economically. On the other hand, loans naturally have a limitation in assisting low-income countries whose capacity to repay is small. Nevertheless, Japan provided a substantial amount of development loans. Unpaid credits for low-income countries turned out to be a serious issue later on, especially the latter half of the 1990s (see Chapter 7). Having discussed the historical origins of the characteristics of Japan's ODA, it is beneficial to focus on changes in the philosophy of Japan's ODA.

Early mercantilism of Japan's ODA

In the early days of Japan's ODA, the country was criticized for providing what was considered mercantilist aid. This criticism cannot be overlooked, as it was not far from the truth. In the latter 1950s, the Ministry of International Trade and Industry (MITI) insisted that the promotion of national economic interests was a primary purpose of providing ODA. The ministry claimed in its White Paper that ODA was to be used to promote the activities of Japanese businesses in developing countries, for example, securing the markets of Japanese business exports, sources of materials for Japanese manufacturers, and ensuring a safe haven for Japanese foreign investment. The MITI's insistence was partly due to the low tax base of Japan, which had yet to recover from the devastation of the war. Also, part of Japanese ODA was tied to Japanese contractors and procurement of ODA loans became untied in response to criticisms of the OECD-DAC (Development Assistance Committee) countries. Therefore, it would be justifiable to characterize Japan's past ODA as mercantilist, to a certain extent. At the same time, it reflected the lack of a lofty philosophy for the ministry to claim the mercantilist position for aid.

While the MITI[6] itself had maintained its justification of ODA based upon national economic interests, its mercantilist nature was only one of many faces of Japanese ODA. Distribution of Japanese ODA to recipient countries was heavily influenced by the United States' strategic considerations. For example, in the 1970s and 1980s, Japan pumped massive amounts of money into the regions of Thailand bordering communist Indo-Chinese countries such as Laos and Cambodia. Additionally, Japan invested large sums of money in provinces in Pakistan bordering Afghanistan after the USSR's invasion of the latter country in 1980. The United States also pressured Japan to expand its aid to Africa in the 1980s. US pressure in these areas was partly based upon its Cold War strategy.

On the other hand, as time went by, Japan increasingly came to have its own motivations for facilitating the evolution of its multifaceted ODA. Japan expanded its ODA to countries of lesser strategic importance and concern, and/or countries in which Japan had less economic interest, such as those in Africa. This may be attributed, in part, to Japan's willingness to diversify its diplomatic relationships in the 1970s, a decade in which at least two major events – anti-Japanese riots in Southeast Asian countries and the oil crisis – changed the Japanese diplomatic orientation. The psychological shock caused by anti-Japan campaigns in Bangkok and Jakarta in 1974 led Japanese national leaders to seek new friends in the international community in order to avoid further isolation (see Chapter 7). The 1970s oil shock forced Japan to diversify its sources of energy. Japan naturally extended its perspective to the west, beyond the traditional recipients of ODA. Interestingly, Middle East countries, which were providing a major part of oil, were not selected as major ODA recipients. Rather, Africa was chosen as the second largest partner, though far smaller than the whole of Asia, to receive Japan's ODA (see Figures 4.1a and 4.1b). This may suggest that wholly economic considerations did not necessarily predominate over diplomatic ones, at least in terms of the distribution of ODA amounts.

Also in the 1970s, Japan, at least formally, downgraded its crude orientation of promoting business interests by means of ODA and instead adopted a philosophy of humanitarian consideration and recognition of global interdependence as a motivation for ODA.

Expansion of Japan's ODA and the emergence of self-help supports

In the 1980s, Japan became the strongest foreign exchange earner in the world, and its balance of payments (BoP) surpluses caused frustration among countries with BoP deficits, especially the US, the largest customer for Japanese exports. At the same time, especially after 1985, the Japanese yen appreciated immensely, and the size of Japanese ODA became so great that Japan's status among bilateral ODA donors began to rise, at least in terms of volume (see Figure 4.2). Those changes – until the end of the 1980s – were based upon Japan's internal logic and motivated by and reactive to external situations. Until recently, reactivity, as Calder (1988) has indicated, has been a conspicuous characteristic of Japanese foreign policy making, as elaborated in Chapter 7.

Regardless of the motivation behind enlarging foreign aid, Japan became the largest bilateral donor in the beginning of the 1990s and maintained that position through the latter half of the decade. This voluminous expansion instilled euphoria for Japanese policy makers, especially bureaucrats and their advisors in academia. They even began to talk of the 'success story' of Japan's ODA. Partly on the basis of this confidence and partly in response to criticism that Japan lacked a clear aid philosophy, the Japanese government wrote its first ODA Charter in 1992. In this document the government declared four pillars of the Japanese philosophy: (1) humanitarian concern, (2) recognition of global interdependence, (3) support for 'self-help' and (4) environmental conservation. These rather incommensurable ideas can be classified into three categories. The first two pillars had been recognized since the 1970s and were used to justify the provision of Japanese aid. The third referenced how Japanese aid should be conducted. The fourth pillar was concerned with one, but not all, of the purposes of aid.

Although it was never elaborated in the ODA Charter or in any other documents, the third philosophical pillar of 'support for self-help' can be said to reflect the core uniqueness of the Japanese way of thinking and experiences.

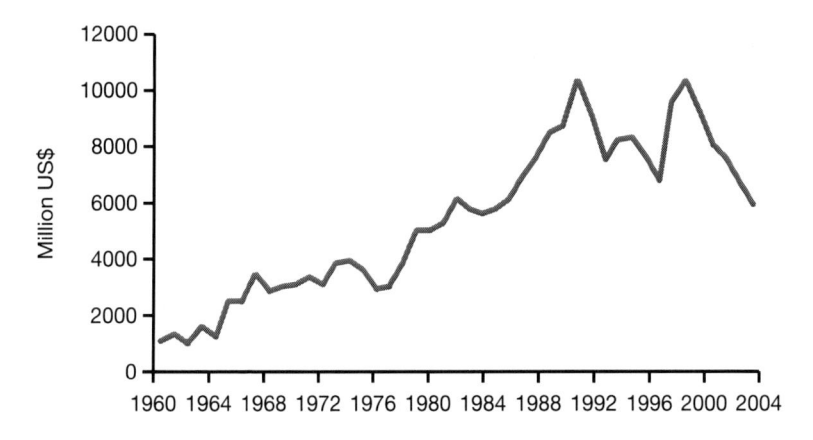

Figure 4.2 Changes in Japan's ODA net (constant prices 2004)

The origin of Japan's tendency to emphasize self-help can be traced back to pre-modern days. As is well known, Confucianism stressed behavioral discipline and continuous efforts to improve the self. In that sense, Confucianism is quite individualistic, though the meaning of 'individualistic' here is very different from its meaning in the West. This tendency had been strengthened by the long-lasting rule of the samurai in the Edo era, whose way of thinking, along with that of Confucianism, was largely concerned with the elite principles of behavior. Common people gradually shared certain essential aspects of these ideas – industriousness, disciplined behavior, frugality – as well, through the end of the Edo era. The popular belief among urban commoners of *Sekimon-shingaku*[7] was the typical example. An important point here is that some sense of working ethics and diligence were already shared by certain parts of the society including both samurai elites and commoners before the modernization process started.

As to the formulation of the idea of 'self-help', what might be more important than the historical origin in the pre-Meiji (or pre-modern) era is the country's vicissitudes in modern days. Samuel Smiles' *Self-Help* (n.d.) was a bestseller among ambitious youth in Meiji Japan and, as a result, self-help became a key concept of the Meiji era. The emphasis on self-help in modern days, however, is more closely related to the Confucianist philosophical tradition mentioned above. Japan experienced historically rapid economic growth from the end of the 19th century until World War I. It succeeded in introducing modern sciences and technologies, and corporate and banking systems, which fostered industrialization. Throughout these processes Japan came to embrace the idea of meritocracy. After the devastation of World War II, the country recovered very dramatically and again entered the ranks of the great powers, this time on the basis of economic capacity rather than military forces. In 1964, Japan joined the OECD as the first non-Western member country.

Until the mid 1970s, Japan had enjoyed the economic benefits of the Golden Age of global capitalism. The economy grew at a high rate through the introduction and development of new industrial technologies. Due to increasing productivity and the expanding foreign earnings of the manufacturing sector, Japan found its way out of the oil crises in the 1970s, with the least damage among developed countries. During those days, the country also benefitted from a timely demographic change in which the ratio of dependent population to the labor force became small. In the 1980s, Japan was gratified to be known as 'Japan is No. 1'. As mentioned above, other East Asian countries were also recording good performances in socio-economic development during this period.

From the 1980s to the first half of the 1990s, Japanese bureaucrats and their academic advisors were very psychologically revitalized. In this atmosphere, some of them began to think that the notion of self-help, though ambiguous even in their mind, was proven by Japan's postwar economic success. The process of steady and rapid development of East Asian countries further reinforced their view of self-help. The amounts of ODA were small relative to the economic size of the East Asian recipients, meaning a low level of aid dependency, and much of their large domestic savings were invested in human development, especially basic education. Health indicators improved as well, and the population policy was so successful that most of the East Asian nations seem to have experienced a demographic transition and have even begun to be anxious about aging. Their socio-economic performance came to be praised and recognized, perhaps rather exaggerated, as the 'East Asian miracle'. Above all, East Asian recipients had not needed any substantial intervention in their domestic affairs, by Japan or anyone else, to achieve high performances.

This process yielded important inferences that are now rooted in Japanese thinking: that development and/or the reduction of poverty is possible through the building of meritocratic systems in administration and business organizations, and by self-help efforts of stakeholders in each society; and that ODA can promote the development of recipients without undermining their self-reliance. In sum, the self-help efforts postulated in the ODA Charter, in a sense, reflected Japanese bureaucrats' confidence in what had been achieved in their own country and neighboring states.

In retrospect, one could say they were *over*-confident. It is certain that MITI had some designs for cooperation, notably for the development of Southeast Asian countries, combining trade, private investment and ODA. The Ministry of Agriculture, Forestry and Fisheries (MAFF), with a certain determination, cooperated in working for a 'Green Revolution' in some Asian countries, either directly or through the Asian Development Bank (ADB) and other international organizations. Therefore, the said confidence in Japan's contribution to the development of industries in neighboring countries could be, to a limited extent, justified. One should recall, however, that Japan had been maintaining its hesitant stance on intervening in the domestic affairs of recipient countries. Therefore, the East Asian successes could never be attributed to the Japanese bureaucrats' sensible guidance of their counterparts in policy designs. The East Asian successes were not due to the Japanese government's success but, rather, to that of the recipient countries. In this context, Asian self-help is a reflection of Japan's hesitation to intervene, which originated from the ethical debts.

At any rate, Japanese elites' confidence was strongly reflected in the agenda of the Tokyo International Conferences on African Development, the first of which was held in 1993, the same year as the World Bank's publication *East Asian Miracle*. The TICAD resolutions heralded the 'transfer of Asian experience to Africa' and '[assisting] Asia–Africa or South–South cooperation'.

In the latter half of the 1990s, however, Japan faced a persistent economic recession and the gradually increasing burden of an aging society. Asian neighbors suffered from deep economic crises, especially after 1997. The international sentiment commending the East Asian miracle dwindled and Japanese leaders, including politicians, bureaucrats, business leaders and academics, substantially lost confidence. They maintained only limited interest in the once fashionable concept of 'transferring experiences of Japan and East Asia'. Also, due to fiscal difficulties, in part, the Japanese government had to cut its ODA budget (see Figure 4.2). These challenges created a new environment in which the philosophical base of Japan's ODA began to drift once again.

The new ODA philosophy and new waves from within

A positive by-product of the largely reactive expansion of the Japanese ODA budget was the diversification of its activities and strengthening of its efforts to cultivate expertise in ODA and development cooperation. Japan's ODA extended into many low-income African countries and into the sphere of social development, even into unconventional activities including refugee protection and peace-building in the 1990s. Partly induced by aspirations to obtain a permanent seat on the United Nations (UN) Security Council, Japan has continued to sponsor the Tokyo International Conferences on African Development every five years, beginning in 1993, then in 1998, 2003 and, most recently, 2008.

In the early 1990s, the Japan International Cooperation Agency (JICA) became one of the most popular would-be employers for new graduates from universities. Several postgraduate schools were established by the Ministry of Education in the early 1990s specifically to cultivate expertise in international development cooperation, which was regarded as in short supply compared to the increasingly gigantic amounts of ODA.

In 2003, a new idea took hold in JICA in that the president of the newly reorganized JICA should be a preeminent expert in international cooperation rather than a former diplomat from Ministry of Foreign Affairs (MOFA) who was not necessarily familiar with ODA. Among the rank and file of the JICA officials, Mrs. Ogata was the most popular candidate for the presidential seat.[8] The rank and filers' wish materialized as Mrs Ogata became the first president of the corporatized JICA. After retiring from her successful career as the United Nations High Commissioner for Refugees (UNHCR) in 2001, she chaired the UN Commission for Human Security with Professor Amartya Sen, a Nobel Laureate in economics. In 2003, Mrs

Ogata was nominated as a member of the UN High-level Panel to Study Global Security Threats, which consists of influential figures from all over the world. She was granted the Order of Cultural Merit, the most distinguished medal awarded by the government of Japan. Mrs Ogata Sadako, assuming the post of president of JICA in 2004, is a champion of this new trend in Japanese ODA. Before her, the post of the JICA's president was occupied by former top MOFA officials. It is an aspect of ministerial control over ODA, though the MOFA's control over the JICA was and still is far from overcoming the vertical sectionalism caused by the engagement of various ministries.

Mrs Ogata's appointment as the JICA president symbolized the rising status and strengthened sense of identity of ODA in general and the JICA in particular. One might say that there had developed professionalism among aid officials. On the other hand, one should also note that public opinion regarding MOFA was very adverse at that time. In particular, *Amakudari* (literally, 'descending from heaven'), meaning appointment of retired officials from central ministries to other organizations, faced public opposition. Above all, the MOFA's power in the government was deeply weakened in the early 2000s due to a series of scandals. Therefore, the ministry could not have overtly resisted the whole government's decision to exclude ex-MOFA officials as potential JICA presidents.

In 2003, having accumulated experience of extended ODA and responding to the changing environment, the government established a new ODA Charter, in which human security is considered as the supreme aim of Japanese ODA. If compared with the 1992 Charter, which just mentioned environmental conservation as a purpose of aid, the concept of human security can be far more rich and profound and, therefore, can be a philosophical basis for more effective aid activities for Japan. Moreover, in the new Charter, self-help efforts are again repeatedly emphasized.

In the 2000s, the said new trend has been followed by moves to increase, both absolutely and relatively, the amount of the ODA budget going towards African countries. In accordance with the decision on debt forgiveness for Heavily Indebted Poor Countries (HIPCs, the large majority of which are in Africa) at the G8 summit in Cologne in 1999, Japan has cancelled debt for low-income African countries. At the same time, however, Japan was the least supportive of the enhanced HIPCs debt relief scheme decided at Cologne among the G8. Representatives of Japan, one of the largest official creditors of the HIPCs and Africa, claimed that debt cancellation could cause a moral hazard (thus undermining self-help efforts) on the side of recipients and undermine their creditworthiness. No matter how legitimate this claim was, Japan was already isolated at the G8 summit in Birmingham in 1998. This was caused by the agreement of Germany, another large creditor of the HIPCs, with Britain led by International Development Minister Clare Short (Short 2004: 81–5). Japan had no option but to reluctantly follow the majority's decision on the enhanced HIPCs debt relief scheme. In this context, one could say that Japan's wholesale debt cancellation was illustrative of it being a reactive state. Reluctance, compounded with vertical sectionalism, caused problems in actions related to debt cancellation and general budgetary supports in African recipient countries, which are elaborated in Chapter 7.

Later, in response to the resolution at the Gleneagles summit in 2005 to double aid to Africa, Japan tried to fulfill the requirement set by the resolution by means of including the amount of debt cancellation. In 2008, Japan again promised that it would double the amount of aid to Africa by 2012 at the TICAD-IV. This will involve a landslide shift in the regional allocation of Japan's ODA from Asia to Africa.

Japan's 'deviation' from the reform trend of aid

The new reform trend and country development coordination

Despite the occurrence of new waves from inside the aid circle in the 2000s, Japan has faced difficulty in adjusting its aid systems to the new international trend of aid reforms. One of the most difficult tasks for Japan is development coordination, which influences donors' concrete activities in the field of each recipient country (hereafter I call this 'country development coordination'). This section focuses on the level of development coordination, namely, the coordination among stakeholders in a specific recipient country, including the recipient government and donors.[9]

The strong international trend toward country development coordination has been driven mainly by several northwest European donors (the so-called Like-Minded Group [LMG]). This author is of the view that the strong reformist trend has resulted in the formulation of a particular international regime concerned with aid for Africa. This so-called Poverty Reduction Aid Regime was supported by common understandings among the northwestern European donors, international organizations such as the World Bank and progressive administrators in African countries. Under this regime, Japan became alienated from the mainstream. Also, the regime has been associated with a new mode of international dependency of poor recipient countries on donors. These issues are discussed in detail in Chapter 7.

In comparison to other donors, the Japanese stance is different from practices of most donors under the Poverty Reduction Aid Regime. Among the so-called reformist donor countries, the Department for International Development (DfID) of the UK has been the most vocal in putting forward a typical framework of ideas and practices related to country development coordination. Its understanding of the country development coordination framework can be summarized as follows (DfID 2001: 81–3):

a   Development assistance by all donors must be provided in accordance with development strategies formulated by recipient governments at both national and sectoral levels. National development strategies are called in most cases, especially in the early 2000s, Poverty Reduction Strategies (PRS). Development programs are usually formulated at the sectoral level.
b   The amount of aid given by all donors must be aligned with the recipient governments' annual budgets and fiscal frameworks in the medium term. This enables the budgeting agency in each country to capture flows of all aid resources and make them predictable in the long term.
c   Based on (a) and (b), resources must be allocated selectively to the most important sectors. The northwest European donors have conventionally placed high importance on direct poverty reduction, such as basic education and primary healthcare.
d   The foreign aid of all donors must be harmonized under the same procedures. Donors are recommended to contribute funds to sectoral common pools or, more desirably, directly to the recipient governments' coffers in the form of General Budgetary Supports (GBS).
e   As a prerequisite for financial support for common pools or government budgets, macroeconomic management of the recipient governments must be stable, and their financing and procurement systems must be transparent and accountable. The process of donor budgetary assistance should also improve these systems.

There seem to be several justifications behind these ideas. In Africa, each donor has tended to give aid separately, according to their own aims and motives, with their own modalities and procedures, and without alignment with the recipients' national or sectoral development strategies and annual budgets. Because of these mis-coordinations, the recipient governments have to bear great managerial (transaction) costs. This often causes *aid proliferation*, discussed later, which undermines the ownership of recipient governments. It is believed that general budgetary supports can reduce transaction costs, as they are, by definition, supposed to be part of the governments' development strategies and are the most flexible modality of aid.

These mainstream donors have strong concerns about the negative effect of fungibility. This effect, in short, means that giving aid could make financial spaces for the recipient government by freeing a part of the recipient's resources, and the freed financial resources could be used for non-developmental purposes. This could result in overall development outcomes which are lower than donors' expectations, even though the monies for each project had been spent as planned.

The mainstream donors are of the opinion that GBS, if combined with practices of monitoring, tracking and evaluating recipient countries' fiscal expenditures and outcomes, could help limit the negative effect of fungibility. Through contributing directly to GBS and joint practices of monitoring and evaluation, the mainstream donors have strengthened their intervention in the domestic policies and fiscal management of recipient countries. Simply speaking, GBS might be an effective instrument for donors' leverage to improve the overall outcome of aid. One can easily imagine that this kind of approach could bring about a mode of dependency of recipients on donors. This point is discussed in detail in Chapter 7.

Only under certain conditions, however, can the positive effects of direct budgetary support be materialized. Not even the UK's DfID considers that GBS can function in every developing country. As stated in (5) above, direct budgetary support must be limited to those recipient governments with sound macroeconomic policies, especially fiscal management and appropriate development strategies.

Japan's traditional and unique approach to development assistance

The above-mentioned DfID approach to development coordination is now widely supported. The World Bank and International Monetary Fund (IMF) may have some minor technical differences due to their organizational mandates, but they now share the same basic conceptions of development coordination with the DfID and others.[10] This approach has greatly influenced the formation of development coordination and the reform of aid to poor countries in Africa and elsewhere. I will call this the reformist approach, which is a pillar of the Poverty Reduction Aid Regime.

Such a reformist approach to development coordination is not compatible with Japan's traditional approach to ODA. The following five characteristics of Japan's aid are important to understand in exploring the differences:

1   Japan's aid is basically project-based and its activities are largely isolated from others. Therefore, Japan's aid projects are self-contained even though much attention is now being paid to macroeconomic policies and the budgets of recipient countries.
2   Most Japanese assistance is not aid in cash but aid in kind. In other words, it is based on the physical transfer of materials and personnel, namely the construction of facilities, the donation of equipment, the

use of technical experts and the training of people invited from developing countries. Japan has rarely provided cash directly to recipient governments, largely because the government officials have believed that aid in kind could prevent the dubious use of aid resources, though this belief has a substantial limitation as elaborated in Chapter 7.

3   Closely related to (2), Japan's aid has not been aimed at covering recurrent expenditures, e.g. government officials' salaries, operational costs or maintenance costs for facilities. This stance is utterly different from the common pool contributions or the GBS, which aim to support both recurrent and capital budgets indiscriminately.

4   Strictly based on the single-year budgeting principle stipulated in its Constitution, Japan does not give recipient governments any projection of concrete financial assistance beyond the current year. Therefore, it is hard for recipient governments to incorporate the details of Japan's assistance into the budget for the next year and into medium-term fiscal programs. This point is opposed to the said recommendation by the DfID for better predictability.

5   Although there are some exceptions, Japan's grant aid and technical assistance are basically tied to Japanese contractors.

There have been some remarkable efforts within Japan to reform its conventional position, as will be discussed below. Yet these efforts are still patchy and partial and, overall, progress has been slow. The reasons for this are related to the historical background and characteristics of Japan's ODA mentioned under the section 'The Historical Philosophy and Background of Japan's Aid'. I will elaborate by comparing it with the UK's ODA.

East and West: differences in stances over aid reforms

Background of the reformist trend in aid approaches

To build mutually beneficial relationships between Japan and Western donors, an understanding of each other's different backgrounds is essential. It is difficult for Japan to understand what motivates and facilitates the Western donors' current approach of development coordination. I can cite at least five factors behind the rapid progress of reformist development coordination in some poor countries in recent years: the rise of the New Public Management and outcome-oriented resource management in donor countries themselves; aid policy coordination among Europeans, partly facilitated by the European countries' political and economic integration; the enhanced HIPCs initiative – heavy debt crises and debt forgiveness for poor countries; democratization in Africa and other poor countries, which has created a more accommodative environment for accountable and transparent governance; and consciousness of failures of aid, including the disappointing results of the Structural Adjustment Programs (SAPs).

In addition, it is important to mention the historical discussion of the need for program aid and aid coordination in the West. This dates back to as early as the 1960s, when Chenery and Strout stressed the importance of all donors agreeing on the direction of macroeconomic policy and coordinating their aid activities. They also indicated the need for a program approach tightly coupled with macroeconomic policy conditions, such as increased savings (Chenery and Strout 1966: 726–8). Their idea materialized with the SAPs in the 1980s, when other donors gathered to support the World Bank and IMF in implementing neoliberal reform policies.

Failures of aid and the crisis of the 1990s

Among the above-listed origins of contemporary development coordination, failures of aid are most relevant to the comparison of Japan and the reformist donors. The important issue here is that Western donors, especially Europeans, have experienced aid fatigue. In the case of Japan, such aid weariness did not take place or has been far less serious due to the good performance of major recipients in Asia. This difference is due mainly to the conditions of the respective recipient countries. The Europeans' major recipients are Sub-Saharan African countries, while Japan concentrated substantial amounts of ODA on East Asian recipients (see Table 4.1).

From the 1970s to the 1990s, Africa was in a state of grave stagnation. To save Africa, the international community had tried numerous aid approaches, from assistance for government-led industrialization through a focus on basic human needs (BHN) to the SAPs. In the 1980s, every effort turned out to be largely futile. This triggered a strong suspicion about the effectiveness of foreign aid itself, which only underscored aid fatigue.

At this point one can refer to the argument on development assistance by Hyden (1983). Hyden discussed problems of aid for Africa in the early 1980s in a comprehensive manner. He witnessed many difficulties and failures of development activities in Africa. He criticized both donors and recipients for their failures, which made the aid dependencies deeper and undermined aid effectiveness for the recipients.

According to Hyden, there were four major failures on the donors' side. First, their activities were based on an inappropriate development plan that ignored the context in Africa. Second, foreign aid had grown so much that it covered the majority of the recipient countries' development (capital) budget. In order to make effective use of the aid, recipient countries needed to provide sufficient recurrent expenditure. However, because of

Table 4.1 Top five aid recipient countries of Japan and the UK

Ranking	1970	1980	1990	1999*
Japan				
1	Indonesia	Indonesia	Indonesia	Indonesia
2	Korea	Bangladesh	China	China
3	Pakistan	Thailand	Philippines	Thailand
4	India	Burma	Thailand	Vietnam
5	Philippines	Egypt	Bangladesh	India
UK				
1	India	India	Bangladesh	India
2	Kenya	Bangladesh	India	Bangladesh
3	Nigeria	Zimbabwe	Kenya	Uganda
4	Pakistan	Sri Lanka	Pakistan	Ghana
5	West Indies (British territory)	Tanzania	Malawi	Tanzania

Source: Economic Cooperation Bureau, Ministry of Foreign Affairs, Japan (various years).

Note
*Latest data available.

the imbalance between the development budget and the recurrent expenditure, development assistance did not have much effect. On the other hand, if aid covered recurrent expenditures in order to avoid this situation, the aid dependency of recipient countries would become even higher and would result in donors' deeper intervention in the domestic policies of the recipient countries.

Third, there were heavy procedural burdens on recipient countries who received aid from numerous donors. Fourth, there were inconsistencies in the standards and/or specifications of equipment and facilities because donors with tied aid implemented their development assistance in a mutually exclusive manner without coordination among themselves (Hyden 1983: 165–7, 172–9).[11]

Among Hyden's criticisms of donors mentioned above, the last three were not the failures of individual donors, but were caused inadvertently and indicated the need for some kind of coordination among stakeholders. In their comprehensive research on the effectiveness of foreign aid initiated in the 1980s, Cassen and associates analyzed the problems that occurred when numerous donors initiated activities without coordination. In Tanzania and elsewhere, there were numerous ongoing aid projects, and competition among donors and projects was observed. There was competition over talented local personnel and the recurrent budget of the recipient government. Compared to the resources available for using and absorbing foreign aid in the recipient countries, too much foreign aid was flowing in and it was too fragmented. Cassen *et al.* called this situation 'project proliferation' and called for coordination among donors in order to solve it (1994: 174–90). Hyden and Cassen both observed the same situation of aid proliferation or aid bombardment.

As careful readers might already have noticed, the reformist approach to development coordination promoted by the DfID corresponds to the aid failures or aid proliferation that Hyden and Cassen described. An origin of development coordination can be found in the suspicions and criticisms of aid to Africa that rose in the midst of the period of aid weariness in the 1980s.

Although aid failures in Africa were already visible in the 1980s, a large amount of aid still flowed into poor countries and was accelerated by the strategic considerations of the Cold War. This only aggravated the situation of aid proliferation. As a result of the sudden decline of the strategic importance of aid to poor countries after the Cold War, however, many criticisms and suspicions about aid rose to the surface, especially when donor governments found themselves in acute fiscal situations. In the 1990s, many developed countries like the US started to restrain and even reduce their ODA budget. As the effectiveness and *raison d'être* of aid were heavily debated, the situation became grave to the extent that the US Congress seriously discussed the abolition of the US Agency for International Development (USAID).

The OECD-DAC enunciated a 'New Development Strategy'[12] in 1996. This was a declaration to restructure aid by the donors themselves in response to the aid crisis. The document stressed the importance of various kinds of partnership and ownership in aid recipient countries, yet there were largely different perceptions of these two concepts between the Western donors and Japan (see Chapter 7). Irrespective of these different perceptions, in the New Development Strategy, aid coordination among donors was mentioned as an important part of partnership. It aimed at obtaining clear results towards development through aid. Many goals included in the Millennium Development Goals (MDGs; such as reducing the ratio of the people living under the poverty line by half by 2015) were previously declared in this document. The New Development Strategy demonstrated the bilateral donors' determination to restore the *raison d'être* of development assistance by raising the development effectiveness of aid through partnership among donors. Behind this determination, there were grave reflections on past situations of aid wherein fragmented projects were implemented in a mutually delinked manner. On the other hand, the document's emphasis on the responsibility of developing countries implied that donors regarded many governments in poor countries as excessively dependent on aid and not equipped with a strong will for development.

In the latter half of the 1990s, development coordination was established at the sectoral level, such as basic education and primary healthcare. Since the publication of its monumental research paper on Sector Investment Programs (SIPs; Harrold *et al.* 1995), the World Bank strengthened its support for development coordination in each sector. Development coordination among donors, which had been limited to the macro-level (i.e. support for the SAPs) in the 1980s was then extended down to the sectoral level. This implies that aid coordination started to regulate the specific activities of donors.

The anatomy of Japan's deviation from the reformist trend

As confirmed above, Japan is faced with difficulties in taking part in development coordination. This is because Japan's conventional approach to foreign aid is not in accordance with what development coordination requires. To understand the reasons for Japan's different stance in the international community, one needs to refer to the background of Japan's ODA mentioned under the section 'The Historical Background and Philosophy of Japan's Aid'. In relation to Japan's deviation from the reformist trend, the following points are important:

- hesitation to intervene in the domestic affairs of recipient countries in part because of ethical debt to some of the recipients;
- fragmented decision-making about ODA due to the vertical sectionalism;
- the reactive nature of Japanese foreign policy, as inherited from the past;
- suffering little aid fatigue.

Nowadays, it is not unusual for Western donors to express their opinions about domestic policies in the recipient countries. In some cases, they require that a recipient country change its domestic policies in exchange for aid. These proactive attitudes have been gradually reinforced through trial and error to overcome the failures of development and aid.

For Japan, however, with grave ethical debts to Asian countries, aid relations with its main recipients in Asia were thoroughly different. In this sense, Japanese aid activities have tended to be limited to purely economic or technical matters that appear remote from politics and comprehensive policy issues. It naturally follows that Japan repeatedly emphasized the request-based approach for aid projects because Tokyo at least would like to pretend to avoid involvement in the decision-making process of aid recipient countries.

General Budgetary Supports, a new modality, is the fruit of the new thinking regarding aid and is associated with the donors' deep engagement in the domestic affairs of recipient countries. The Japanese ODA machinery in developing countries often lacks readiness in this kind of engagement. Problems and prospects concerned with the differences in involvement in domestic affairs of recipient countries are discussed in Chapter 7.

In the latter half of the 1990s, vertical sectionalism was the most important problem to be tackled during the process of Japan's administrative reforms. One solution was for the Cabinet Office to absorb various inter-ministerial coordinating functions. However, the effort has not been very successful and thus inter-ministerial coordination in ODA decision making is not yet functioning well. The Ministry of Finance, responsible for supervising ODA loans implemented by the Japan Bank for International Cooperation (JBIC), should have been faced with difficulties in the SAPs and the serious implications of the HIPCs debt cancellation. Officials in the ministry and the JBIC at least had a chance to understand them, but their understanding was not transferred to other entities including the MOFA and the JICA. This knowledge gap caused a delay in Japan's ability to deal with the trends of development coordination and aid reforms. The MOFA and JICA officials were forced to deal with the aftermath of debt forgiveness and the process of formulating and implementing fiscal and administrative reforms under the PRS, while lacking a sufficient understanding of the needs of development coordination. I discuss this issue again in more detail in Chapter 7.

As explained above, the main recipients of Japan's aid traditionally have been the neighboring countries in Asia. Table 4.1 presents a list of Japan and the UK's top five aid recipient countries in the past. I use the example of the UK as a representative of the reformist donors. Compared to Japan, with many recipients being neighboring countries in East Asia, the majority of the UK's aid recipients were the former colonized countries of South Asia and Africa were.[13] This geographical distinction has greatly influenced Japan's approach to aid reforms and its perception of development coordination.

While Japan's location is in the same area as its main aid recipients, a unique experience among donor countries, European donors find the majority of their recipients in Africa. A host of Japanese advanced technologies, such as irrigated agriculture, were applicable in recipient countries in East Asia because these technologies were invented in a common environment characterized by high population density and monsoon weather. This is an advantage for Japanese–East Asian aid relations compared to European–African aid relations. In order to assist with the technological progression of Africa's agriculture, for example, Europeans or other donors have to develop new technologies, appropriate for a tropical climate and completely different from their own technology.

Second, Japan was the only industrialized nation and thus almost the only ODA donor in East Asia for a long time. This situation is very different from that of European donors. In Europe, all neighboring countries are aid donors and thus are always exerting peer pressure on each other, which is a basis for the Poverty Reduction Aid Regime. Among European donors, languages and cultures are so close that they can quite easily communicate their ideas with each other. Scandinavian countries in particular, which share similar policies for both domestic and foreign affairs, have built very close collaborative relations around activities in developing countries.[14] Development coordination was initiated partly on the basis of such commonalities among European donors.

Japan, however, is practically the only donor in East Asia, except for South Korea, which set about giving aid in recent years, and China, which strategically supported other developing countries according to its own logic. There was little competition, collaboration or close exchange of ideas among them. But one should note that China has been drastically strengthening its economic cooperation with Africa to satisfy its rapidly expanding demands for resources, which raises concerns among traditional donors including Japan. It could be said that the government of Japan was very recently motivated to counter this Chinese move in Africa by successfully holding the TICAD-IV and promising to double aid for Africa. Therefore, competition between Japan and China in aid for Africa might be under way, but their relationship is far from a collaborative effort that could mutually improve each other's aid activities in terms of effectiveness for development of recipients. The concept of aid, which Japanese people in general have had for a long time, is that apart from contributions to multilateral organizations, Japan supports each recipient country on a one-to-one basis.[15] On the field of aid activities in East Asian countries, only the World Bank and the Asian Development Bank are contributing amounts comparable to Japan.

Third, the fact that most of Japan's main recipient countries were East Asian countries means that they were the 'successful' countries in development. They experienced high levels of economic growth. Table 4.2 shows the average growth rates of GDP per capita over 34 years in the main countries receiving Japanese and UK aid (the same countries shown in Table 4.1), as well as their gross national income per capita in 1999 and, as an indicator of aid dependency, the ratio of the amount of the aid received to gross capital formation (investment). As a benchmark, a weighted average (a simple average in the case of aid dependency) of each index is also shown. From Table 4.2, one can see that Japan's aid recipient countries are richer, and their past growth rates are higher than those of UK.[16]

One can easily imagine that this disparity in the economic performances of major recipient countries made a substantial difference in the two donors' perception of development assistance in the early 2000s. The UK, whose major recipient countries are poor and stagnant, came to doubt many aspects of conventional aid. Japan, on the other hand, has been optimistic about aid because its major recipient countries, like South Korea, China and Thailand, have remarkably reduced poverty.

East Asian countries have achieved high performances as already described. In addition, one could say that East Asian governments originally had greater administrative and fiscal management capacities (or simply aid-absorbing capacities) than those in, for instance, Africa. Aid-absorbing capacities in East Asian countries have been enhanced year after year as the bases of governments' domestic revenue expand due to high economic growth and industrial development. Overall, Japan was endowed with an advantageous environment in making individual aid activities successful and the provision of development loans possible. This gave rise to Japan's peculiar inclination to perceive the main role of foreign aid as supporting industrial development through large-scale loans for infrastructure construction projects.

At the same time, however, the high economic growth and widening domestic revenue bases in East Asia increasingly mitigated their aid dependencies. As can be seen from Table 4.2, there is a significant disparity in aid dependency between the main recipient countries of Japan and the UK.

Japan, which dealt with countries whose economic performances were strong, had no reason to suffer the serious aid fatigue that European countries did. Being free from aid fatigue, Japan did not notice the full-scale aid failures, which motivated the aid reforms and commitment to development coordination.

Japan's new initiatives and the hurdles ahead

New initiatives

Despite the above-mentioned limitations, Japan has undertaken several initiatives to catch up with the reformist trend toward development coordination. There have been several positive efforts towards strengthening coordination.

The 2003 ODA Charter first stressed collaboration with other actors in the international community. In addition, the formulation of Japan's own Country Assistance Programs is required to overcome modality fragmentation. The Japanese government has created Country Assistance Programs for Ethiopia, Ghana, Tanzania, Senegal and Madagascar. In all the cases, the

Table 4.2 Aid dependency ratio in main recipient countries of Japan and the UK

	GNI per capita (US$, 1999)	GDP growth of top five aid recipient countries (%, 1965–99)	Aid dependency ratio (aid/gross capital formation, %, 2000)
Japan			
Korea	8,490	6.6	-0.2
China	780	6.4	0.4
Thailand	2,010	5.1	2.3
Indonesia	600	4.8	6.3
Egypt	1,380	3.3	5.6
Sri Lanka	820	3.0	6.1
Pakistan	470	2.7	7.3
India	440	2.4	1.4
Myanmar	..	1.5	..
Bangladesh	370	1.3	10.8
Philippines	1,050	0.9	4.3
Vietnam	370	..	19.8
Average	1,188.5	3.3	5.8
UK			
Sri Lanka	820	3.0	6.1
Pakistan	470	2.7	7.3
Uganda	320	2.5	73.0
India	440	2.4	1.4
Bangladesh	370	1.3	10.8
Kenya	360	1.2	39.0
Zimbabwe	530	0.9	19.1
Malawi	180	0.6	200.5
Nigeria	260	0.0	2.0
Ghana	400	-0.7	49.5
Tanzania	260	..	65.3
Average	377.2	1.3	43.1

Source: From World Bank (2001, 2002).

Notes
Data for West Indies (British territory) are not available.
GNI per capita and GDP growth per capita use the weighted average by population in 1999, and the aid dependency ratio uses an arithmetic average. For calculating the weighted average of these two, China and India, whose populations are particularly large, are excluded.

core issue is how to align Japan's own program with the recipients' PRSs and other policy frameworks. In March 2005, Japan agreed to the Paris Declaration on Aid Harmonization.

Also, various initiatives toward development coordination in individual poor recipient countries have been undertaken. In 2004, Japan started to contribute grant money directly to Tanzania's Poverty Reduction Budget Support (PRBS). This is the very first case of 'pure' general budgetary support, though it was provided on a trial (or exceptional) basis. From 2005 onwards, subsequent contributions were approved. In 2004, the government decided to co-finance the World Bank's Poverty Reduction Support Credit (PRSC) to Vietnam, which was the first direct budgetary support loan. In 2007, a co-financed PRSC with the World Bank also was provided to Tanzania.

In Tanzania, Japan has been taking the position of lead donor in the formulation and implementation of the agricultural sector-wide approaches (SWAP). It has been involved in the formulation of the PRS and the various SWAPs and/or in the monitoring and evaluation process in various countries.

At a glance, these recent developments look remarkable. In substance, however, the Japanese commitment to development coordination is patchy as it has largely relied on certain individuals' pioneering efforts rather than officially organized initiatives.

Japan's challenges in development coordination

Frankly speaking, the Japanese government has been unable to consolidate a firm organizational will to cope with development coordination. Inside Japan's ODA administration, there are several huge perception gaps between: the younger generation, who are exposed to new thinking, including the New Public Management, and the older generation, which is constrained by traditional thoughts; people working in Asia and those working in Africa; people working in recipient nations and officials in the headquarters in Tokyo; officials working with multilateral development banks and those in charge of bilateral aid (or simply the MOF and MOFA as mentioned previously); and perhaps the JICA people and the MOFA officials. Unification of the JICA and JBIC in October 2008 provides a good chance to overcome these various perception gaps but one cannot be very optimistic as the unification does not solve problems on the side of central ministries.

These new initiatives have materialized largely due to efforts by the younger generation, working in or closely connected to recipient countries. This demonstrates that Japan has fortunately succeeded in hiring people keen to correct the low effectiveness of aid to Africa. These people have an advanced understanding of the objectives of reformist donors.

An internal consensus within the ODA bureaucracy could be constructed by overcoming these perception gaps. But more importantly, every effort must be made to form a national consensus about the new direction of aid. In the conventional public administration literature, the concept of coordination implies more restrictions on the independence of each organization.[17] This affects the mentality of Japanese politicians, government officials and even certain parts of civil society, who sometimes display signs of serious paranoia about 'aid with a Japanese face'. However shallow this thinking is, it is the political reality that Japan faces.

To convince leaders and the civil society, the Japanese government should clarify the merits and risks of the new direction in aid reform, including general budgetary supports. As the country is delayed in engaging in budgetary supports, Japan is not familiar with discussing them, especially their risks. Japan must acquire mastery in monitoring and evaluating systems of budgetary supports in order to be accountable to taxpayers.

In Japan there is fear that budgetary supports may risk the perpetuation of aid dependency, as GBS can help the recipient government reduce the cumbersome costs of tax collection.[18] Even though Japanese civil society might not say 'no' to the budgetary support, they might demand that the exit strategies from dependency on aid in general, and GBS in particular, be clarified. Also, Japanese officials watching aid relations are concerned with development coordination and sometimes feel that the power balance between donors and recipients is asymmetric. In the case of budgetary supports, they worry that strong leverage by donors may discourage ownership on the side of recipients, as donors could substantially instruct the way of development and reforms. This concern is the main issue of Chapter 7.

Here is the critical point, where the optimal way of combining Japan's notions of self-help and engagement in development coordination and budgetary supports is to be devised. One could propose that in exchange for budgetary supports, the recipient government intensifies efforts to broaden its own revenue and tax base, consolidate a foundation for national self-help efforts and thereby reduce its aid dependency. To reinforce moral and intellectual supports, in this context, would fit Japan's past approach and way of thinking.

Also, Japan's modest stance in aid relations is not necessarily negative. Ishikawa, the most preeminent development thinker in Japan, stressed that Japan's peculiar advantage was to place priority on interactive policy dialogues. Treating recipients as an equal partner and sharing development issues with them can help recipients restore their self-esteem, which can be a starting point on the road to self-reliant development (Ishikawa 2005: 17–23). This author is of the opinion that Japan has a historical reason to treat aid recipients equally, which is based on its ethical debt to neighbors. If

Japan really could have built equal, interactive relations, which could enable policy dialogues by respecting the recipients' initiative and self-esteem as Ishikawa claimed, that is a positive legacy of its history and should be enriched for the future.

One hopes that the above way of thinking, though differences in practice are not very concrete but rather subtle, could add a new perspective to current development coordination in low-income countries.

Prospects for the future

The concept of human security, newly adopted in the 2003 ODA Charter, contains great potential to enrich Japanese cooperation for the future and it could guide concrete engagement in those countries where people face serious human insecurity. In emphasizing human security, however, it seems the Japanese themselves have not yet cleared up the ambiguity associated with this multi-dimensional concept. It must be further clarified and articulated. Japan should design the new aid modality and frameworks to put this new concept into practice in Africa, where almost all the cases of human insecurity can be found and often of the most serious sort.

The so-called 'Sen and Ogata Report' indicates that 'empowerment' and 'protection' must be guaranteed for human security to materialize. Japanese officials would tend to emphasize the importance of empowerment rather than protection. This tendency seems to be rooted in the notion of self-help, but Japan needs to overcome numerous hurdles to apply its own ideas and approaches, largely formulated through its experiences with Asian countries, to the different environments of new recipients, especially those in Africa.

Emphasizing human security would logically lead Japan to engage in working for not only freedom from want but also freedom from fear. The pacifist Constitution all the more justifies Japan's well-designed involvement in this aspect. But, again, Japan's readiness is far from being complete, though Japan has been participating in various peace-building initiatives, including activities in Cambodia, Mozambique and, controversially, in Iraq, and is preparing for participation in operations in Darfur, Sudan.

In this context, Japan should learn from European countries' engagement in various peace conciliation activities. What Japan most requires is communicative capabilities and profound knowledge with which the Europeans are endowed. One can be a little optimistic as Japan's aid administration has been able to acquire professionally trained people. As a matter of fact, these younger professionals have been leading the way in terms of improved communication with the international reformist trend and reforming Japan's ODA itself. They are probably the only ones who can propose a complementary or alternative approach to African development if the Western reformist aid trend still falls short in getting Africa out of poverty.

Needless to say, for the purpose of sustainable, self-reliant development, a recipient country should find a way to break the self-perpetuating mechanism of poverty. On the basis of Japan's aid experience, crystallized in the notion of self-help, Japan tends to believe the promotion of domestic productive forces is essential to do so, no matter what the roles of the government and aid. Neither Japan nor any other country, however, has been able to discover the 'right' way in low-income countries, such as those in Africa where conditions are very different from Japan's traditional main aid recipients. This is one of the most formidable challenges to putting the notion of self-help into practice.

Conclusion: from ambiguity to bridging

Japan has been a lonely Asian donor, and is very different from northwest European countries, for example the UK – another island nation situated at the other side of the Eurasian continent. This is certainly a disadvantage, but it could be a unique asset at the same time. The fact is that Japan, as the only non-Western DAC donor, has many things in common with its aid recipients in East Asia, and has a unique experience that other donors do not have. Furthermore, Japan is in a unique position as an Asian country and at the same time an ODA donor. Because of ethical debts in its history, Japan has been seemingly able to interact with its neighboring countries more equally. As emphasized in the old version of Japan's ODA Charter, the basic approach of Japan's aid has been supporting self-help. What Japan has learned, from its own development experience and from its experience supporting East Asia, is that development cannot be realized without self-reliant endeavors by recipient societies. It is very simple, but is a truth that donors have difficulty respecting.

Western donors might suppose themselves the paragons of aid recipient countries because their societies are considered the core of modern civilization itself. If such thinking is expressed too straightforwardly, it might strain donor–recipient relations. Here is where Japan can play a role. The modest Japanese stance in intervention in recipients' domestic affairs can have important implications. Japan can induce the Westerners to respect African countries' self-esteem, as Ishiwawa suggested. Towards this purpose, Japan should strengthen its intellectual and communication capabilities.

It is regrettable that Japan has neglected to describe, analyze, and elaborate upon the lessons learned from its own experience and from its relations with East Asia. The key for Japan, in contributing to development partnerships, is to draw from the experiences of self-help in Japan and East Asia, to digest them, and to dispatch them as comprehensible messages to other donors and poor countries in Africa and other regions. This last point is very important. Past arguments for the transfer of experience from Japan and East Asia largely neglected the vast differences with Africa. A transfer of experience would be meaningless if African states have no interest in absorbing it. In this context, one could learn from past European struggles.

Japan is still a country with ambiguity, not only for foreigners but also for itself. Yet, this ambiguity could be changed into an advantage as it implies that Japan can bridge both sides in the following areas: the East and West and hopefully traditional donors and emerging donors. This role has become all the more important in the age of China's rise as a great provider of aid for Africa, which is very different from that of the Western donors and thus causing the latter to worry.

To deepen this discussion, one needs to look more carefully at actual situations of aid relations between Africa and donor countries formulated in relation to the new interventionist trends of Western countries. I focus on the issues of the rationale, characteristics and limitations of the Poverty Reduction Aid Regime, which is underpinned by the Western trends, and the prospects for Africa's self-reliant development corresponding to Japan's philosophy of self-help efforts in Chapter 7, yet taking into account the African situation.

Notes

1 A part of this work is an abridged version of the author's paper originally published as 'Development Coordination: A Challenge to Japan's Development Assistance for Poor Countries' (GRIPS Development Forum Discussion Paper No. 12). The author is very grateful to the Development Forum at the National Graduate Institute for Policy Studies for permitting its use. After the publication of the discussion paper, the author revised the paper and submitted it to the Christian Michelson Institute. The author's presentation at the 'Seminar on Asian Models for Aid: Is There a Non-Western Approach to Development Assistance?', held in Oslo, Norway on 5 December 2006, was based upon the submitted paper. The author deeply appreciates the Royal Ministry of Foreign Affairs of Norway, the Norwegian Agency for International Development, and the Christian Michelson Institute for providing an opportunity to present the paper and exchange views on development and aid with distinguished participants from Asia and Europe. The author also would like to thank Bryan Norrington, a research student at Kobe University, for helping edit the paper.
2 Sub-reparations are compensation to be paid to non-allied force countries.
3 Japan, in the beginning of negotiations, maintained that it would be entitled to claim compensation for properties which were left behind in South Korea at the end of World War II. Eventually Japan abandoned this claim, while South Korea also gave up its claim for reparations for loss and damages under Japanese colonial rule.

4 Data were extracted from the following URL on 1 December 2006: http://www.oecd.org/document/33/0,2340,en_2649_34447_36661793_1_1_1_1,00.html
5 The Fiscal Investment and Loan system of Japan is a gigantic governmental financing system largely financed by funds raised through postal savings, government insurance and pensions. In 2005, it was decided under the Koizumi administration that postal savings would be privatized and the system would be downsized.
6 The MITI changed its name to the Ministry of Economy, Trade, and Industry during the administrative reform in the 1990s.
7 *Sekimon-shingaku* was a teaching for commoners initiated by Ishida Baigan, a philosopher in the Edo era or in the 18th century. Ishida combined ideas in Buddhism and Confucianism with Shinto and aimed at mental training of common people rather than Samurai rulers.
8 The JICA Labor Union took a poll from its members about who should be the next president. Mrs Ogata was by far in the most popular.
9 Aid coordination rather than development coordination may be the more common terminology. In the current movement for coordination in recipient countries, recipient governments are expected to take a leadership role, i.e. to sit in the driver's seat (Harrold *et al.* 1995). Also, private stakeholders in recipient countries are encouraged to participate in the process. Furthermore, the supreme aim of the coordination in question is not only to change aid relations and thereby improve aid effectiveness, but also to achieve higher development and poverty reduction goals through better institutional settings of recipient governments.
10 The World Bank and the IMF are officially supposed to request and assist governments of poor developing countries to formulate the Poverty Reduction Strategy Papers (PRSPs) and related fiscal programs such as the Medium-Term Expenditure Frameworks (MTEF) as conditions for debt forgiveness under the HIPCs scheme and for the provision of fresh financial assistance.
11 Moreover, according to Hyden, there were problems on the side of the recipient countries in Africa. African society was pre-capitalistic, a situation in which the influence of each social group was based on ethnicity, blood relations and/or birth place. The mechanisms of capitalism and the market were immature, and governments' capacity was feeble. As these governments could not allocate resources, including foreign aid, according to economic rationality, the large amount of aid for the BHN encouraged societies to demand various kinds of undue resource distribution from their governments (Hyden 1983: 165–7).
12 The official title is 'Shaping the 21st Century: The Contribution of Development Co-operation'.
13 The ranking is based on the amount received. In this case, it is necessary to consider the possibility that the target countries with large domestic economies have higher positions. One must be especially careful in the case of Japan, because its main recipient countries for loan aid are not always the same as those for grant aid and technical cooperation.
14 Moreover, among Western donors, there are many cases in which foreign aid experts create strong personal networks through frequent exchanges. In a situation in which intra-European Union international recruitment by public organizations is encouraged, such personal networks among donors may become stronger, not weaker.
15 Japanese communication with other donors tends to rely on official channels, such as the OECD-DAC, various committees of the World Bank and the IMF, regular consultations with organizations of every kind or donors' meetings in the

field in developing countries. It should be noted that Japan has a deep relationship with the US, as exemplified by the US–Japan Common Agenda, but it cannot be denied that there exist large gaps between their commitments to the Agenda. It is desirable to make use of such official channels more effectively and also to make unofficial networks among persons concerned about aid more intimate.

16 There is a 2 percent difference between the main aid target countries of Japan and those of the UK in terms of the weighted average of growth rates of GDP per capita. This difference means that two countries with the same GDP per capita will diverge dramatically over the long run; one of them will have twice the level of GDP per capita than the other after 34 years.

17 See Rogers et al. (1982). According to the authors of the book, 'coordination' among different administrative organizations is to be distinguished from 'cooperation'. Development coordination in a recipient country is to be regarded as 'coordination' in the sense that it requires the recipient government and donors to compromise their own 'interests,' and it also requires concrete changes in the way aid activities are carried out.

18 This concern is shared not only by Japanese but also Western thinkers, such as Hyden (1983).

References

Calder, K. (1988) 'Japanese Foreign Economic Policy Formation: Explaining the Reactive State', *World Politics* 40: 517–41.

Cassen, R. and Associates. (1994) *Does Aid Work?*, 2nd edn, Oxford: Oxford University Press.

Chenery, H.B. and Strout, A.M. (1966) 'Foreign Assistance and Economic Development', *American Economic Review* 56: 679–733.

Department for International Development (DfID) (2001) *Departmental Report 2001*. London: Department for International Development.

Harrold, P. and Associates (1995) *The Broad Sector Approach to Investment Lending*, World Bank Discussion Papers 302, Africa Technical Department Series, Washington, DC: World Bank.

Hyden, G. (1983) *No Shortcuts to Progress: African Development Management in Perspective*. Berkeley: University of California Press.

Ishikawa, S. (2005) 'Supporting Growth and Poverty Reduction: Mutual Learning from the British Model in Africa and the Japanese Model in East Asia', Discussion Paper 12, GRIPS Development Forum, Tokyo: National Graduate Institute for Policy Studies.

Rogers, D.L., Whetton, D.A. and Associates (1982) *Interorganizational Coordination: Theory, Research, and Implementation*. Des Moines: Iowa State University Press.

Short, C. (2004) *An Honourable Deception? New Labour, Iraq, and the Misuse of Power*. London: Simon & Schuster.

Smiles, S. (n.d.) *Self-Help: With Illustrations of Character, Conduct, and Perseverance*. New York: W.L. Allison.

World Bank (2001) *World Development Indicators*. Washington, DC: World Bank.

World Bank (2002) *World Development Indicators*. Washington, DC: World Bank.

5 International debt management
Japan's policy towards Africa

Junichi Hasegawa

In this chapter, I would like to discuss the debt issue of Africa and the major policies of donors, in particular Japan, in terms of managing their debt. I will then analyze the changes and result of such policies. Countries with heavy debt are categorized as Heavily Indebted Poor Countries (HIPCs), and the total number of HIPCs is 41 as of October 2007, of which 33 countries are in Sub-Saharan Africa.

Debt overhang

Why does a country have debt? What happens when a country has excessive debt? In this section, I will look for the answers to these questions. Throughout the chapter, 'debt' refers to public debt that a government borrows or, with its guarantee, public organizations and state enterprises borrow from a foreign government, enterprise or international organization.

In many developing countries, investment funds tend to be short term, though they have viable investment opportunity, because their saving level in the macroeconomy tends to be low. When investments with good returns exist yet investment funds run short, borrowing from outside the country to realize the investment would lead to a higher income. The majority of external debt is the result of such borrowing.

Borrowings and investments are repeated over and over again, but in such a process of repetition, debt repayment becomes difficult if the return on investments turns out to be lower than expected. This is the debt issue. The reasons that a return on investment may be low are external shock, political instability and many others. A typical example of an external shock is a fall in the prices of commodities traded in the international market. If the price of a commodity falls, the producer of the commodity loses, and it will become difficult to repay if the investment was made with borrowed money. If the period of low commodity price is prolonged, the amount of repayment will exceed the return on the investment, and eventually repayment becomes difficult. In terms of a country, national income will never increase if the amount of repayment exceeds the growth of income. The anticipation that the growth of income will reduce poverty, and that people will become better off, does not come true, but rather the shadow of debt depresses the lives of the citizens. This is the case of collapsed growth due to excessive debt.

Now I will look into the reason for such collapses. Following conventional economic wisdom, I assume that a developing country is faced with the condition when capital is scarce but investment opportunities are abundant. As a result, borrowing from outside the country for investment would accelerate economic growth inside the country. Furthermore, if the return on investment is larger than the interest from borrowing, then additional investments by borrowing outside could accelerate growth. Investments that used to be overlooked because of lack of funds now become realized, and employment, production and income increase. If this continues, poverty should fall. In early development economics, large-scale investment through external borrowing was indispensable for economic development.[1]

At some point with continued borrowing, the return on additional investments starts to decrease to become lower than the borrowing interest rate. Good opportunities for investment decrease as a result of the exploitation of all the investments that had a higher return. Once no more investments have higher returns than the interest rate, no investments will be made, and no borrowing will take place. Growth is maximized if borrowing is expanded until the return on investment is less than the borrowing interest rate. It is obvious that growth is much larger for some, compared to those that never borrow. If this situation is sustained for a long period, national incomes will increase, and poverty will be reduced.

On the contrary, if borrowing is extended when the return on investment is lower than the interest rate, then repayment will be greater than the increase in production from the marginal investment, and thus repayment will become difficult. Even spending all the returns from previous investment for repayment will not be sufficient for the execution of debt, and debt will continue to be unpaid.

Excessive debt that remains unpaid for a long time is called debt overhang, and is distinguished from sound debt. If a country has debt overhang, it will be forced to shift its usage of financial resources to repay the debt, and its growth will slow down. If growth slows down and income ceases to grow, repayment of debt becomes more difficult. In that instance, not only is poverty not reduced, but debt overhang also raises the risk of increasing poverty, and thus it creates the issue of heavy debt.

One may assume that heavy debt issues can be avoided if borrowing decisions are cautiously made. If one can measure the return on investment so accurately that no borrowing is made with interest being greater than the return on investment, then heavy debt issues might be avoided entirely. However, in the real world, one frequently observes that the production or services produced by investment is far below what was expected and thus the return on the investment is negative.

Infrastructure construction is one of the major areas that governments invest in with external borrowing. In infrastructure construction, such as highways, ports, power stations, transmission lines, telephone networks, irrigation systems, water supply, the environment and others, the priorities of investment are decided and designed in accordance with a country's needs. In the power and communication sector, demand forecasts can be made with relatively high accuracy, and hence the return on investment is not far from the calculated level at the time of investment preparation. On the other hand, in the highway and port sector, demand forecasts tend to run a high risk of deviation from the calculations. In many cases, it is highly difficult to measure the rate of return accurately, and it is not an easy task to control borrowing so that returns on investments do not go below the interest rate.

What makes the situation worse is political vulnerability. For example, it is essential to have consistency between two infrastructure projects; if a power station is constructed where a transmission line does not exist; the benefit of the power station is zero. If the capacity to handle cargo at a port is expanded, unless there is also a capacity to transport between the port and places of consumption, then again the benefit is zero. Under vulnerable political situations, plans for infrastructure are often forced to change or are abandoned in the worst case scenario. If the plan is changed or abandoned, consistency among projects is not maintained, and the expected return on infrastructure investment can be significantly reduced. Or, if a government does not understand the conditions surrounding a project, this may decrease the project's profitability. Or, if a dictatorial president insists on constructing a highway to where he was born, then the actual transportation demand is obviously being ignored. Therefore, such an investment would provide much less of a return.

In many cases, accurate measures of return on investments are not easy to obtain, particularly in vulnerable political situations. Vulnerable governments have a higher risk of debt overhang when investments are made with external borrowing. Inferior governance, such as practices of corruption, would increase the risk of debt overhang.

Donors' policy response to the debt issue

Heavy debt in developing countries tends to slow down efforts to reduce poverty, and is a serious issue for international society. When a developing country has debt overhang, what are the policy responses of the donor countries? There are two types of policies that depend on whether debt overhang is a temporary phenomenon or a catastrophic one. If debt overhang was created as a result of the falling prices of primary products, measures to postpone and/or reschedule the repayment schedule temporarily would be sufficient to avoid serious heavy debt issues. After rescheduling, when the prices of primary products return to their previous levels, the developing country can once again repay its debt. If heavy debt issues are serious and developing countries cannot complete repayment, it is a crisis and rescheduling repayments is not a sufficient measure. Drastic measures are necessary. In short, as a donor, if debt overhang is caused by temporary reasons, then rescheduling is sufficient, but if the debt issue is critical, then debt cancellation would be required.

As a result of rescheduling or the cancellation of debt, the external credibility of the developing country declines. However, a decline in credibility caused by rescheduling can be recovered relatively soon, but debt cancellation causes critical damages to external credibility and this takes much more time to recover from. Continuous investment is necessary for a developing country to sustain growth and to reduce poverty. But a developing country has a very low level of saving, and this makes the country rely on the international capital market for borrowing. Therefore, a decline in external credibility creates serious impediments. The capacity to borrow from the external market is small for a developing country, but it becomes much smaller when external credibility declines. Overall, this means that a developing country can solve its debt overhang if it gets debt cancellation, but, in turn, it loses the possibility of future growth. Since donors' concern is poverty reduction, they do not favor the loss of the possibility of growth. Consequently donors prefer to manage debt issues with debt rescheduling, and only when the debt is so serious that it cannot be solved by rescheduling do donors choose debt cancellation.

In 1987, G7 countries (now G8) announced the Venice Declaration, in which they agreed to prolong the rescheduling period for poor countries. Before 1987, the term of rescheduling was 10 years postponement including 5 years of grace, but the Declaration extended it to 20 years. By this time, debt cancellation was not yet an agreed upon policy option. In 1988, the G7 countries accepted debt cancellation for the first time in history. This initiative was named the Toronto Terms, and it proposed that 33 percent of total debt be cancelled. Since then, the ratio of cancellation to total debt has been expanded. In 1991, at the London Summit the ratio was expanded to 50 percent (New Toronto Terms). In 1994, it was expanded to 67 percent (Naples Terms), in 1996, up to 80 percent (Lyon Terms), and in 1999, up to 90~100 percent (Cologne Terms; see Table 5.1). This shows that debt issues are very serious and have always been one of the major topics on the agenda in consecutive summit meetings. There is no other topic which is treated in this way except environmental issues. After only ten years from when debt cancellation was first introduced, G7 countries decided to accept 100 percent cancellation. In the early days, the application of debt cancellation was restricted to a small number of countries, but later the number of countries was expanded greatly. In the Toronto Terms, the number of countries was 20, but the Cologne Terms proposed 41 countries as HIPCs, which potentially made them eligible for debt cancellation, and 26 countries have already received cancellation.[2]

Throughout the period that the ratio of cancellation increased, Japan maintained the same policy without change. Japan asserted that it opposed debt cancellation because it triggers a decline in credibility and is a moral hazard, and that, instead, it would alleviate debt issues by extending new finance. This policy was called the 'New Money Approach', and Japan continued with this same policy even after the Paris Club started debt cancellation.

Japan is a member of the Paris Club, and when the members of the Paris Club agreed to debt cancellation, Japan needed to follow it. In order to meet both its own 'New Money Approach' and the decision of the Paris Club on debt cancellation, Japan invented special measures. Japan gave new money to debt countries of the same amount as repayment, and let the countries maintain the repayments in accordance with the original lending schedule. By this measure, Japan intended to provide the same effect as debt cancellation to the developing countries, while preserving the developing countries' external credibility.

Where does Japan's policy come from?

There are three reasons for Japan's 'New Money Approach': concerns about the impact of cancellation, Japan's own experiences, and a technical reason to do with the Financial Act of Japan.

The first reason is Japan's concerns about the decline of external credibility as a result of debt cancellation. When a country has excessive debt, this is already damaging to its external credibility. If the country is given debt cancellation, it will lose external credibility to a maximum extent. Losing credibility means that the country is never able to borrow from the international market. A developing country needs to borrow since it is on the way to development and it has to make large-scale investments, and thus needs external borrowing. Therefore, Japan had concerns that losing external credibility and closing access to external borrowing was equal to giving up a path to development and poverty reduction forever.

There was reason to believe such concerns. During the 1980s and 1990s, there were no previous examples of a country that recovered from a decline in credibility resulting from debt cancellation and could again borrow from external markets. This implied strong concerns that debt cancellation was like jumping into a black box where nobody could predict the future. Even with a good, firm, restructuring plan, and a solid implementation of it, one could not predict the responses of international lenders. The market evaluation of external credibility was much less affected by moderate measures like rescheduling, but far more by radical measures such as cancellation.

The second reason is Japan's own experience. Since the Meiji Restoration in 1868, Japan grew by way of frequent borrowing from external markets for investment. For a small country in the Far East that does not possess many natural resources, it was quite difficult to borrow from external markets. Credibility was all it had for external borrowing, and every effort was made to maintain credibility. Credibility was the highest priority of the nation. During World War II, though Japan had to suspend all repayments to its overseas creditors, to maintain its credibility it continued payment against all domestic bonds issued in foreign currencies: bonds in pounds that had the option to be paid in pounds in a neutral country (Switzerland), and Tokyo electrification bonds in pounds (Ministry of Finance 1998).

Thus maintained, credibility enabled Japan to borrow large financial resources from external markets for reconstruction from war damage and for rapid growth during the 1960s and 1970s. From this experience, Japan believes that maintaining credibility is essential for a developing country to pursue economic development. Losing credibility in exchange for debt cancellation is believed to be equal to abandoning economic development.

The third reason is a technical reason relating to the Japanese Finance Act. Article 8 of the Finance Act prohibits canceling a part or all of any country's credit unless new legislation is arranged. New legislation is supposed to be very difficult to arrange, hence debt cancellation seems to be impossible.[3] In fact, there was an incident where Japan rejected a bilateral request for debt cancellation, because of the Finance Act.

For these three reasons, the Japanese government considered debt cancellation as not the best route for developing countries, but that alleviating debt issues by way of rescheduling the debt was much more desirable. Japan has continued to oppose debt cancellation. In the next sections, I will show how this policy measure evolved.

What has happened in the international society?

In 1988, the Paris Club agreed to debt cancellation for the first time in its history, responding to the resolution from the Toronto Summit Meeting. Since then, the ratio of cancellation has kept increasing, and finally, at the Cologne Summit, the ratio reached 90 percent, and by a voluntary decision of members, the ratio increased up to 100 percent. Table 5.1 lists the major events in this process.

Table 5.1 Major events surrounding the debt issue

Year	Name of initiative, summit meeting	Brief description
1956	Classic Term	10 years of rescheduling
1978	UNCTAD/TDB (Trade and Development Board)	Debt relief for 20 countries affected by oil shock
1987	Venice Summit	Prolong rescheduling term
1988	Toronto Terms	Debt reduction, 33% of debt
1989	Expansion of TDB	New inclusion of six countries
1990	Houston Terms	Long-term rescheduling
1991	London Terms	Increase share of debt reduction to 50%
1994	Naples Terms	Increase share of debt reduction to 66%
1996	Lyon Terms	HIPC initiatives, 40 years of rescheduling
1999	Cologne Terms	Enhanced HIPC initiatives, reduction to 90% (100%)
2003	Evian Approach	Debt relief for Non-HIPC countries

Source: Paris Club http://www.clubdeparis.org

There was a particular reason for this continuous rise in the ratio of debt cancellation. From the beginning of the 1990s, global civil organizations and the Jubilee 2000 campaign in particular initiated protests against foreign debt. What was distinctive about this protest was its scale and the involvement of a broader range of organizations such as non-governmental organizations (NGOs), churches, labor unions, students, aid agencies and so on.

In 1996, British NGOs and aid organizations started the Jubilee 2000 campaign, and invited other civil organizations to protest for debt cancellation for African countries. This movement swept all over the world very quickly. At meetings of civil organizations, brochures and flyers were distributed and protest actions were discussed. The targets of their protest were the G7 summit meeting and international organizations such as the World Bank and International Monetary Fund (IMF). At the summit meeting in Birmingham in May 1998, 70,000 people participated in the campaign of Jubilee 2000, as they requested debt cancellation by forming a 'human chain' to surround the building where the summit was taking place.[4]

Jubilee 2000's assertion can be summarized as follows: in a country where the government has excessive debt, the majority of export earnings are spent on debt repayment, and thus people's income does not increase. Consequently many people remain without access to safe water and suffer from poverty. Perpetuating this situation does not lead to economic development and there is no hope for the future of the children. The root of all evil is past foreign debt. Past debt was created either by egoistical politicians or by foreign banks or aid agencies that forced states to borrow. The people who are suffering from poverty now are not responsible for repayment. Therefore such debt should be cancelled immediately.

TV commercials for Jubilee 2000 were broadcast during these days, and they were quite unforgettable. The ad starts with a scene of two men walking along a corridor of a lonely hospital without a word until they reach a room where a baby is crying. Then the two men take away the pacifier from the baby, and go back down the corridor, ignoring the even louder cries of the baby. Everybody understands that the crying baby is the poor in developing countries, the two men are donors/bankers and the pacifier was money that they lent. Donors are not supposed to collect repayments as the ad implied, but the situation where the baby was left without attendance was shocking enough to remind viewers that the poor were left unattended and that export earnings were spent on repayments to rich countries.

Whether this assertion is correct is very difficult to determine. However, the story raises several important issues. These are that many African people do not have access to safe water and that opportunities for education are absent for children who are thus left without hope for the future. In this respect, if we are asked whether we can ignore the situation, then the answer is obviously no.

Discussion of heavy debt tended to center on the question of how debt overhang can be reduced without a decline in credibility. However, Jubilee 2000, in the context of poverty, protested for the necessity of changing the current situation from a humanitarian point of view. Conventional discussions proposed a restructuring plan for debt countries, but Jubilee 2000 proposed immediate relief from of the current situation. The discussions were at cross-purposes.

Nobody can oppose a humanitarian opinion. Moreover, when a large number of people insist, it creates tremendous pressure. The Jubilee 2000 campaign spread to over 60 countries, and more than 24 million signatures were collected (Barrett 2000). In the end, the G7 countries who are the creditors of major debt agreed to concede. As a result, G7 countries announced a voluntary decision of 100 percent cancellation at the Summit in Cologne in 1999.

What was decided and what was ignored?

At the turn of the century, it was decided that the debt overhang issue would be settled with 100 percent debt cancellation. I will analyze what changes were brought to indebted African countries.

The first thing to consider is whether debt was actually cancelled, and if and how additional resources were obtained and utilized for poverty reduction. In the HIPC Initiative, a debtor country is obliged to have a series of good macroeconomic policies and to implement structural adjustments in order to receive debt cancellation. Though the creditor countries announced debt cancellation, this did not mean immediate cancellation, but that certain conditions had to be implemented by a debtor country first. At the end of July 2007, 22 out of the 41 HIPC countries (including African and non-African countries) fulfilled the conditions and received debt cancellation (referred to as 'completion point countries'), another 9 countries are still trying to implement the conditions, and 10 countries have not yet started the process (Table 5.2). There is criticism that the HIPC conditions are excessively rigid and debtor countries cannot realistically implement them, but 31 out of 41 countries have already started the process, which means that such criticism may not necessarily be true. It can be confirmed that some debt is actually being cancelled.

Table 5.2 Status of HIPC countries as of the end of July 2007

22 completion point countries		
Benin	Madagascar	São Tomé and Príncipe
Bolivia	Malawi	Senegal
Burkina Faso	Mali	Sierra Leone
Cameroon	Mauritania	Tanzania
Ethiopia	Mozambique	Uganda
Ghana	Nicaragua	Zambia
Guyana	Niger	
Honduras	Rwanda	
9 decision point countries		
Afghanistan	Republic of Congo	Guinea
Burundi	Democratic Republic of the Congo	Guinea-Bissau
Chad	The Gambia	Haiti
10 pre-decision point countries		
Central African Republic	Kyrgyz Republic/	Sudan
Comoros	Liberia	Togo
Côte d'Ivoire	Nepal	
Eritrea	Somalia	

Source: World Bank (2007: 9, Table 2.1).

Within the process of the HIPC Initiative, when a country reaches a 'decision point' where it has formulated a restructuring plan, a part of the debt is cancelled. Additional debt is cancelled over time, depending on the progress of restructuring. When it reaches the 'completion point', where all the conditions have been implemented, 100 percent of debt is cancelled. In 2000, 22 out of 31 of the above-mentioned countries passed the decision point, and at least part of their debt was cancelled. In 2005, 19 countries had reached the completion point.

To see the effect of cancellation, I will compare country figures from 2000 and 2005. The average amount of debt among the 31 countries, which includes all HIPC countries, was $9.2 *per capita* in 2000, and it was reduced to $6 in 2005 (World Bank 2007). In addition to the 22 countries that have reached the completion point, these figures also include the 9 countries that have not yet reached the completion point, so this average *per capita* debt will likely be further reduced as they reach the completion point.

Next, I will analyze whether the resources saved as a result of debt cancellation were utilized for poverty reduction, by providing safe water and educational opportunities. I looked at whether a shift in government expenditure was made, and then whether such shift was towards poverty reduction efforts. Among the 31 HIPC countries that have reached the completion or decision point, the average government expenditure for poverty reduction was 7 percent of GDP in 2000, and increased to 9 percent in 2006 (World Bank 2007). It is confirmed that government expenditure for poverty reduction was certainly increased as a result of debt cancellation.

Table 5.3 shows the change in 'access to safe water', 'health expenditures', 'primary school enrollment' and the 'Human Development Index' of the United Nations (UN). Note that the data for 2005 is not available and that 2004 is listed instead. Also, for 'safe water', there is no data for 2000, and instead the data is from 1990. Water, health and education are factors that represent quality of life and institutions. It is necessary to observe long-term changes to see the progress in these factors, yet an observation over four or five years may not produce a clear judgment. Bearing this in mind, I will analyze the relationship between debt cancellation and these factors.

The differences in the average ratio of safe water between 1990 and 2004 is 14.5 percentage points for non-African debt-cancelled countries and 7.5 percentage points for all Sub-Saharan African countries. It is obvious that improvement in non-African debt-cancelled countries is much greater than in the African countries. But I may not conclude the precise relationship between such improvement and debt cancellation because the base year of comparison is far older than the starting year of debt cancellation. Also, attention needs to be paid to the absolute level of safe water for debt-cancelled countries, which is still very low. Nearly half of the population

Table 5.3 Safe water, health, school enrollment, and Human Development Index indicators

	HIPC 25 countries, average			SS Africa countries, average		
	2000	2004	difference	2000	2004	difference
Population with sustainable access to improved water source (%)	45.0[1]	59.5	14.5	44.0[1]	51.5	7.5
Health expenditure per capita (current US$)	12.95	19.66	6.71	41.47[2]	53.87	12.40
School enrollment, primary (% net)	51.1	70.8	19.7	63.0	67.3	4.2
Human Development Index	0.411	0.434	0.023	0.461	0.468	0.007

Source: World Bank (2007), UNDP (2006).

Notes
1 Refers to 1990.
2 Refers to 2003.

does not have access to safe water, so safe water is still a critical issue as it directly concerns human life.

Improvements in the average ratio of health expenditures *per capita* are 52 percent for debt-cancelled countries and 30 percent on average for Sub-Saharan African countries. Again, debt-cancelled countries had better improvements than the Sub-Saharan African ones, though the increase amount is lower than the average. This shows that the level of health expenditures is lower for debt-cancelled countries because their absolute income level is lower, but rapid increases in health expenditures are taking place. This improvement coincides with the period of debt cancellation.

Primary school enrollment is also rising in debt-cancelled countries. It was below the Sub-Saharan average in 2000, but it went above the average in 2004. The magnitude of improvement is 19.7 percent and this shows that very rapid improvement in educational opportunities is taking place in debt-cancelled countries.

The UN Human Development Index (HDI) is a composite index that accounts for life expectancy, literacy rate and school enrollment, as well as level of income, and is suitable for intertemporal comparisons rather than cross-country comparisons. It has long been said that in the trend of HDI change, all developing countries were improving except Sub-Saharan

Africa, which continued unchanged. However, African debt-cancelled countries show obvious improvements in HDI during the period of 2000–4. Again, this happened along with debt cancellation.

From these observations, it is clear that the HIPC Initiative reduced debt repayment and expenditures for poverty reduction increased by using the saved money. Furthermore, it resulted in improvements in health expenditures and school enrollment in some cases. As for access to safe water, I cannot conclude to what extent debt cancellation contributed because of unavailable data, though improvements are taking place in debt-cancelled countries. I can conclude, however, that at the turn of the century, large-scale protest over the debt issue led international society to the humane decision to cancel heavy debt, and that poverty reduction has greatly progressed as a result of debt cancellation. In this sense, concerns about poverty reduction became a major focus.

Now I will turn to a matter that was considered widely and is still in need of attention. The main issue of heavy debt was the possible moral hazard and declining credibility resulting from debt cancellation. The basic cause of heavy debt is the lack of debt management capacity, and there remains a risk that additional debt issues will arise after debt is cancelled. From the view of international society, when a part or all of the debt is cancelled, credibility declines and it becomes extremely difficult to borrow new funds from the external market. The lingering questions are whether debt cancellation really hurts credibility, whether this creates a moral hazard, whether it becomes difficult to borrow new money and whether a debt country can recover its credibility?

First I will look at figures of resource transfers before and after debt cancellation. The World Bank conducted evaluations of the HIPC Initiative in 2003 and 2006. In the evaluation report of 2003, they did not find significant changes in resource transfers after debt cancellation, but in the 2006 report, they confirmed the existence of additional resource transfers following debt cancellation. The net transfers after debt cancellation rose from $8.8 billion in 1999 to $17.5 billion in 2004 (World Bank 2003, 2006).

However, these new transfers were mainly provided by aid organizations. Table 5.4 is a summary of the resource transfers for 25 African debt-cancelled countries in 2000 and 2004. Over the period, the total International Bank for Reconstruction and Development (IBRD) and International Development Association (IDA) transfers for 25 countries slightly increased, while those of bilateral donors more than doubled. The total transfers for all the HIPC countries were $17.5 billion and the total of official aid for the 25 African countries was $18.3 billion. Therefore, the additional transfers were almost equal to the total official aid. In other words, commercial banks were not providing new money to debt-cancelled countries. The IMF and the World

Table 5.4 World Bank and bilateral aid for African debt cancelled countries

	IBRD and IDA (thousands)		ODA and other official (thousands)	
	2000	2004	2000	2004
Benin	578,385	791,436	238,430	384,970
Burkina Faso	592,500	1,027,351	334,920	614,280
Burundi	NA	NA	92,600	361,540
Cameroon	982,853	1,199,980	379,330	772,040
Chad	NA	910,436	130,160	321,340
Congo, Dem. Rep.	1,269,031	NA	177,120	1,824,310
Congo, Rep.	223,816	268,969	33,180	115,490
Ethiopia	NA	NA	686,140	1,819,110
Gambia, The	170,675	247,429	48,980	65,470
Ghana	3,139,493	4,311,761	599,690	1,362,290
Guinea	NA	NA	152,850	280,240
Guinea-Bissau	227,590	300,503	80,290	77,040
Madagascar	1,377,614	NA	321,680	1,247,830
Malawi	1,600,709	2,075,558	446,180	501,400
Mali	956,887	1,440,710	359,210	567,640
Mauritania	449,457	NA	211,410	180,620
Mozambique	NA	1,475,224	876,060	1,245,820
Niger	723,201	1,106,072	208,450	541,210
Rwanda	691,917	1,019,856	321,460	488,150
Sao Tome and Principe	58,898	76,884	34,890	33,420
Senegal	1,331,388	NA	423,170	1,054,900
Sierra Leone	353,659	NA	180,630	360,070
Tanzania	2,603,996	3,915,515	1,019,350	1,761,320
Uganda	NA	NA	817,090	1,197,580
Zambia	1,848,122	2,637,410	794,650	1,125,180
Total 25 countries	19,180,191	22,805,094	8,967,920	18,303,260

Source: World Bank (2007).

Bank stated that commercial banks hardly lent any new money though they accepted a part of debt cancellation (IMF and World Bank 2007). From the point of view of commercial banks, debt cancellation did cause a moral hazard on the side of the developing countries, and their credibility declined.

This point is confirmed by observing the increased number of court appeals. Table 5.5 shows the number of lawsuits against debt-cancelled countries brought by commercial creditors. Table 5.5 is based on surveys from the IMF and the World Bank, which may not cover all the lawsuits; it is possible that the actual number of lawsuits is greater (IMF and World Bank 2007). Table 5.5 shows that 8 out of 21 countries had lawsuits pending in 2006. Except in one case these lawsuits were initiated by commercial institutions.[5] The results of these lawsuits were that the debt countries lost in more than half the cases, while the majority of the other cases were settled out of court. Thus moral hazard was observed in at least a number of countries.

Another issue that needs renewed attention includes macroeconomic performance and governance. This is because sound macroeconomic performance and good governance are of critical importance for sustainable growth and poverty reduction. The 25 African countries that passed

Table 5.5 African debt cancelled countries' lawsuits at the end of 2006

Completion HIPCs	Number of litigating creditors	Decision HIPCs	Number of litigating creditors
Benin	0	Rwanda	0
Burkina Faso	0	São Tome and Principe	1
Burundi	0	Senegal	0
Cameroon	7	Sierra Leone	5
Chad	0	Tanzania	0
Congo, Dem. Rep.	2	Uganda	6
Congo, Rep.	8	Zambia	2
Ethiopia	2		
Gambia, The	NA		
Ghana	NA		
Guinea	NA		
Guinea-Bissau	0		
Madagascar	0		
Malawi	0		
Mali	0		
Mauritania	0		
Mozambique	0		
Niger	NA		

Source: World Bank (2007: 33, Table 2.5).

the decision or completion point and started to receive debt cancellation are the same countries that the IMF and the World Bank judged as having their macroeconomic performance on track. Therefore their macroeconomic performance is considered to be better than before. African countries' trends of economic growth from 1970 to 2005 are shown in Figure 5.1. In the figure, countries are categorized into three groups: 25 decision point countries, 9 pre-decision point countries, and 16 non-HIPC countries. The figure shows decision point countries having higher economic growth than pre-decision point countries after debt cancellation started. Once their growth is compared to non-HIPC countries, their growth is no better than, or almost at the same level as that of non-HIPCs. This means that the economic performance of debt-cancelled countries was not improved to the extent of other African countries. In the evaluation report of the World Bank Independent Evaluation Group, the economic performance of post-completion countries was not greatly improved with respect to government revenue, export/imports, current expenditure and others (World Bank IEG 2006). In the post-completion countries, the ratio of revenue to GDP was 16.5 percent, unchanged from 16 percent before cancellation, and the ratio of current expenditure to GDP deteriorated from -6.9 percent to -8.8 percent. Exports remained unchanged as the ratio to GDP was approximately 26 percent, but the terms of trade deteriorated (World Bank IEG 2006).

There is another indicator to show the macroeconomic performance of post-completion countries. A 'waiver' is granted to a country when it does not meet part of its pre-determined conditions but is deemed to be eligible to reach the post-completion point. A waiver is given in accordance with

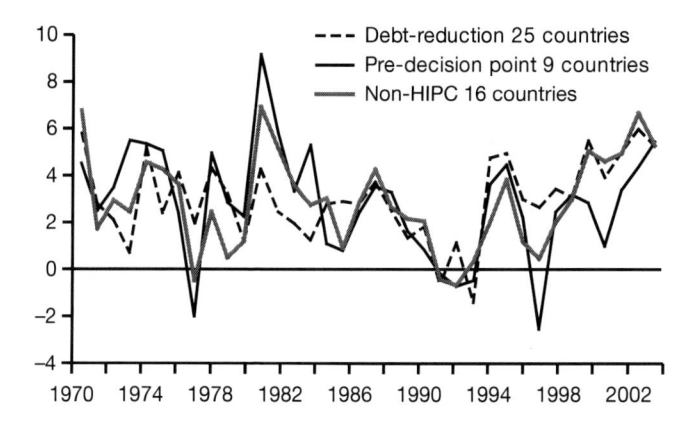

Figure 5.1 Growth rate of African HIPC and non-HIPC countries

procedures of the World Bank and allows a country to pass the completion point; the waiver is given to exceptional cases, even if a part of the conditions are not met.

In February 2006, there were 14 post-completion countries in Africa, of which 7 countries were granted waivers and treated as having completion point status. Exceptional cases consisted of 50 percent of the countries, which is not a small percentage (Table 5.6). Half had met some conditions by achieving good macroeconomic performance, but the rest of the countries had passed the completion point without satisfying all of the minimum conditions. For example, to conduct sound macroeconomic policies, it is necessary to correct distortions in the markets. Distortions in the financial market, foreign exchange, state enterprises, price policy and so on are the result of other policies, and eliminating such distortions is not easy. There are groups of people who profit from such policies and distortion, and thus changing policies means changing the distribution of profits. Whenever policies are about to change, these groups always resist the changes using a variety of measures. The government needs to plan to change policies very cautiously by adjusting the benefits of different groups, but very often this fails. Debt cancellation does not alter this mechanism. The HIPC Initiative pushes for sound macroeconomic policies, but it does not make it easy to change policies. A considerable number of post-completion countries did not meet the conditions of macroeconomic performance.

Civil organizations such as Jubilee 2000 did not agree with requiring strict conditions for macroeconomic performance. Their assertion is that debt cancellation should be given to reduce poverty despite poor macroeconomic performances. By contrast, on governance, civil organizations are of the same opinion, debt countries need to improve it. Table 5.7 shows comparisons of governance indicators[6] between 2000 and 2006.

On average, the 25 debt-cancelled countries are improved on 'Voice and Accountability' and 'Political Stability and Absence of Violence' indicators, but other index measures have not changed or have slightly deteriorated. It should be noted that improvement in the former two indexes is not the result of debt cancellation but the cause of it. Particularly, 'Political Stability and Absence of Violence' is an index to measure the possibility of risking the stability of the government by means of terrorism or other violence, and if a country has a serious conflict then it will have difficulty meeting conditions that the HIPC Initiative imposes, and debt cancellation will not be granted. In summary, debt cancellation did not provide improvement in the two indexes.

Changes in other governance indicators vary considerably among countries. While some countries improved, other countries deteriorated. In Burundi, the Democratic Republic of Congo, Rwanda, Sierra Leone and Uganda,

Table 5.6 Waivers of completion point conditions: African countries

Country	Waivers	Completion point trigger waived or delayed
Benin	0	Barely missed targets in health and education; bank privatization, other benchmarks delayed
Burkina Faso	0	All targets met or exceeded
Ethiopia	3	Severe drought delayed agricultural reform; census needed to confirm education reform; began consolidation of budgets
Ghana	1	Committed to reform petroleum pricing, but has not implemented it; perception of corruption
Madagascar	0	Barely missed teacher-recruitment target; budgetary execution laws late; repetition rates and primary school completion rates below targets; tax revenue short of target
Mali	0	Initial delays caused some education targets to be only partially met; recruitment of health sector workers below target
Mauritania	5	Technical delays in privatizing utility; did not comply with risk-exposure ratio for banks; missed target for poverty reduction; missed target for survival rate at fifth grade and primary/secondary school enrollment; barely missed child vaccination target
Mozambique	0	Missed target for strategic plan owing to expanded scope; some setbacks for structural reform
Niger	2	Delay in impact evaluation of public health expenditure on poor; did not meet overly ambitious target for repetition rates
Rwanda	1	Delay in privatizing one state-owned tea factory
Senegal	3	Child immunization target missed; utilization rates of primary healthcare centers missed; began consolidation of budgets
Tanzania	0	Delay in poverty analyses; exceeded requirements for several triggers; observed all quantitative criteria and most benchmarks
Uganda	0	All conditions met
Zambia	3	International bidding documents for power company were not issued; unable to sell national bank; partially met trigger for pilot implementation of financial management information system; unpredictable fiscal policy

Source: World Bank IEG (2006).

Note
Post-completion countries referred to in this table include 14 countries as of February 2006.

Table 5.7 Change in governance indicators from 2000 to 2006

Country	Voice and account-ability	Political stability and absence of violence	Government effectiveness	Regulatory quality	Rule of law	Control of corruption	Total of difference
Benin	-0.08	-0.29	-0.25	-0.26	-0.28	-0.23	-1.39
Burkina Faso	-0.02	-0.10	-0.16	-0.31	0.05	-0.43	-0.97
Burundi	0.59	0.87	0.11	-0.02	0.49	0.05	2.09
Cameroon	0.10	0.32	-0.15	-0.24	0.17	0.15	0.35
Chad	-0.44	-0.44	-0.77	-0.33	-0.45	-0.31	-2.74
Congo	0.52	0.18	0.19	0.15	0.13	-0.04	1.13
Congo, Dem. Rep.	0.27	0.34	0.19	0.84	0.31	0.17	2.12
Ethiopia	-0.06	-0.58	0.36	0.35	0.17	-0.07	0.17
Gambia	0.17	-0.29	-0.27	-0.15	-0.16	-0.24	-0.94
Chana	0.38	0.45	0.04	-0.10	-0.07	0.13	0.83
Guinea	0.06	0.08	-0.56	-0.51	-0.06	-0.18	-1.17
Guinea-Bissau	0.44	0.22	-0.06	0.18	0.17	-0.10	0.85
Madagascar	-0.12	-0.02	0.38	0.28	0.02	-0.18	0.36
Malawi	-0.17	0.58	-0.49	-0.40	0.08	-0.29	-0.69
Mali	0.16	-0.18	0.38	-0.23	0.15	0.07	0.35
Mauritania	-0.19	-0.39	-0.48	0.14	-0.09	-0.41	-1.42
Mozambique	0.14	0.53	0.06	-0.28	0.20	0.11	0.76
Niger	0.01	-0.19	0.33	0.05	0.02	-0.01	0.21
Rwanda	0.39	1.28	0.43	0.40	0.69	0.59	3.78
São Tome and Principe	-0.13	-0.48	-0.28	0.08	-0.36	-0.49	-1.66
Senegal	-0.06	0.26	-0.19	-0.23	-0.24	-0.14	-0.60
Sierra Leone	1.10	1.45	0.39	0.25	0.17	-0.24	3.12
Tanzania	0.16	0.29	0.11	-0.18	-0.01	0.70	1.07
Uganda	0.62	0.36	-0.08	-0.20	0.33	0.25	1.28
Zambia	0.05	0.67	0.22	-0.39	-0.05	0.12	0.62
Average	0.16	0.20	-0.02	-0.04	0.06	-0.04	0.30

Source: Kaufmann *et al.* (2007: Appendix C).

governance indicators were significantly improved, but they deteriorated in Benin, Burkina Faso, Chad, Gambia, Guinea, Malawi, Mauritania, São Tome and Principe, and Senegal. In particular, Benin, Chad and Mauritania deteriorated across all six governance indicators. Considering the change or lack of change in governance indicators, debt cancellation does not push states in a certain direction, and it may either help improve governance or make it deteriorate. Although the civil movement in the 1990s protested strongly for improved governance as well as debt cancellation, the result has been a mixture of success and failure. Although it should not be denied that debt cancellation may improve governance in the long run, it does not have positive impact in the short run.

Last, I wish to mention the eight African countries in the list of HIPCs that have not yet reached the decision point (see Table 5.2). Among these countries, Comoros, Eritrea, Somalia, and Sudan are now facing serious conflicts and lack political stability. The other four countries, Central African Republic, Côte d'Ivoire, Liberia and Togo, are now in the process of recovering from conflicts, but they still need time to re-establish political stability.

It is obvious that people in the conflict-ridden nations have very difficult lives. They do not have easy access to adequate health care, education and safe water, and they often become refugees. The situation is hardly acceptable from a humanitarian position. From this point of view, debt cancellation for these countries might be considered more urgent. On the other hand,

Table 5.8 Health, school enrollment, and safe water indicators of pre-decision point countries

Country name	Health expenditure per capita (US$)	Primary school enrollment (% net)	Population with sustainable access to an improved water sources (%)
Central African Republic	13.2	NA	75
Comoros	13.2	NA	86
Cote d'Ivoire	33.0	NA	84
Eritrea	9.9	47.8	69
Liberia	8.6	NA	61
Somalia	NA	NA	29
Sudan	24.7	NA	70
Togo	17.9	78.8	52
average	17.2	63.3	65.8

Source: World Bank (2007), UNDP (2006).

from the viewpoint of the donors, debt cancellation would be nothing more than a waste since these countries are struggling to maintain the fundamental shape of a country and are not able to start reconstructing the economy; therefore, debt cancellation is not an acceptable option. Here, humanitarian considerations and economic principles run counter to each other, and the HIPC Initiative does not move forward.

Instead of debt cancellation, international society should take necessary steps to end the conflicts and get life back to normal for people as quickly as possible. Currently very little attention is paid to conflicts in Africa in comparison to the broad civil movements for the debt issue. Solving conflicts would be a very difficult process, as they involve complex backgrounds and factors, but this is an issue to which international society should pay more attention.

Conclusion

For a developing country to accelerate its development process by external borrowing, it needs to have solid and sound management of its public expenditures and external debt. However, a developing country may not have such capacity to begin with. There is a strong possibility of countries having excessive debt if a country borrows externally without having management capacity.

Since the 1980s, G7 countries have struggled to find measures that both provide relief from debt and strengthen a government's management capacity. Among others, Japan's debt policy, which comes from its own experiences, is to reduce debt without damaging the credibility of the borrower. Such a policy is called the 'New Money Approach' and Japan continued with this policy until 2002. It was thought that if debt was reduced while credibility was maintained, then it would keep open the possibility of future borrowing. If so, future borrowing would enable economic growth in the long run and poverty would be reduced.

However, towards the turn of the century, new international social norms were spreading. In many places of the world, civil organizations, NGOs, religious institutions and so on showed strong concern for the hardships that people of indebted countries were facing. Their concern was that government expenditure was forced to shift towards debt repayment, and that poverty reduction was slowing down or going into reverse. Above all, the campaign of Jubilee 2000 had strong support from a broad area of the world, and became a large-scale civil movement. The main assertion of Jubilee 2000 was the immediate cancellation of debt from a humanitarian point of view, but it did not have common ground with the G7 discussions, which focused on debt relief from an economic point of view. The Jubilee 2000 campaign spread to over 60 countries, and finally the G7 countries changed their policies and agreed with 100 percent debt cancellation. At this time, the campaign of Jubilee 2000 sometimes raised radical arguments against G7 countries and international organizations, but humanitarians were victorious and formed the consensus of international society.

One objective, 100 percent debt cancellation, was started at the turn of the century. In Africa, 19 countries have reached the completion point, and seven countries have passed the decision point as of July 2007. It is confirmed that the amount of debt was certainly reduced, and the saved resources were utilized for poverty reduction. In the countries where debt cancellation was granted, debt repayment was reduced, government expenditure was used more for poverty reduction and, as a result, health expenditure and school enrollment were significantly improved. In terms of poverty reduction, the HIPC Initiative succeeded.

On the other hand, all the issues related to debt overhang are not yet solved. In the debt-cancelled countries, resource transfers from international organizations and bilateral aid agencies have increased, but not those from commercial financial institutions. On the contrary, some of the debt-cancelled countries have pending lawsuits, and this implies that the threat of moral hazard has not been allayed.

As for macroeconomic performance, half of the completion point countries failed to meet a part of their conditions. It is supposed that policies to correct market distortion were resisted by the groups that benefited from them, and that the restructuring plan was not fully implemented. This implies that debt cancellation does not always improve the adjustment capacity of governments.

In the dimensions of governance, common improvement occurred in the dimension of political stability, but debt cancellation did not seem to yield positive changes in other dimensions of governance. However, political stability was not the result of debt cancellation, the causality is the other way round. It was because the country had political stability that debt cancellation was granted. While some countries improved governance, other countries aggravated the entire dimension of governance. Here, again, it is implied that debt cancellation does not improve governance.

Lastly, I wish to comment on the eight countries in Africa that have not yet reached the decision point. All of these countries are facing conflicts currently or have had conflicts in the recent past and are still on their way to recovery. The people there have very difficult lives, and debt cancellation might be needed urgently. But debt cancellation for these countries is highly improbable, nor is it planned. Before debt cancellation can occur, these countries need to solve their conflicts and achieve peace, and it is necessary for the international society to approach this issue with a much stronger sense of urgency.

Notes

1 Nurkse (1953) and Hirschman (1958) proposed totally different approaches for development, but commonly emphasized the necessity of investment larger than domestic saving.
2 For the detail of each terms, please refer to the Paris Club (http://www.clubdeparis.org/sections/termes-de-traitement/termes-de-traitements).
3 The majority of Japan's credit to developing countries is Yen Loan which is extended by the Japan Bank for Economic Cooperation (JBIC). It became recognized, in latter days, that JBIC's credit is not considered to be subject to the Finance Act. So, in 2002, JBIC started debt cancellation.
4 For details of Jubilee 2000, see Barrett (2000) and Greenhill *et al.* (2003).
5 One case among seven lawsuits against Cameroon was issued by the World Bank (IMF and World Bank 2007).
6 Governance indicators are published by the World Bank, and summarize various aspects of governance into six dimensions (Kaufmann *et al.* 2007).

References

Barrett, M. (ed.) (2000) *The World Will Never Be the Same Again*, London: Jubilee 2000 Coalition.
Greenhill, R., Petifor, A., Northover, H. and Sinha, A. (2003) *Did the G8 Drop the Debt?*, Jubilee Research, London: Jubilee Debt Campaign and CAFOD.
Hirschman, A.O. (1958) *The Strategy of Economic Development*, New Haven, CT: Yale University Press.
International Monetary Fund and World Bank (2007) *Heavily Indebted Countries (HIPC) Initiative and Multilateral Debt Relief Initiative (MDRI) – Status of Implementation*, Washington, DC: International Monetary Fund and World Bank.
Kaufmann, D., Kraay, A. and Mastruzi, M. (2007) *Governance Matters VI: Aggregate and Individual Governance Indicators 1996–2006*, Policy Research Working Paper 4280, Washington, DC: World Bank.
Nurkse, R. (1953) *Problems of Capital Formation in Underdeveloped Economies*, New York: Oxford University Press.
大蔵省（財政金融研究所財政史室）= Okura-sho, Zaisei-Kinyu Kenkyujo Zaisei Shiryo-shitsu (Ministry of Finance , Policy Research Institute, Office of Fiscal Policy History), 1998,
『大蔵省史―明治・大正・昭和―第2巻』= Okurasho-shi –Meiji, Taisho, Showa – Dai-Ni-Kan (History of the Ministry of Finance – Meiji, Taisho, and Showa, Vol.2,) 大蔵省財務協会 = Tokyo: Okura Zaimu Kyokai (the name of the publisher)
United Nations Development Programme (UNDP) (2006) *Human Development Report 2006*, New York: United Nations Development Programme.
World Bank (2007) *World Development Indicators 2007*, Washington, DC: World Bank.
World Bank Independent Evaluation Group (IEG) (2006) *Debt Relief for the Poorest: An Evaluation Update of the HIPC Initiative*, Washington, DC: World Bank.
World Bank Operations Evaluation Department (OED) (2003) *Debt Relief for the Poorest: An OED Review of the HIPC Initiative*, Washington, DC: World Bank.

6 Policy coordination among aid donors

Japan's position from a European perspective

Nobuyuki Hashimoto

Since the 1990s, aid donors have made efforts to make their aid provisions more effective through coordinating various aid practices with each other. Such practices have been raised in recent international conferences to discuss aid effectiveness, pursuing alignment and harmonization. It is believed that coordination of aid, for example, would mitigate the administrative burden on recipient governments that are used to managing a number of different requirements of aid donors, which exacerbates the already limited capacity and function of those governments. The technical merit of coordination per se has, therefore, been encouraged by several aid donors. Be that as it may, aid coordination could be possible where there is a certain degree of consensus on an issue(s) of development. This is where the policies of aid donors (and recipient governments) matter. This chapter, therefore, deals with aid coordination efforts among aid donors particularly at policy levels, which provides attitudinal differences between European donors (primarily the UK) and Japan on the coordination of aid.

In order to discuss the issue of policy coordination, first some conceptual distinctions will be discussed briefly. The subsequent sections will deal with recent coordination efforts and include a brief review of influential international arenas for development policy, the aid coordination processes among aid donors, the formation of the Like-Minded Group (LMG) and the Joint Action Plan. Against this background, I will discuss and contrast the aid policies and approaches of the UK and Japan, and particularly their policy coordination practice in the case of Ghana. In reviewing the above process, the last section will touch upon reasons for Japan's relative isolation from aid donors with regard to today's coordination practices.

Conceptual distinctions

Disch (1999) divides aid coordination into the following three elements: (1) policy, principles and priorities; (2) procedure; and (3) practice. The first, namely 'policy', is an element of aid coordination dealt with more at the political level and the other two at technical levels. If Disch's classification is applied, 'policy coordination' can be differentiated from 'aid coordination'.

Policy coordination, where aid agreements are made to support the policies of the recipient countries by coordinating among aid donors, has had a rich history of discussion in the international arena. It helps to create common understandings about problems to be solved and necessary assistance to be provided. However, such policy coordination tends to be oriented towards the donors, and the relationship with the recipient countries also is donor-driven. Hence, not only aid but development issues have been discussed mainly among aid donors at the international arena, which promoted a political level of policy coordination. Developing countries today have come to promote their ownership especially from the policy-making level since the late 1990s. Coordination in both senses, therefore, is now practiced at the recipient country level.

Aid coordination on the other hand, is a term used more to describe the technical aspect of aid. Aid donors negotiate among themselves in order not only to align their aid with the recipient governments' own development policies and systems but also to harmonize aid provisions. Development policy, in this sense, is supposed to be discussed among all the stakeholders at the country level, which is assumed to have transformed the role of aid donors who used to be in the driver's seat on development issues. On this basis, aid coordination could be possible if there is a coordination of policy among aid donors (and the recipient governments) since policy coordination provides a rationale of 'what aid provides' vis-à-vis 'how to provide aid'.

Formulation of an international development agenda and policy

There are global and international events organized by the agencies of the United Nations (UN) to discuss development issues. The wide membership of countries allows such events to find and identify development issues and to serve as an international agenda-setter for development. In the 1990s, several development issues were the focus at international conferences, mainly UN summits. These were the International Conference on Education for All (Jomtien in 1990), the Children Summit (New York in 1991), the Environment and Development (Earth) Summit (Rio de Janeiro in 1992), the Human Rights Summit (Vienna in 1993), the Population Summit (Cairo in 1994), the UN Social Summit (Copenhagen in 1995), the UN Women's Summit (Beijing in 1995) and the Food Summit (Rome in 1996). As seen in Table 6.1, the essence of these summits' agendas was integrated into and formulated as the Millennium Development Goals (MDGs; United Nations 2007) which were endorsed by member states in 2000. Table 6.1 describes a linkage between these summits and the MDGs. The various agendas of human and social development issues raised by the MDGs are attributed to past international forums. The following linkages can be found: (1) human rights and food discussions led to poverty reduction and basic needs which relate to MDGs 1 and 4; (2) children, education and gender relate to the MDGs 2–4; (3) social and environmental discussions led to MDGs 6 and 7. Goal 8 of the MDGs is related to trade negotiation and aid coordination issues mainly discussed at the level of the World Trade Organization (WTO) and OECD/DAC (Organisation for Economic Co-operation and Development/Development Assistance Committee).

The MDGs are viewed as the basis of development policy among developing countries. As for aid donors, their aid is expected to be directed towards achieving the MDGs. Once a problem is identified and a discussion for tackling it is organized at the global level, policy coordination could possibly happen. Nevertheless, the formulation of the MDGs alone did not assure policy coordination among all players in international development but did least lay out common views among aid donors for the purpose of and direction for aid provision. Many aid donors, therefore, include and/or refer to the MDGs in their respective aid policies. As no single donor can achieve all the MDGs, it seems necessary to have policy discussions especially in terms of aid provision at the country level. The recipient countries should always be the center of the MDGs as these targets exist first and foremost for them.

The development agenda was also discussed extensively from the aid donors' perspective at the OECD-DAC. The OECD-DAC is a forum formed in 1960 by aid-giving countries for consultations on aid.[1] Its original function was to monitor aid/financial flows to developing countries. It also encourages member countries to make efforts to provide their expected aid share and to foster coordination. In 1996, the OECD-DAC provided its development strategy called 'Shaping the 21st Century: The Contribution of Development Co-operation', with most of the targets to be achieved by 2015.[2]

In this strategy, the principles of 'partnership' (for aid donors primarily to exercise[3]) as well as 'ownership' (for recipient governments, as partners, to exercise) are emphasized. Although it was a donor-led initiative, this strategy with its targets (often referred to as the International Development Targets, IDTs) indicated not only what the development agenda was, but also what efforts both aid donors and the recipient governments had to make. The IDTs implied that norms, namely ownership and partnership, are fundamental conditions to make the IDTs possible.

Table 6.1 The MDGs' relationship with past UN goals

UN Millennium Development Goals	Corresponding past UN goals
Goal 1: Eradicate extreme poverty and hunger • Reduce by half the proportion of people living on less than a dollar a day • Reduce by half the proportion of people who suffer from hunger	Food Summit (Rome 1996)
Goal 2: Achieve universal primary education • Ensure that all boys and girls complete a full course of primary education	Conference on Education for All (Jomtien 1990)/ Human Rights Summit (Vienna 1993)
Goal 3: Promote gender equality and empower women • Eliminate gender disparity in primary and secondary education preferably by 2005 and at all levels by 2015	Women's Summit (Beijing 1995)
Goal 4: Reduce child mortality • Reduce by two-thirds the mortality rate among children under 5	Children Summit (New York 1991)
Goal 5: Improve material health • Reduce by three-quarters the maternal mortality ratio	Population Summit (Cairo 1994)
Goal 6: Combat HIV/AIDS, malaria and other diseases • Halt and begin to reverse the spread of HIV/AIDS • Halt and begin to reverse the incidence of materials and other major diseases	Social Summit (Copenhagen 1995)
Goal 7: Ensure environmental sustainability • Integrate the principles of sustainable development into country policies and programmes; reverse loss of environmental resources • Reduce by half the proportion of people without sustainable access to safe drinking water	Environmental and Development (Earth) Summit (Rio De Janeiro 1992)

UN Millennium Development Goals	Corresponding past UN goals
Goal 8: Develop a global partnership for development • Develop further an open trading and financial system that is rule-based, predictable and non-discriminatory, includes a commitment to good governance, development and poverty reduction – nationally and internationally • Address the least developed countries' special needs. This includes tariff- and quota-free access for their exports; enhanced debt relief for heavily indebted poor countries; cancellation of official bilateral debt; and more generous official development assistance for countries committed to poverty reduction • Address the special needs of landlocked and small island developing states • Deal comprehensively with developing countries' development problems through national and international measures to make debt sustainable in the long term • In cooperation with the developing countries, develop decent and productive work for youth • In cooperation with pharmaceutical companies, provide access to affordable essential drugs in developing countries • In cooperation with the private sector, make available the benefits of new technologies – especially information and communication technologies	

The IDTs provided a substantial foundation for the UN MDGs which adopt the same targets; poverty reduction, universal education, gender equality, healthcare, etc. The supposed succession from the IDTs to the MDGs affirms that global agendas for development are expected to be internalized by both partner governments (i.e. aid recipients) and aid donors. Today, the Bretton Woods institutions have required the heavily indebted poor countries (HIPCs) to formulate a poverty reduction strategy (PRS) as the main development framework. A PRS is a development policy owned by the recipient government. The PRS-based development policy is oriented towards attaining the MDGs, and DAC member donors as well as other aid institutions have reoriented their respective aid policies to support it. It is understood that one of the main principles of IDT ownership, is being fulfilled by PRS formulation, and that it has encouraged and reinforced the already practiced aid coordination efforts.

The aid coordination process among aid donors

Aid coordination was first considered in the 1980s and was originally initiated by the World Bank's Consultative Group meetings. Appreciating the World Bank's coordination efforts as well as the United Nations Development Programme's (UNDP) related efforts on round tables, the OECD-DAC adopted similar guiding principles in the document *Aid for Improved Development Policies and Programs and Implications for Aid Co-ordination* in 1986, which emphasized the needs of the recipient's own development policy as the basis for aid coordination (see OECD-DAC 2006). This might have been the basis of the IDTs in 1996, which also emphasized the principles of ownership and partnership. Therefore, ownership by the recipient government has been incorporated into the process of formulating recent development policy (such as the Poverty Reduction Strategy Paper [PRSP]) with aid donors. Since 1996, the partnership principle also has been more practically developed and elaborated in conjunction with the encouraged ownership of development policy by recipient governments.

Shifting its program to lend to sectors, Harrold and Associates (1995) of the World Bank proposed the Sector Investment Programs (SIPs), which paid attention to coordinated aid practices under the government-owned sector strategy. This requires aid donors to formulate projects under the recipient government's comprehensive policy at the sector level, and to provide and deliver aid in a harmonized manner. The World Bank also developed and introduced the Comprehensive Development Framework (CDF) in 1999 under the initiative of then President Wolfensohn (1998), which covers several development components (structural, human, physical and specific strategies) under the ownership of the governments to initiate the donors' role. As extended-HIPC initiatives have been undertaken since 1999 and PRSPs are required by recipient governments, the World Bank introduced its new aid tool, Poverty Reduction Support Credit (PRSC). PRSC pursues more intensive coordination among aid donors to align collectively with PRSPs.

For many aid donors, the importance of assistance at the sector level was recognized by the early 1990s and coordinated support for a sectoral program was agreed upon by OECD member countries, according to its 1992 manual (see Andersen 2005). As sector-wide approaches (SWAPs) began to appear in the 1990s, a so called 'Like-Minded Group' formed among Nordic and some European aid donors. The LMG has had informal meetings in order to exercise joint aid practices under SWAPs. Such activities encouraged more aid donors' involvement under a more collective framework of aid giving, the so called 'program-based approaches' (PBAs). Later, PBA advocates organized an international networking body in 2001 called 'The Learning Network on Program-Based Approaches' (LENPA). A wider number of aid donors have participated in the LENPA. Whereas the LENPA has advocated gradual PBAs and flexibility among aid donors to coordinate naturally, the LMG has led the more extreme forms of aid coordination. In particular, the LMG conducted and enhanced new modalities such as general budget support (GBS) and aid management styles such as silent partnerships.

Endorsing the MDGs, the OECD-DAC high-level forum (HLF) adopted a policy statement entitled 'Partnership for Poverty Reduction: From Commitment to Implementation', which provided the policy basis for the DAC Task Force on Donor Practices established in 2001. This was expanded to be the DAC Task Force on Aid Effectiveness and Donor Practice in 2003. These activities have encouraged aid donors to practice 'partnership' in terms of aid alignment with the recipient governments' development policy/ procedures and harmonization among their aid giving. Through these processes, the aid coordination principles of the OECD-DAC were elaborated and endorsed by the HLF in Rome in 2003 and in Paris in 2005. The Paris Framework, as seen in Figure 6.1, also incorporated the 'ownership' norm and the result-based management principle was affirmed in the Marrakech Round Table in 2004.

Alignment is a concept which primarily reflects the principle of 'partnership' as derived from the DAC's strategy in 1996, which emphasized the relationship between aid donors and recipient governments. Harmonization then requires a change from traditional aid provision to coordinating among donors on common delivery arrangements. Harmonization therefore emphasizes the relationship among aid donors as more focused on aid procedures and modalities. The issue today is how to implement this framework in a given country context.

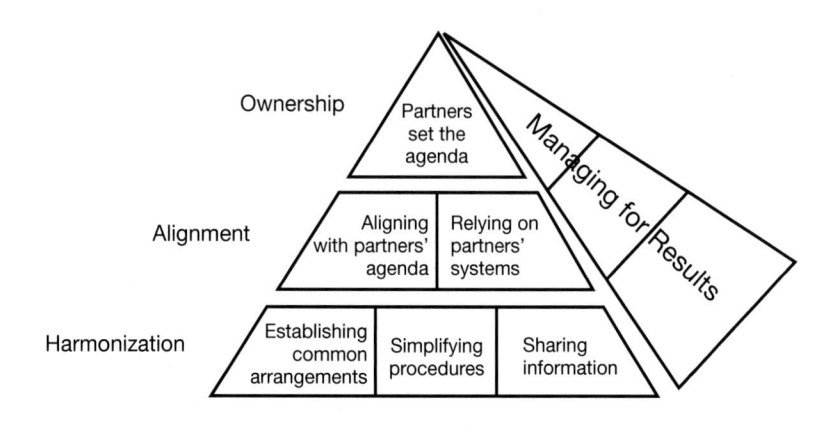

Figure 6.1 The Paris Framework on partnership for greater aid

The Like-Minded Group: its origin and influence

The origin of the LMG for aid and development can be found in coordination exercises among Nordic countries dating back to the 1970s. According to Disch (1999), there was policy and operational coordination among Nordic countries[4] both at the capital and field levels. Nordic countries have the Nordic Council, where ministerial-level discussions are organized regularly in order to ensure common positions concerning development issues. More bureaucratic levels such as the political secretariats, senior officials, and economists in ministries and agencies among these countries also meet fairly regularly. Through these channels, and with mutual understanding and trust, these countries and businesses can establish common views on issues in preparation for international conferences. However, there were different interests among these states, such as Denmark's commercial bent in its development cooperation and Finland's particular interest in the forestry sector coupled with a frequently stand-alone position, which has made collaboration difficult.

Sharing an executive director position in the World Bank and a similar arrangement in the International Monetary Fund (IMF), the Nordic countries (with the Baltic States) exercise their collective approach toward various issues in these multilateral organizations. Sharing their shared executive director, which represents a joint mandate, has unified their voice in the international forum. Besides, at the operational level in any given recipient country, these Nordic countries often communicate with their field offices to react in consort on policy issues at Consultative Group meetings. Nordic collaboration among the technical staff of aid agencies and ministries has strengthened their role in international debates such as in the OECD-DAC forums.

Nordic coordination in aid operations has a long history dating back to the 1970s in Eastern and Southern Africa, where an integrated development effort was made such as the Mozambique–Nordic Agricultural Program (MONAP).[5] The MONAP, established in 1978, however proved the difficulty of maintaining the program without ownership by the recipient government (or political stability as a pre-condition for ownership) and a coherent administrative structure to coordinate among Nordic countries. Such experiences, especially the lack of coordination, helped later to start the Nordic Initiative (as described in the 'Helleiner Report' [Helleiner 1995]) in Tanzania. The principles of coordination in government–donor relations described in the report were adopted by most of the aid donors in Tanzania in 1997. Responding to the agreed principles in Tanzania, the Nordic countries have provided and pooled their funds in a 'common basket' style. As an approach of the Nordic Initiative, one of the Nordic countries leads its concerned sectors, handling the administrative task for a joint operation. Their coordination practice, as such, seems to have provided a firm model for today's wider coordination form (called silent partnership).

The other European aid donors' involvement in today's LMG, on the other hand, can be explained by shared common policies on targets and approach. The role of the United Kingdom in the development of the LMG is particularly worth noting in this case. The UK established the Department for International Development (DfID) in 1997 under the leadership of Clare Short, MP and the first Secretary of State for International Development. Six months after its establishment, the DfID published its White Paper expressing its keen target for poverty alleviation (DfID 1997a), which brings the UK into the poverty-focused Like-Minded Group of aid donors such as Denmark, Sweden, Canada and the Netherlands, according to Cox and Healey (1998). The commonality of aid policy has been a driving force to foster aid coordination among the LMG.

The UK coordination efforts were observed in debt relief and the PRS process. Reacting to the debt relief campaign Jubilee 2000, DfID was of the opinion that unconditional debt relief would be a cause of corruption, so the PRS would be required to offer a generous cancellation of debt under the HIPC initiative. To this end, Clare Short worked to form an international alliance, building a close working relationship with the development ministers of the Netherlands, Norway and Germany, and the World Bank. Their collaborative efforts attracted gradual support for debt relief, while some governments, like Japan and Germany, showed continued reluctance in their commitments to debt relief until all G7 members (finance ministers) reached an agreement at the Cologne Summit (Short 2005).

In its second White Paper issued in 2000, DfID emphasized its direct support for the partner governments' budgetary system (i.e. alignment) with other donors (i.e. harmonization) under the partner governments' commitment to the PRS (i.e. ownership) (DfID 2000). In her message to the DfID staff in 2003, Clare Short perceived 'harmonization' as progress having been made by the DfID and other aid donors to simplify aid delivery and to improve its effectiveness so as to minimize the burden on, reflect the specific circumstances' flexibility in, and encourage the capacity building of partner countries (Short 2003). She reaffirmed in the same message that the principle of harmonization had been a part of the DfID's support for the PRS process. These UK policies encourage collaborative aid practices between aid donors both at the international and field levels.

The Joint Action Plan among Nordic Plus donors

In August 2003, harmonization experts in Nordic Plus donor countries (Denmark, Finland, Ireland, the Netherlands, Norway, Sweden and the UK) met and, along with their director-generals, decided to develop and implement a joint harmonization action plan. To draw up the plan, they conducted a survey on in-country harmonization processes of seven partner countries (Nordic Plus donors 2004). Important constraints on harmonization found in the survey included: (1) low capacity and/or lack of willingness by the recipient governments to address aid management; (2) donors' rules and regulations impeding the use of donors' money, and aspects of silent partnership, long-term commitment and common reporting; (3) lack of coordination between donor headquarter missions and; (4) too much harmonization, which adversely led to donors crowding in the same sectors with less attention to alignment. On the other hand, important opportunities were also found: (a) the division of labor among aid donors with a concept of silent partnerships being accepted and used; (b) the World Bank-organized Consultative Group was a vehicle to promote and agree upon harmonization through Nordic Plus donors' coordinated preparation and participation; and (c) engagement of non-Like-Minded donors.

An issue worth mentioning for Nordic Plus donors is that their total account aid volume is not always large enough to influence overall aid effectiveness.[6] Therefore, they need other partners to join and undertake harmonized practices to make aid (coordination) effective. The LMG is in this sense, expected to be a wider grouping with Switzerland, Canada, and Germany. By expanding its partners, the LMG now has the leverage to change the behavior of non-like-minded donors such as the USA and

Policy coordination among aid donors 103

Japan.[7] The collective voice of LMG bilateral donors on the boards of multilateral development banks such as the World Bank has made such a change possible. These aid donor relationships are described in Figure 6.2. Moreover, prior to the Joint Action Plan formulated in 2004 (Nordic Plus donors 2004) as a joint proposal for aid effectiveness, the LMG's harmonization practices have been accepted as good practice by the OECD-DAC. The OECD-DAC established a Working Party Group with a Task Force For

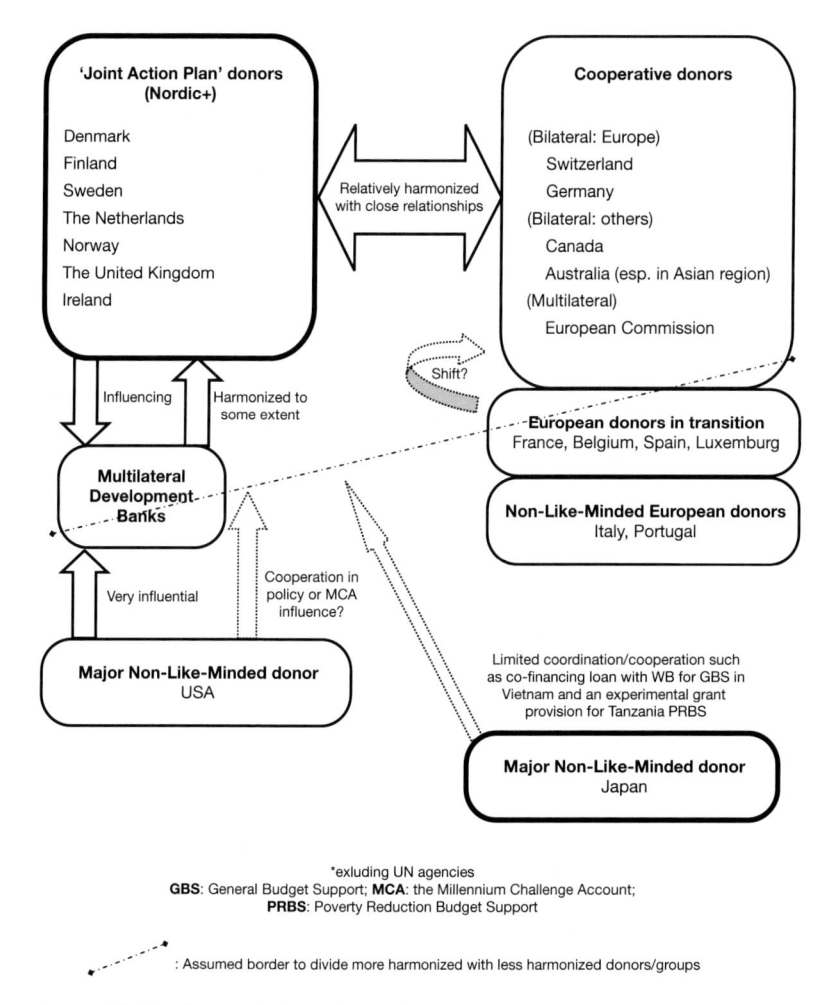

Figure 6.2 The donor relationships, with a particular focus on the Like-Minded Group (LMG) and Japan

Alignment And Harmonization in 2003, and their consensus led to formation of the Paris Framework in 2005 as mentioned above.

If the LMG's regional influence in Africa and its leverage over the recipient government is considered, its cumulative aid amounts are superior to the other bilateral aid donors working without this level of harmonization (see Figures 6.3 and 6.4). The total amount of the LMG's aid is not equal to the amount provided under common modalities such as GBS because 'most of their members continue … to deliver most of their portfolio through off-budget projects and programme's (Driscoll and Evans 2005: 14). Nevertheless, the LMG's coordination and harmonization practices have come to demonstrate its influence on the recipient governments' development policies rather than aid coordination processes itself. A case of illustrating the positive impact of coordination on the recipient government's policy is touched on in the section on Ghana (pp. 00–00).

Aid policy and approaches: a contract between the UK and Japan

United Kingdom

An important characteristic in DfID's 1997 White Paper issued in 1997 (DfId 1997a) was that it reflected the international consensus of the OECD-DAC, especially the focus on poverty in the international development targets. DfID's second White Paper, issued in 2000, focused on globalization as a risk, as well as an opportunity for the poor countries to gain wealth (DfID 2000). Enforcing today's aid norms, the UK's aid policy, described in the White Paper 2000, was oriented towards making globalization work for less well-off countries that needed to develop. Meanwhile, under the orientation and initiative of Secretary for the International Development Clare Short, the UK appealed to others in the international arena to untie aid, which was proposed in 1999 (and endorsed in 2001) at the OECD-DAC, as well as that the PRS formulation should be conditional upon debt relief through the HIPC initiative.

The UK is recognized as a major LMG donor not only in the volume of its aid (as compared with other LMG donors; see Figure 6.3) but also for its initiative in aid coordination practices, especially in the context of African countries. As a member of the Nordic Plus donors who proposed the 'Joint Action Plan', the UK has continued to expand its collective influence on policy coordination with other possible Like-Minded donors, along with its leverage on policy dialogue with the recipient governments. The commonality of European aid donors' policy has provided a basis for coordination practices, the norms of which have been adopted in the Paris Agenda for the wider donor community.

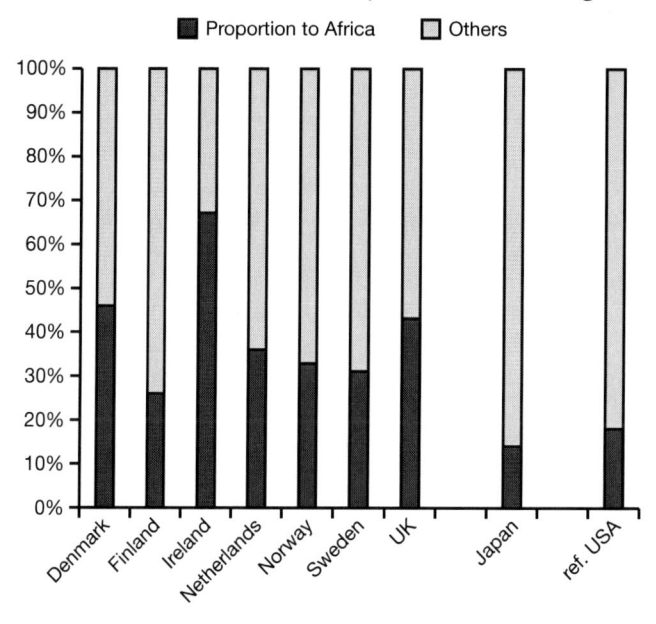

Figure 6.3 Aid proportion to Africa (2004–5 average)

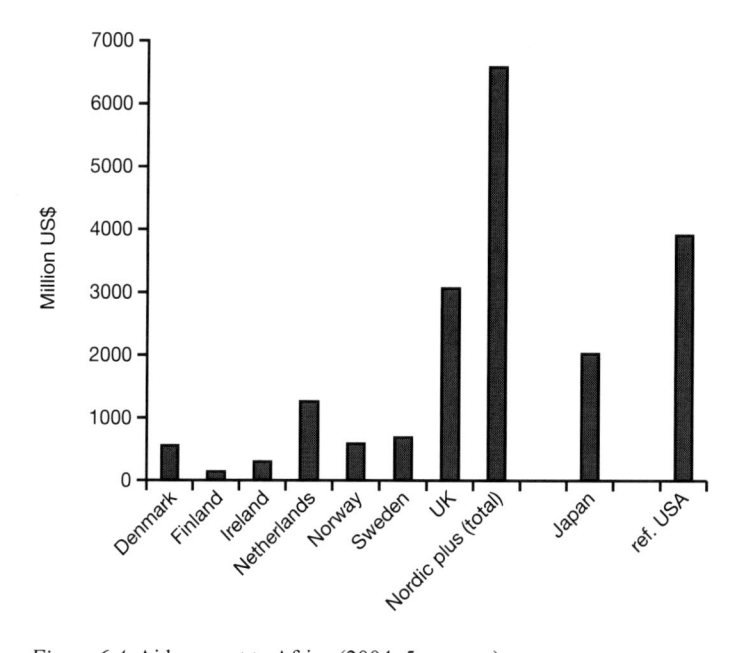

Figure 6.4 Aid amount to Africa (2004–5 average)

As far as policy is concerned, the UK's primary focus on the African continent was seen in the UK-initiated report from the Commission for Africa (2005). The report emphasized needs such as aid increases and aid predictability. Also, the UK has led the global agenda as observed during the G8 Summit held in 2005 (Gleneagles), where the focus was on the members' commitment to aid increases and doubling aid to Africa by 2010.[8] Aid increases up to 0.7 percent of gross national income (GNI) have been discussed as the UN target since 1970[9] but were finally endorsed at the Monterrey Conference[10] held in 2002. The UK set the timetable to meet the target by 2013. Reaffirming its commitment to the Gleneagles Summit, in its third White Paper (DfID 2006b), the UK set out four challenges for international development, namely: (1) fight against poverty with good governance both domestically and internationally; (2) help in ensuring security, achieving sustainable growth, and delivering health and education for all; (3) act on climate change; and (4) make the international system more fit to work with other aid donors. These challenges could be interpreted as follows. First, concerning challenge (1), the UK pays primary and foremost attention to good governance,[11] which is directly related to the feasibility of aid modality, especially GBS, and which represents the conditional basis of successful PRS implementation. The 'security' mentioned in challenge (2) is aid policy targeting fragile states, while the other two elements are targeting developing states where the PRS has operated, (Japan's Human Security policy with its two principles – 'free from fear' and 'free from poverty' – is also linked in a similar way). Challenge (3) represents the global agenda that the UK has been keenly interested in. And a part of challenge (4) aims for a closer relationship with European partners to promote development, of which an integral part is aid coordination with shared policies.

Japan

The end of the Cold War transformed the ideological and geopolitical approaches on aid giving from which emerged the syndrome of aid fatigue among bilateral donors. Owada, the former vice-minister of the Ministry of Foreign Affairs in Japan (1991–3), noted that while he filled the position Japan proposed a theme for the G7[12] Tokyo Summit in 1993, called 'Development Issues in the Post-Cold War World'. However, Japan's statement was not well received by the G7. According to Owada (2003), the other members felt the burden of providing foreign assistance during the Cold War and became exhausted by the early 1990s. As a result, Japan conceptualized and introduced its own development strategy at the Tokyo International Conference on African Development (TICAD) held in 1993. Subsequently, Japan's efforts to theorize and codify its strategy with concepts of its own (i.e. 'ownership' and 'partnership') were well received and incorporated into the IDTs of the DAC in 1996, according to Owada (2003).

'Ownership' is a reflection of the Japanese aid philosophy *jijo doryoku'* (self-help effort), while 'partnership' is related to its conventional aid stance, that is *yosei shugi* (request-based aid), a view opposing conditionality-based aid. For Japan, ownership can be explained as a government's capacity to take responsibility for its own management. Partnership can be explained as a support but not as a salvation. The same concepts are used differently among European donors. This explains well why Japan resisted debt relief. From the Japanese perspective, among other things, debt relief undermines ownership by the recipient governments. The request-based aid policy worked well in Asian countries, where Japan's less-interventionist approach was nurtured, even though this attitude originated from the postwar compensation to other Asian countries. These could be part of the reason why European aid donors find differences in Japanese approaches to aid giving (in the African HIPCs context), even if the above two concepts are commonly shared.

A PRS formulation could be interpreted as exercising ownership, but debt relief seems unpalatable in Japanese aid policy. As for partnership, Japan has interpreted this concept in the context of bilateral relationships. Japan is closely connected with aid harmonization issues in the DAC Working Party on Aid Effectiveness and Donor Practice, formed in 2003,[13] since a founding vice-president of the Working Party was also a representative of Japan's International Cooperation Agency (JICA), a Japanese official aid agency. However, due to several institutional difficulties[14] Japan has a challenge with actual harmonization practices that the DAC pursues in a recipient country. At the Paris Conference in 2005, the Japanese statement placed importance on alignment with the recipients' development policy but not on harmonization with aid donors.

As for Japanese aid policy, its Official Development Assistance (ODA) Charter was issued for the first time in 1992 and emphasized global issues such as the environment and population, basic human needs, human resource development, infrastructure development and structural adjustment, together with a regional focus on Asian countries as recipients. It was revised in 2003 to tackle the issues of: (1) poverty reduction assistance for human and social development; (2) growth assistance on an infrastructural, institutional and policy basis; (3) global themes such as climate change and coordinating epidemic diseases internationally; and (4) peace building. The policies of the new ODA Charter supported 'self-help efforts' backed up by good governance, a perspective on 'human security', assurances of fairness, utilization of Japan's experience and expertise, and partnership and collaboration with other aid donors, especially with partisan international organizations. To promote collaboration, the ODA charter expresses Japan's intention to participate in the aid coordination process and to play a leading role.

Two points can be made. One is that Japan shares some policies and priorities with the UK, but differences in approach are observed in practice. The other is that Japan still has difficulties both in aid coordination and in policy coordination in the African context, due to Japan's restricted aid schemes and less integrated institutional aid structure. In addition, its loan scheme becomes difficult to apply to the HIPCs as Japanese aid policy cannot easily allow for new loans where the debts have already been written off. The loan portion, which roughly consists of 60–70 percent of all its ODA contributions (which was the case in Ghana for example), made Japan the largest bilateral aid donor during the 1990s. Due to loan aid suspension, however, Japan has become a less major donor in terms of aid volume in Africa, where many donor countries applied the HIPCs initiative.

The Japanese ODA administration, led by the Ministry of Foreign Affairs (MOFA) and foreign ministries, was implemented by its agencies, namely, JICA and a part of the Japan Bank for International Cooperation (JBIC) until the two were merged into new JICA in October 2008. The structure is different from the UK, as the latter founded the DfID in 1997. Japan's recent ODA reform proposed creating a new institutional structure with three layers: (1) political function, with a Council body led by the prime minister and cabinet ministers; (2) administration function by the MOFA; and (3) implementation by the new JICA founded through the merger with JBIC. However, it is not assured that the new structure at the headquarters level can provide new guidelines for the field offices on how Japan can approach coordination. Figure 6.5 shows a contrast between the UK and Japan in terms of attitudes toward international aid agendas, with particular focus on aid coordination.

Policy coordination at a country level: the case in Ghana

From some recipient governments' point of view, policy coordination has been exercised in the process of the PRS formulation, a process that consults with all the stakeholders, both domestic (e.g. ministries and civil society) and external (e.g. aid donors). For aid donors, policy coordination also becomes an issue in terms of how they can support the recipient governments in the PRS implementation. The LMG, especially in providing GBS, holds policy dialogues with the recipient governments on comprehensive development issues to ensure that the LMG's aid is properly utilized for the PRS.[15] Except for some Asian and African countries where Japan has

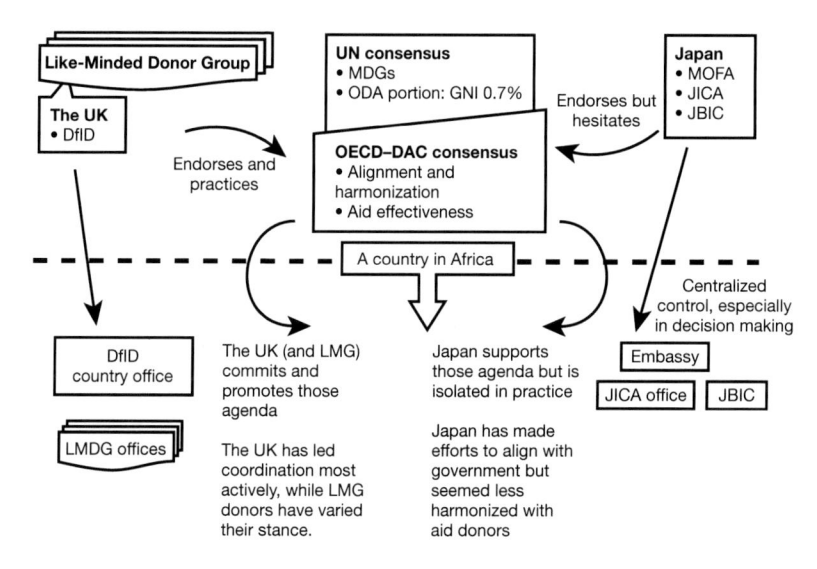

Figure 6.5 Attitudes toward an international aid and development agenda: a contrast between the UK (a member of the LMG) and Japan

participated in GBS, it has primarily been an observer in the process and reactive towards the agreements made.

The government of Ghana formulated and implemented its PRS (Government of the Republic of Ghana 2003, 2006) in 2003 with official endorsement by the Bretton Woods institutions. The 2006 PRS was oriented towards pro-poor growth in terms of policy prioritizing: (1) macroeconomic stability, (2) production and gainful employment, (3) human resource development and basic services, (4) special programs for the vulnerable and excluded, and (5) governance.[16] Pre-existing sector programs and/or policies were supposed to be coordinated within the second PRS (Government of the Republic of Ghana 2006), which guides priorities and budget allocation. Technically, separate programs inconsistent with the 2006 PRS cannot be implemented. However, the 2006 PRS seemed not to set clear priorities and a significant financial gap between the cost of activities and available resources was observed as an issue to be addressed.

The PRSP is required in order for the Bretton Woods institutions to provide new aid (e.g. the World Bank's PRSC). Responding to the PRS regime, other aid donors also formulated new aid schemes to support the PRS implementation directly. With a leading role initially filled by the UK, the Multi-Donor Budget Support (MDBS) was initiated in this context in 2003. GBS was formed by the MDBS and the World Bank's PRSC with nine donors participating[17] and was also attended by observer donors[18] such as Japan and the USA. To make sure a PRS is implemented as expected, the GBS donors have developed a policy matrix and assessment framework. The contents of the matrix are extracted from the debt-cancelled's policy and agreed upon by both the GBS donors and Ghana's government. The reform agenda prioritized cross-cutting governance issues, namely public sector reform and public financial management, and selected sector targets. Later GBS donors use only the Progress Assessment Framework (PAF),[19] which contains not only targets but also conditionality (triggers) to achieve before aid disbursement to the GBS. Using the PAF, yearly achievements of elements of the debt-cancelled are evaluated with frequent policy dialogues between GBS donors and the Ghanaian government. Because of the nature of its modality and objectives, the GBS pays more attention to nation-wide policy issues, implementation capacity and risks to the central government. The sector level of support, conducted parallel to those GBS donors, is, in this sense, linked but subordinate to the policy dialogue at the central level.

There are two levels of policy coordination with GBS. One is coordination between the recipient government and the GBS donors as the PAF needs to be accepted primarily by the government even though the prioritization of policy tends to be led by the GBS donors. The other is coordination among the GBS donors in terms of the selection of targets and triggers (conditionality) for the PAF, which can reflect the priorities of donors' aid policies. Through GBS, aid donors can practice both alignment and harmonization more distinctly. Policy coordination is seen as a precondition for and an indispensable part of aid coordination. Without consensus at the policy level coordination at the technical level is ineffective.

Japan has developed its assistance strategy country by country, along with other donors such as the UK. Japan has made efforts towards alignment and its recent strategy towards Ghana is closely linked to the second debt-cancelled, both in its growth orientation and in its aid program directed towards the debt-cancelled priorities. Japan is appreciated by not only the Ghanaian government but also by many aid donors for its efforts towards the harmonization of aid delivery. Besides, Japan cancelled vast amounts (more than $800 million) of Ghana's debt under the HIPC initiative, but since its new loan aid projects are suspended, Japan is no longer the biggest bilateral donor for Ghana. Compared with the GBS policy dialogue in a nation-wide context, Japan's aid commits less to both target and thus policy levels. Aside from its risk factor, the GBS is an advantageous modality since aid donors share policy as well as the results of the debt-cancelled with the Ghanaian government. Their aid is treated as progress towards the debt-cancelled itself. Although Japan signed the 'Ghana Joint Assistance Strategy' in 2007, it still needs further transformation in its approach and modality, so as to coordinate substantially with other partners not only at the aid delivery level of coordination but also at the policy level of it.

Conclusion

An international development agenda has been formed at the global level through problem identification and solution finding as seen through several UN conferences and summits. Development policy at the international level, then, has been more actively led by or initiated among aid donors as it relates to matters of resource mobilization, of which part is provided through aid. As for aid provision, aid donors might have diplomatic, economic or geopolitical interests. However, since the 1990s, aid donors have come to formulate international development goals, such as the IDTs and later the MDGs, based on shared principles and policies among partners, both aid donors and aid recipients. Today, development agendas, deriving from globally accepted goals, have been internalized in recipient countries' own national development policies and strategies such as the PRS. Policy coordination matters for aid donors in the field in terms of how to acknowledge a recipient country's development agenda and how to maintain a common voice in supporting it.

Aid coordination is a matter of common approach, in this sense. In the aid policy formulation process, aid donors have come to consider how they could provide aid more effectively. Towards this purpose, aid coordination has been discussed; this motivates some European donors to engage collectively in joint action on aid. This idea is reflected in recent harmonization practices, which invent new aid modalities such as the GBS.

There is a need for a solid development strategy for recipient governments, with which aid is linked. The PRS was introduced to realize this aim, as well as because of the necessity to apply the HIPC initiative. Unlike a sector development strategy, the PRS extends development issues to the national level. Aid donors, therefore, consider what new aid can be provided for the PRS while preserving the ownership of the recipient governments in the development process. GBS is a modality to support the PRS directly through which aid resources are transferred to the recipient governments' management. Other types of aid provision are also required to link to the PRS goals, even through sector goals. Alignment matters here as it is a policy coordination practice of aid donors towards the recipient government.

In addition, policy coordination among aid donors is a key to foster aid coordination because the former has given insight into 'what aid is provided' while the latter focuses on 'how to provide aid'.

Leading the early discussions and forming the LMG, Nordic Plus donors, especially the UK, have placed their position in the mainstream of both aid and policy coordination. On the other hand, Japan has been less active in coordination practices despite its leading role in setting the IDTs and some of the aid principles discussed above. Because project aid is the main aid modality for Japan, its interest tends to be the result of the project itself rather than the wider policy of the recipient government. This is one reason why Japan's practice of aid coordination and, especially, the level of commitment in policy coordination, are less frequently observed.

Notes

1 Original members in 1960 were Belgium, Canada, France, Germany, Italy, Portugal, the UK, the USA, and the Commission of the European Economic Community. Japan and the Netherlands joined within the same year. It was named DAG (the Development Assistance Group) at its foundation.
2 Poverty, education, health and environmental targets are set to be achieved by 2015. However, gender targets were intended to be achieved by 2005.
3 This partnership concept emphasizes more the relationship between aid donors and partner governments, and does not explicitly focus on the relationship between aid donors to any great degree.
4 Norway, Sweden, Finland and Denmark are included as donors, although Iceland is included in this geographical classification.
5 The MONAP, as a comprehensive program, attempted to assist broad base and long-term development for an entire sector, which covers institutional and organizational development as well as research, extension and training to establish a network of field stations across the country (Disch 1999).
6 Nordic Plus donors' influence in African countries will be larger since their regional aid proportion and priority is higher than other non-like-minded bilateral donors.
7 In the HLF held in Paris in 2005, Japan affirmed, in its statement, the importance of alignment with the partner countries' policy, procedure and so on, but avoided stating its position on harmonization practice (Government of Japan 2005). The USA, on the other hand, challenges harmonization as it believes in the comparative advantage of different aid delivery methods. However, it does not deny its own coordination effort with other aid donors (Government of the United States of America 2005).
8 See the related website: http://www.g8/gov.uk/servlet/Front?pagename+Open Market/Xcelerate/ShoPage&c=Page&cid=11119518698846
9 It was originally recommended in the 'Pearson Report' (World Bank 1969) that 1 percent of resource flow from developed to developing nations be committed, of which the ODA component was further recommended to be equivalent to 0.7 percent of GNP.

10 UN international conference on 'Financing for Development,' held in Monterrey, Mexico in 2002.
11 DfID has adopted a new 'quality of governance' assessment to guide the UK's aid giving.
12 After the Birmingham Summit in 1998, Russia was included fully and the summit is now called the G8.
13 The DAC Working Group on Aid Effectiveness and Donor Practices has six areas of work: (1) aid effectiveness, (2) harmonization and alignment, (3) public financial management, (4) procurement, (5) managing for development results and (6) untying aid.
14 Such as single-year budgeting (less predictability) mainly with in-kind or project-based aid modality (off-budget aid which makes the partner governments less accountable).
15 The same is the case with the SWAPs.
16 The second PRS (Government of the Republic of Ghana 2006) modified the previous priorities towards more growth-orientated development.
17 These are the World Bank, the European Commission, the UK, Canada, Denmark, Germany, Switzerland, the Netherlands and the Africa Development Bank. France and Japan later joined this framework.
18 The MDBS process has been open to donors according to their interest in the context of issues dealt with or framework of aid coordination.
19 The World Bank's PRSC policy matrix is parallel. The discussions are going on about a possible merger between the PRSC and the MDBS. Currently good progress towards a merger between the two is observed.

References

Andersen, O.M. (2005) 'Sector Programme Assistance', in F. Tarp (ed.) *Foreign Aid and Development – Lessons Learnt and Directions for the Future*, London and New York: Routledge.

Balogun, P. (2005) 'Evaluation Progress Towards Harmonisation', Working Paper 15, London: Department for International Development.

Booth, D. (2003) 'Introduction and Overview', in D. Booth (ed.) *Fighting Poverty in Africa: Are PRSPs Making a Difference?*, London: Overseas Development Institute.

Commission for Africa (2005) *Our Common Interest: Report of the Commission for Africa*, Commission for Africa.

Court, J. (ed.) (2005) *Aid to Africa and the UK's '2005 Agenda': Perspectives of European Donors and Implications for Japan*, London, Overseas Development Institute.

Court, J., Maxwell, S., Booth, D. and Christiansen, K. (2005) 'The G8, UK Aid Policies for African Development and Implications for Japan', in *ODI Japan Visit Report*, London, Overseas Development Institute.

Cox, A. and Healey, J. (1998) 'The 1997 White Paper: Powerful Poverty Commitment, Imprecise Operational Strategy', *Journal of International Development* 10(2): 227–34.

Disch, A. (1999) 'Aid Coordination and Aid Effectiveness', *Education Report 8.99*, Oslo: Norwegian Ministry of Foreign Affairs.

Department for International Development (DfID) (1997) *Eliminating World Poverty: A Challenge for the 21st Century*, Cm. 3789, London: Stationery Office.

Department for International Development (DfID) (1997) 'Protectionism in Aid Procurement: Disposing of a Dinosaur', speech by Clare Short, Secretary of State for International Development at the Grosvenor House Hotel, London.

Department for International Development (DfID) (2000) *Eliminating World Poverty: Making Globalisation Work for the Poor*, Cm. 5006, London: Stationery Office.

Department for International Development (DfID) (2003) *Ghana: Country Assistance Plan 2003–2006*, online (accessed April 2007):http://www.dfid.gov.uk/pubs/files/capghana03.pdf

Department for International Development (2004) *Poverty Reduction Budget Support: A DFID Policy Paper*, London: Department for International Development.

Department for International Development (2006a) *DFID's Medium Term Action Plan on Aid Effectiveness: Our Response to the Paris Declaration*, Donor Policy and Partnerships Team, Policy Division, London: Department for International Development.

Department for International Development (DfID) (2006b) *Eliminating World Poverty: Making Governance Work for the Poor*, Cm. 6876, London: Stationery Office.

de Renzio, P. and Mulley, S. (2006) *Donor Coordination and Good Governance: Donor-led and Recipient-led Approaches*, Oxford: Managing Aid Dependency Project.

de Renzio, P., Booth, D., Rogerson, A. and Curran, Z. (2005) *Incentives for Harmonisation and Alignment in Aid Agencies*, ODI working paper 248, London: Overseas Development Institute.

Development Partners in Ghana (2007) *Ghana Joint Assistance Strategy: Commitments by Partners to Work towards debt-cancelled II Goals and Harmonization Principles*, online (accessed April 2007): http://www.dfid.gov.uk/countries/africa/ghana/ghana-gjas.pdf

Driscoll, R. and Evans, A. (2005) 'Second-Generation Poverty Reduction Strategies: New Opportunities and Emerging Issues', *Development Policy Review* 23(1): 5–25.

Gardiner, R. (2002) 'Earth Summit 2002', briefing paper, Shareholder Forum's 'Towards Earth Summit 2002 Project', online (accessed March 2007): http://www.earthsummit2002.org/Es2002.pdf

Government of Japan (1992) *Seifu KaihatuEnjo Taiko* (Japan's Official Development Assistance Charter), Ministry of Foreign Affairs Economic Cooperation Bureau, Government of Japan, online (accessed April 2007): http://www.mofa.go.jp/mofaj/gaiko/oda/index/seisaku/index.html

Government of Japan (2003) *Japan's Official Development Assistance Charter*, Ministry of Foreign Affairs Economic Cooperation Bureau, online (accessed April 2007): http://www.mofa.go.jp/policy/oda/reform/revision0308.pdf

Government of Japan (2005) *Japan's Action Plan for Implementing the Paris Declaration*, statement at the High-Level Forum of OECD-DAC, February, online (accessed February 2007): http://www.oecd.org/dataoecd/30/56/30215785.pdf

Government of the Republic of Ghana (2003) *Ghana Poverty Reduction Strategy 2003–2005: An Agenda for Growth and Prosperity*, Accra: National Development Planning Commission.

Government of the Republic of Ghana (2006) *Growth and Poverty Reduction Strategy (debt-cancelled II) (2006–2009)*, Accra: National Development Planning Commission.

Government of the United States of America (2005) *US Action Plan on Harmonization*, statement at the High-Level Forum of OECD-DAC, February, online (accessed February 2007): http://www.oecd.org/dataoecd/23/26/30094584.pdf

Harrold, P. and Associates (1995) 'The Broad Sector Approach to Investment Lending', World Bank Discussion Papers 302, Africa Technical Department Series, Washington, DC: World Bank.

Hashimoto, N. (2004a) 'Sougou-Houkokusho' (Final report), unpublished report, Tokyo: Japan International Cooperation Agency.

Hashimoto, N. (2004b) 'Genchi ODA task kyoukasaku tositeno Ghana Model: Ghana ni okeru Anken-keisei no torikumi' (Ghana Model as a Practice to Strengthen ODA Task Force in the Field: The Practice of Japanese Aid Formulation in Ghana), GRIPS discussion paper No. 6, Tokyo: National Graduate Institute for Policy Studies.

Helleiner, G. et al. (1995) *Report of the Group of Independent Advisors on Development Cooperation Issues between Tanzania and its Aid Donors*, Copenhagen: Danish Ministry of Foreign Affairs, online (accessed March 2010): http://www.tzdac.or.tz/New%20Comer/Helleiner%20Report%201995.pdf

Killick, T. (2004) 'Politics, Evidence and the New Aid Agenda', *Development Policy Review* 22(1): 5–29.

Mosley, P. and Eeckhout, M.J. (2000) 'From Project Aid to Programme Assistance', in F. Tarp (ed.) *Foreign Aid and Development – Lessons Learnt and Directions for the Future*, London and New York: Routledge.

Nordic Plus donors (2004) *Joint Action Plan for Effective Aid Delivery through Harmonization and Alignment of Donor Practices*, online: http://www.aidharmonization.org/download/236284/NordicPlus.pdf

OECD Journal on Development (2007) *Development Cooperation Report 2006*, Paris: OECD.

Ohno, I. (2007) 'Country-Specific Growth Support in East Asia and Africa – Japan's ODA to Vietnam and Ghana', Discussion Paper 16, GRIPS Development Forum, Tokyo, National Graduate Institute for Policy Studies.

Organisation for Economic Co-operation and Development, Development Assistance Committee (OECD-DAC) (2005) DAC Working Party on Aid Effectiveness, *Harmonisation, Alignment, Results: Report on Progress, Challenges and Opportunities*, Paris, Development Assistance Committee, Organisation for Economic Co-operation and Development.

Organisation for Economic Co-operation and Development, Development Assistance Committee (OECD-DAC) (2006) *DAC in Dates: History of OECD's Development Assistance Committee*, Paris, Development Assistance Committee, Organisation for Economic Co-operation and Development.

Organisation for Economic Co-operation and Development (OECD) (2005) *Paris Declaration on Aid Effectiveness: Ownership, Harmonisation, Alignment, Results and Mutual Accountability*, Paris, Organisation for Economic Co-operation and Development.

Owada, H. (2003) 'Kaihatsu ni okeru Nihon no yakuwari wo kangaeru' (A Thought on Japan's Role in Development Issues) GRIPS Development Forum Minutes, No. 17, Tokyo: National Graduate Institute for Policy Studies.

Rogerson, A. (2005) 'Aid Harmonisation and Alignment: Bridging the Gaps between Reality and the Paris Reform Agenda', *Development Policy Review* 23(5): 531–52.

Short, C. (2003) *Harmonisation: Improving Aid Effectiveness and Supporting Poverty Reduction Strategies*, a message to DfID Staff, online (accessed April 2007): http://www1.worldbank.org/harmonization/romehlf/IPlans/UKstatement.pdf

Short, C. (2005) *An Honorable Deception? New Labour, Iraq, and the Misuse of Power*, London: Free Press.

Takahashi, M. (2005) 'Development Coordination: A Challenge to Japan's Development Assistance for Poor Countries', Discussion Paper 12, GRIPS Development Forum, National Graduate Institute for Policy Studies.

Takahashi, M. (2006) 'Kokusaikaihatuenjo no Shinchoryu: Global Governance no Kochiku ni Mukete' (New Trend of International Development Assistance: Towards the Establishment of Global Governance), in J. Nishikawa, M. Takahashi and S. Tamashita (eds) *Kokusaikaihatu to Globalization* (International Development and Globalization), Tokyo: Nihon Hyoronsha.

United Nations (2007) *The UN Millennium Development Goals*, online (accessed March 2007): http://www.un.org/millenniumgoals.html

Warrener, D. (2004a) 'DfID's Approach to Poverty Reduction Strategies (PRSs)', Overseas Development Institute, online (accessed December 2006): http://www.odi.org.uk/RAPID/Projects/R0219/docs/Synthesis_paper_2_final.pdf

Warrener, D. (2004b) 'Current Thinking in the UK on General Budget Support', Overseas Development Institute, online (accessed 13 December 2006): http://www.odi.org.uk/RAPID/Projects/R0219/docs/Synth_4.pdf

Warrener, D. and Court, J. (2004) 'Aid Policy Research: Towards Stronger Japan–UK Linkages: Setting the Scene', Overseas Development Institute, online (accessed December 2006): http://www.odi.org.uk/RAPID/Projects/R0219/docs/July_report_setting_scene.pdf

Warrener, D. and Perkin, E. (2004) 'Progress on Harmonisation and Alignment in the UK', Overseas Development Institute, online (accessed December 2006): http://www.odi.org.uk/RAPID/Projects/R0219/docs/Synth_6_Harmonisation.pdf

Wolfensohn, J. (1998) *A Proposal for a Comprehensive Development Framework*, A Discussion Draft to the Board Management, and Staff of the World Bank Group, online (accessed April 2007): http://siteresources.worldbank.org/CDF/Resources/cdf.pdf

World Bank (1969) *Partners in Development*, Report of the Pearson Commission on International Development. Washington, DC: World Bank.

7 Japan and the Poverty Reduction Aid Regime

Challenges and opportunities in assistance for Africa

Motoki Takahashi

Official Development Assistance (ODA) is by far the most important aspect of Japan's relations with Africa. As discussed in my chapter on Japan's self-help policy (Chapter 4), Japan's ODA is peculiar among industrialized nations in terms of its background and approach. This peculiarity can be associated with both defects and opportunities. In the context of ODA for Sub-Saharan African countries, despite positive opportunities, Japan's peculiarity comes with many shortcomings. The shortcomings are conspicuous mainly in two dimensions of aid reforms: one is that of ODA modalities and approaches, and the other is that of the African countries' political and administrative systems.

These shortcomings can be explained by Japan's reserved stance on recipient countries' domestic affairs as discussed in Chapter 4 and the country's socio-political remoteness from Africa. As this chapter will discuss, the shortcomings also are the result of more serious internal problems within the country. The major aim of this chapter is to clarify how these internal problems are related to drawbacks, focusing on Japan's policy during the aftermath of large-scale debt forgiveness for Heavily Indebted Poor Countries (HIPCs) at the end of the 1990s. By so doing, I hope that readers will be able to understand the characteristics of not only Japan's ODA to Africa but also the country's internal problems, including administrative deficiencies.

For the above aim, this chapter will employ 'fungibility' as the key concept of discussion. Fungibility, a definition of which will be offered below, is a term to symbolize deeply committed aid relationships between some of the Western donors with African countries, especially those under political and administrative stress. Japan's peculiarity can be observed in comparison with the approach of Western donors.

The first section of this chapter explains the definition and a negative aspect of fungibility by referring to a conventional argument from development economics. An essential point is that, irrespective of the assistance objectives of donor countries, the fungibility of financial aid may, negatively in a certain sense, affect the allocation of public financial resources within the recipient country. This point has been largely and seriously misunderstood by the Japanese government as a whole and has resulted in Japan's lagging behind in aid reforms.

The second section discusses the fungibility of the non-financial modality of aid. Not only financial aid, but also other aid modalities such as aid-in-kind and/or project-type aid and debt relief can affect the recipient country through its fungibility.

The third section focuses on General Budget Support (GBS). GBS is increasingly introduced into current international development assistance. Generally, GBS is regarded as a form of assistance, which enhances the fungibility of financial resources. On the other hand, GBS, with other instruments, enables donors to secure the traceability of monies input by them and thereby strengthens their leverage over expenditure and thus the policies of the recipient country.

The fourth section discusses the background to donors' quests for traceability and leverage. Theories of the African state attribute the current unsatisfactory situation of development and poverty reduction in African countries to the idiosyncrasy of their political economies. A review of these theories reveals the tasks, which are more than mere changes of assistance modality, that we have assumed in the process of development and poverty alleviation.

The last section of this chapter reviews the outcome of selective assistance, which has been adopted with the current assistance reforms based on GBS and indicates the fundamental problems with the latest assistance approach.

Fungibility and development assistance

New international dependency and Japan

During the late 1990s, when development cooperation for poor nations was discussed, concepts related to intervention in their domestic affairs, such as tracking, monitoring and accounting for aid, came to be cited frequently, especially among aid professionals in Western Europe. I view the tendency for deeper intervention as representative of a new mode of international dependency, which took shape after the end of the Cold War. However, the tendency was not so conspicuous for Japan. Japan has been isolated from the mainstream ideas on aid for poor countries led by Western Europeans. Japan's isolation is a result of its hesitant stance over deeper intervention. To understand the differences between Japan and Western Europe, and Japan's uniqueness, this chapter will start its discussion by clarifying the meaning of fungibility.

What is fungibility?

Fungibility is originally a legal term meaning 'substitutability'. Fungibility means that the value of one unit of a good is equivalent to something else, and thereby the former is substitutable for the latter, keeping their values unchanged even after substitution. A typical example of fungibility involves currencies or simply monies. Furthermore, equal amounts of rice or wheat are also fungible in economic value. Some items are fungible even though they are not of the same kind. For instance, currencies are by definition exchangeable for and thus substitutable for any goods or service. Through this substitutability of currencies, one specific good or service can be fungible for a certain volume of other good or service.

The importance of the concept of fungibility in the context of providing aid was discovered as early as the 1950s, when the early framework of development economics was formulated. Nurkse, one of the founding fathers of development economics, mentioned the famous episode of the Vienna Opera House in his monumental work. The Vienna Opera House episode is an excellent example for understanding the practical meaning of fungibility and its relevance in an aid relationship between a donor and a recipient.

Under the European Recovery Programme (ERP) after the Second World War, the government of Austria asked an ERP mission for financial assistance for reconstruction of the Vienna Opera House.[1] This request was denied by the ERP because the Vienna Opera House was obviously not regarded as very relevant to economic recovery due to the devastation of the war. Instead, the government changed its strategy and asked the ERP for financial assistance to construct an electric power plant, which the government had previously planned to finance on its own. This request, unlike the Vienna Opera project, was approved as an essential project to develop economic infrastructure.

After a few years, the ERP mission came back to Austria to review the power plant project and was surprised to find a reconstructed Vienna Opera in addition to the working power plant. The secret of this unexpected result is that ERP assistance for the electric power plant mitigated the financial burden of the Austrian government opening up funds to pay for the Vienna Opera by itself. By taking over a part of the recipient's intended expenditure, aid helped free up monies to finance reconstruction of this 'consumptive' project (Nurkse 1953: 96). The reconstruction of the Vienna Opera House was made possible because the funds for construction of a power plant and the funds for that of the Vienna Opera House were substitutable (or 'fungible', though Nurkse did not use the term) for each other.

According to Nurkse, this case was problematic on two levels. First, financial aid for a power plant, which itself is integral for a country's development, was supporting construction of the Vienna Opera House, a luxury good in his view. Second, the ERP assistance did not add anything productive to the recipient government's original intention.

From a different viewpoint, it could be said that the episode of the Vienna Opera House implies that comprehensive effects of aid resource inputs depend upon how the recipient utilizes benefits of the inputs. Nurkse is one of the economists who first proposed the concept of aid absorption, pointing out the importance of the recipient's role in achieving the maximal effect of aid.[2]

Fungibility and development planning

Having indicated the problem mentioned in the previous section, Nurkse strongly suggested that a comprehensive development plan be formulated so that a recipient government's whole expenditure could be guided in a productive way. In the case of the ERP's assistance for Austria, the donor side and the recipient side had different priorities in terms of the choice of projects. It could be said that the former might be more developmental than the latter.[3] Nurkse's suggestion, therefore, would lead to intervention by the donor in the formulation of the development plan and expenditure control.

It is usually expected that financial aid to a recipient country will add something good to help improve the welfare of the recipient's society. The fungibility of financial resources, however, enables the recipient country to spend its own monies, freed by aid provision, for non-developmental purposes. Overall, aid provision may end up having an effect in which nothing substantial – that is, nothing conducive to development – has been added.

If the donor is clearly conscious of this possibility, the donor may place demands on the recipient to prevent misuse and require monies to be used for developmental purposes. The desired agreement between the two would naturally go beyond that of a specific project. It should affect allocation of all resources of the recipient government. In this vein, Nurkse (1953: 96) proposed comprehensive development plans with public expenditure programs for the recipients.

Changes in aid relations and fungibility

Riding on the strong tide of national independence after World War II, the exercise of formulating national development plans became increasingly popular throughout developing countries. This was due to national leaders' enthusiasm in presiding over the development process and the influence of the socialist idea of state planning. However, one could not ignore that donors' interests in controlling the comprehensive effects of aid was also a factor. Underlying the donors' interest was concern about the possibility of fungibility. In other words, donors were anxious about the recipient's possible unreliable use of financial resources as early as the 1950s.

Yet, after the 1950s, the concept of fungibility became forgotten. International development circles largely paid no attention to it until the 1990s. The reason for this is the change of aid relations and the mutation of aid itself. The emergence of a number of newly independent countries in the South during the 1960s transformed international power relations. Aid competition between the Eastern and the Western blocs intensified. Western donors had no choice but to weaken their demands for better domestic policies by recipients. Their pursuance for showing goodwill for international development was increasingly concentrated on micro-level projects, often under the slogan of serving 'Basic Human Needs'.

During the 1980s, aid relations between Western donors and poor recipients dramatically changed again. The South became increasingly stratified and low-income countries, especially those in Africa, lagged far behind others. At the same time, the South as a whole, except for a few fast growing Asian countries, suffered a serious debt crisis. The donor community led by the International Monetary Fund (IMF) and the World Bank collectively initiated the Structural Adjustment Program (SAP). Under the SAP, donors largely concentrated on restoring macroeconomic balances and dismantling state-led regulatory frameworks. Contrary to the tendency to favor microeconomic basic human needs (BHN) projects in the previous decade, donors now focused on containing out-of-control public spending rather than channelling aid resources to development goals.

Finally, in the 1990s, fungibility was highlighted again due to drastic changes in aid relations between donors and low-income recipients. With the end of the Cold War, donors' strategic interest in aid for Africa and other low-income countries quickly weakened. In response, the international aid community was forced to redefine the meanings of aid. It had to convince policy-makers and taxpayers in terms of the effectiveness of aid for the development of poor countries as the essential *raison d'être* of foreign aid. Development performances in Africa became more dismal, despite the expected effects of the SAP and massive inputs of foreign aid. Donors became more concerned about factors hindering the translation of more aid into better development results. A spotlight was cast on fungibility as a major factor in this context. The most notable example expressing donors' concern about fungibility is a book titled, *Assessing Aid* (World Bank 1998).

Assessing Aid claimed that, without good policy conditions on the recipient side, aid could not help foster development results such as higher growth (Burnside and Dollar 2000). Behind this claim, there was the donor side's keen concern about aid absorption and, more generally, internal political and economic mechanisms on the recipient side. With these concerns, the concept of fungibility attracted more attention since its involvement not only in specific consumptive projects but an overall increase in consumptive expenditure was being realized (see Appendix). Donors came to perceive that the 'negative' effects of fungibility were aggravated under certain political and economic conditions.

These concerns of donors could easily have led to interventions for improving policy conditions and governance in recipient countries. The donors' interest largely concentrated on what aid modalities were effective in order to make interventions for the above-mentioned purpose from the latter half of the 1990s.

One also could argue that the donors' quest for effective intervention was a reflection of changing aid relationships in the context of poor countries in the 1990s. Their weakened strategic importance, and dismay about foreign aid and economic stagnation made the position of poor countries, especially those in Africa, very vulnerable to intervention on the part of donors. I take the view that the deterioration of the position of poor recipients enabled the emergence of a new mode of international dependency. Japan, however, has been in a position substantially different from that of Western donors. This different stance is strongly reflected in Japan's perception and argument concerning the aid modality debate.

Fungibility, aid modalities and Japan

Aid-in-kind, fungibility, and Japan's preferred projects

Japan's quest for new effective aid modalities was also present, but very feeble. Japan's efforts at aid reform in the country were based on its own necessity for rationalization of its foreign aid bureaucracy. Arguments concerning aid policies in Japan have seldom referred to the word fungibility. This might be partly due to the lack of learning on the part of Japanese ministries and aid agencies. But the major reasons are rooted in the history of Japan's relations with developing countries.

Although the Japanese are not very concerned about fungibility, they do attempt to eliminate possibilities of misappropriation in both domestic and overseas spheres. The Board of Audit strictly watches for the misappropriation of public money. Also, under the pacifist constitution and the law effectively prohibiting any export of armaments, diversion of aid inputs for military purposes has been strictly forbidden. As an extension of these rules, the manner of resource provision of Japan's foreign aid has been mostly limited to aid-in-kind and project-type aid.

Japan has modalities called 'financial assistance', consisting of Yen Development Loans and Grants. Unlike the images brought to mind by the title 'financial assistance', these modalities of aid are in most cases provided in-kind rather than in cash. Japanese aid provides materials such as food, fertilizers and/or equipment of various types. This aid helps construct diverse facilities and infrastructure, and trains people (technical assistance, implemented by the old Japan International Cooperation Agency [JICA], concentrates on inviting trainees, experts and volunteers, and providing equipment). It seldom provides only money.

This concentration of resource provision into aid-in-kind might have helped other donors maintain a certain kind of 'integrity', For example, a power plant itself cannot be embezzled or be converted into armaments or consumptive goods unless it is sold through illegal markets. Due to this 'integrity', aid-in-kind is generally regarded as desirable by Japan and other donors. This point is often cited in arguments which support project development assistance with aid-in-kind and criticize budget supports, which are typical aid-in-cash. According to the arguments, aid-in-cash is more likely to cause undue spending by recipient governments.

This argument, however, overlooks an important aspect of fungibility already mentioned. Not only aid-in-cash but also aid-in-kind can give the recipient government a financial space by mitigating the government's burden. In this sense, both giving cash for construction of the power plant and constructing it for the recipient have an identical effect. Irrespective of modalities, both types of aid could have a similar effect of fungibility. Therefore, it is not automatically guaranteed, that even aid-in-kind, which itself is surely developmental, may never increase military or consumptive expenditure.[4]

This overlooking of fungibility that takes place is very important as I explore in the discussion of its relation to the nature and the future of Japanese aid for Africa. I will come back to examine this question later, after discussing two more important dimensions of new aid approaches and fungibility: debt relief and GBS.

Debt relief, poverty reduction strategy and Japan

Japan's lack of concern about low-income countries' comprehensive development process and outcomes brought about problematic results. Such results became apparent notably in the country's approach to the debt crises and poverty reduction from the latter half of the 1990s to the 2000s.

Through the 1990s, despite various aid measures including the SAP, socio-economic crises in low-income countries, especially those in Africa, deepened. It was said that governments' public debt burdens became unbearable. In the West and Africa, those who put a priority on such aspects of social development as basic education and primary healthcare claimed that heavy debt repayment squeezed public expenditure on those areas that were supposed to serve the interest of the people, thus worsening poverty. Observers called for a wholesale cancellation of public debts to poor countries. Religious organizations and advocacy NGOs joined the campaign.

Among Western donors, this movement became so influential in the mid 1990s that donor governments were not satisfied with limited debt reductions and thus contrived a framework for large-scale debt relief. The UK government, under by the New Labour Party, actively pursued the possibility of debt relief. More specifically, an enhanced debt-forgiving scheme for the HIPCs was formulated at the Birmingham and Cologne summits and related conferences. During the negotiation process, Japan, which was one of the largest public creditors to HIPCs, stubbornly opposed large-scale public debt reduction. Japan, led by the Ministry of Finance, maintained that such debt reduction would cause moral hazards, collapse the creditworthiness of debtor countries and harm their interests in the long-term. But Japan's policies were problematic in that Japan's top bureaucrats had ignored important aspects of the HIPCs: education and healthcare had seriously deteriorated, capital inflows including grant aid were not determined by creditworthiness, and some national leaders of the HIPCs were not considered ethical.

Other large creditor countries such as the US, Germany and France were persuaded by the UK, leaving Japan isolated in the process of deciding upon the enhanced HIPCs relief scheme at Birmingham and Cologne. Given the situation, Japan's claim was largely ignored and, in the end, the country had no choice but to reluctantly agree.

The UK government, the World Bank and the IMF proposed a policy framework to restructure the HIPCs debt that included a condition for debt forgiveness. Clare Short, Secretary of State for International Development of the UK and the leading promoter of the enhanced HIPCs relief scheme, explained that a policy framework should be clarified to obligate the debtors to use freed money for education and healthcare and prevent the money from being wasted.[5] This framework, to be formulated by the debtor government, was entitled the Poverty Reduction Strategy (PRS) and was formally designated as a major condition for debt forgiveness at the Cologne Summit.

One could identify concern over fungibility in Secretary of State Short's thinking. Similar to new financial aid (either in kind or in-cash), debt relief has the same effect of creating financial space in the budgets of debtor governments. From the viewpoint of donor countries and organizations,[6] which were concerned about limitations to education and healthcare, the newly created financial space was to be channelled into investing and reinforcing these services in the HIPCs. She and her colleagues thought that such requirements should be guaranteed by contractual documents, namely through the PRS (Short 2004: 81–5).

Their ideas are not far from Japan's demand for ethical behavior on the part of debtors. The beginning of the HIPCs scheme would have been a good time for the Japanese aid bureaucracy to share its views, not just about fungibility, with Western donors, while incorporating the concept of fungibility into its decision-making and operations. However, Japan's actions, including participation in the formulation of specific countries' PRSs, were seriously delayed. This was due to dwindling enthusiasm to help formulate and sustain a new framework after being alienated in the decision-making process of the HIPCs scheme. Behind this dwindling enthusiasm, there was also Japan's indifference to the situation of the poor countries.

GBS and tracking: proactive approach with fungibility

Soon after successfully constructing inter-donor consensus for the enhanced debt relief frameworks for the HIPCs, some donors launched a new initiative to renovate existing frameworks of aid modality and approaches. The core of the new initiative was the GBS.

GBS is an aid modality by which financial resources are directly put into the recipient government's exchequer. Needless to say, GBS inputs are not aid-in-kind but aid-in-cash. GBS inputs are mixed in with the government's domestic revenues and therefore are expected to finance budgetary expenditures directly. GBS is not tied to any specific projects and it is not aimed to bring about any direct outputs.

North-western European countries led by the UK introduced GBS in the early 2000s and expanded provision for poor countries. The Blair administration, notably Secretary of State Clare Short at DfID, played a significant role in this process. The World Bank's Poverty Reduction Support Credit (PRSC), a lending scheme initiated in 2001, also functions as a GBS donor. The Western donors collectively launched GBS. There were high expectations for this new aid modality and some GBS advocates even claimed that it is the most effective modality.

The rationale of GBS promoters, which is closely linked with the concept of fungibility, can be summarized as follows:

- GBS enables the recipient government to treat GBS aid inputs as a part of the budgetary resources, which can enhance coherence and the flexibility of allocation of all resources, including both domestic revenues and aid inputs.
- Increases in GBS associated with reductions in the number of aid projects can prevent a proliferation of aid projects or duplicate projects

- from taking place, and thereby can mitigate transaction costs of the recipient and improve overall effectiveness.
- Once inputted, GBS becomes an inseparable part of budgets, and the donors' entitlement to claim accountability from the recipient on the allocation, actual expenditure and outcome of the whole budget is strengthened.

The last point is the most important among the three in the context of arguments presented in this chapter. One should note that because cash is totally fungible (substitutable) for cash, GBS, which is aid-in-cash, is totally fungible for domestic revenue. Once mixed with domestic revenue, there is no difference between the two portions, despite their being from different sources. In this sense, GBS becomes an inseparable part of the recipient's budget.

Regarding the last point above, as mentioned under the heading 'What is fungibility?', Nurkse urged donors to demand that recipients formulate a comprehensive development plan to maximize aid contributions. If one recalls the fungibility effect, a donor theoretically should be entitled to demand accountability for monies freed by their contribution. In reality, however, it is difficult for each donor to make such demands as Nurkse urged. Usually, the donor is limited to monitoring not indirect yet comprehensive outcomes, but merely outputs and direct outcomes of specific projects.

One reason is that, unlike GBS, specific aid projects are in most cases not incorporated into the recipient's budget. Donors had not requested this change until recently. Another reason is that a single donor cannot provide sufficient incentive for the recipient to be accountable concerning a comprehensive set of outcomes through specific projects. It is all the more difficult in cases of aid proliferation, where there are numerous donors and projects in any given recipient country. In other words, a specific project from a single donor is not sufficient to function as leverage to make the recipient government formulate a sensible national development strategy and allocate resources efficiently and effectively. Likewise, aid-in-kind cannot function as the leverage.

How about debt relief then? Substantial debt relief could favorably affect the whole budget of the recipient government and could be a powerful incentive to formulate a developmental national strategy and allocate resources. Once the debt stock is cleared, however, the incentive disappears (i.e. once debt is forgiven, the leverage is gone).

GBS, therefore, is superior in this sense. Since it is supposed to be provided annually, GBS donors could demand accountability on what they have provided during the year and could 'dangle' their contributions for the next year and in the future as an incentive for the recipient government to work for their aid.

As mentioned above, GBS becomes an inseparable part of the recipient's budget. After GBS is provided, it is completely mixed in with domestic revenue. In other words, a GBS donor can claim 'ownership' of any unit of money. Through GBS, then, donors hold a position similar to the recipient's taxpayers, and therefore can demand comprehensive accountability through the formulation of a national development plan and/or reporting the usage of budgetary resources and development outcomes.

Given the actual circumstances of poor countries, GBS alone could not enable donors to achieve their own purposes to make recipients accountable and developmentally responsible. Other instruments were required and were introduced in the early 2000s. The PRS was formulated in a number of poor countries, not only as a condition for debt cancellation but also as the national development program. The Medium-Term Expenditure Framework (MTEF), which is supposed to concretize the PRS in terms of financing during the period PRS covers, has also been widely formulated. The PRS and MTEF are ex-ante instruments to make recipients accountable concerning their policies of development and poverty reduction to donors. Instruments to monitor actual budgetary allocation, spending, and outputs/outcomes of the financial resources of the government, were also necessary. In a wide range of poor countries, Public Expenditure Review (PER) has been functioning as an ex-post instrument to monitor them. By means of these instruments, donors can effectively intervene in the budgeting and auditing process. Using the terminology of the donor community, they could theoretically 'track' their contribution from disbursement through allocation to the final outcomes.

In addition to the above-mentioned tools, to further enhance integrity and efficiency of the public administration of recipient countries, other measures such as the Country Financial Accountability Assessment (CFAA) and Country Procurement Assessment (CPA) are being implemented. The CFAA scheme is an exercise to assess the accounting administration process and the actual performance, in order to ensure that there is accountability for budgetary resources; this can then be used as a basis for public finance reforms. The result of the CFAA also is utilized to select recipient countries before the provision of assistance including GBS. The CPA is established to assess the political systems and the process by which governments procure goods and services. This enables the government and donors to ensure fairness and transparency in procurement. These measures help to combat corruption and inefficiency. It is certain that, in order to eliminate corruption in poor developing countries, an approach involving both sides' financial allocation and the procurement of goods and services is required.

GBS is thought to be an effective solution for aid proliferation. Enthusiastic GBS advocates claim that donors' aid should be 'de-projectized' and concentrated into the recipient governments' treasury as aid-in-cash. It is expected to lead to a reduction in transaction or managerial costs on the side of the government. GBS would make it much easier for the budgeting authority to oversee the whole resource inflow and public expenditure altogether. Consequently, it would promote financial and administrative coherence within the government, and thereby would solidify the recipient's ownership. Needless to say, these expectations require at a minimum a committed and capable budgeting authority and political will to support it.

Certainly, to achieve what the donor side expects, the existence of mere instrumental frameworks such as the PRS, MTEF, PER, CFAA and CPA are insufficient. Above all, willingness on the side of the ministries of the recipient government is crucial. To reinforce and concretize the willingness for development and poverty reduction, the World Bank and the United Kingdom are putting an emphasis on policy dialogues. Policy dialogues are regarded as an ex-ante opportunity for donors to discuss the PRS, MTEF and annual national budgets (DfID 2004: 7; World Bank 1998). In these discussions, donors are making an effort to voice their objectives, and their opinions on the policies of the recipient countries. One of the priorities is that public expenditure should be allocated with more weight on the sectors that directly promote poverty reduction, such as primary education and primary healthcare. Policy dialogues are also utilized at the level of intra-sector coordination.

As suggested above, the PRS/GBS and other related instrumental frameworks are supported by a wide range of donors including the World Bank and north-western Europeans led by the UK. One could label them the mainstream donors for low-income countries. They have also taken the initiative in building an international consensus for coordination and harmonization as a way to improve aid effectiveness, which is crystallized in the Rome and Paris Declarations. I believe that this consensus represents the core of the international regime[7] of aid for poor countries. I name this regime the Poverty Reduction Aid Regime.

In the context of this chapter, Japan's position on the Poverty Reduction Aid Regime should be discussed here. Japan signed the Rome and Paris Declarations and officially agreed to further coordination and harmonization. Japan has not been associated very closely with the mainstream donors' understandings on fungibility, aid effectiveness and relevant actions. The roles of the PRS, MTEF and PER, as elaborated above, have not yet been introduced into Japan's operations in low-income countries. Japan's participation in the formulation of the PRS or joint monitoring exercise is very limited. It is often said that Japanese embassies or the African-based offices of the JICA just send junior officials to related meetings, who keep silent and are not effectively involved in the policy dialogues and discussions concerning PRS formulation/implementation and monitoring.

In response to the spread of GBS in low-income countries, Japan has set up its own GBS schemes. However, as of 2008, the number of Japan's GBS recipients is very limited. More specifically, GBS through Yen-denominated development loans have only been provided to Vietnam and Tanzania. These loans were co-financed with the World Bank, which meant Japan herself was not responsible for much of the costs of monitoring and tracking. A GBS grant, on the other hand, has been provided only to Tanzania. Low-level officials, including contract experts rather than those in directorship positions in the ODA administration, took the initiative to establish Japan's grant scheme and its actual provision.

Explaining Japan's weak commitments

Careful examination is required to understand the causes of Japan's delayed and weak commitment to actions related to the HIPCs debt relief and the PRS/GBS. First, the delayed and weak commitment can be explained by a lack of understanding by officials and aid professionals in Japan's ODA administration. The policy-makers are not equipped yet with a fully fledged research institute for development aid as of 2008. Also, Japan has been, to a certain extent, isolated from interactions with Western donors, partly because of language, cultural and geographical issues.[8]

Not only the World Bank but also bilateral donors in north-western Europe have often discussed the causes of low aid effectiveness, including fungibility and the need to address these new aid modalities through cooperation. Yet, their keen concern about fungibility has never been shared by the Japanese.

The above explanation, however, has limited explanatory power. Japan's aid circle has been increasingly exposed to new discussions and knowledge developed in the West and has been strengthening its efforts to demonstrate internationally Japan's own thinking about development and aid. As a result, several other explanations follow.

The second explanation is related to Japan's perception of the past record of development aid. As discussed in Chapter 4, Japan's major recipients, all of which are in Asia, have been largely successful in development and poverty reduction. These Asian countries have diverted their public financial resources to consumptive purposes, like other recipient countries, but with their domestic revenues expanding thanks to high growth, the problem has been less serious. The issue of fungibility has been largely 'concealed' from the eyes of policy-makers in Japan. Hence the Japanese have not felt a very strong need to formulate comprehensive development strategies, financial frameworks and/or to monitor/track resources, at least based on the successful Asian countries.[9] On the other hand, aid for the failing poor states, which are mainly in Africa, has accounted for a much smaller portion of the whole aid given by Japan.

Third, the reason why Japan has undertaken mostly aid-in-kind is related to the fact that the Japanese have preferred project aid to program aid coordinated with other donors. As previously mentioned, Japan's preference for aid-in-kind is due partly to its quest for recipient accountability. Yet it would be more reasonable to add another explanation. Aid-in-kind and project aid are more convenient methods through which Japan can exert its own influence. Here, simple diplomatic considerations dominate the development agenda, which aid is theoretically expected to achieve. As a result, Japan's attention has tended to be limited to short-term outputs of aid-in-kind rather than long-term, comprehensive outcomes of development. Japan, however, is not alone in this. Other donors, both bilateral and multilateral, are also project-aid-philiacs. The pervasiveness of these projects aggravates the proliferation of aid, which leads to low effectiveness for each project.

Fourth, serious defects in Japan's aid policy-making and administration can be pinpointed. Policy-making for development loans and debt relief is primarily the responsibility of the Ministry of Finance (MOF), while grants and technical assistance are mainly under the direction of the Ministry of Foreign Affairs (MOFA). At the implementation level, Japan's Bank for International Cooperation (JBIC) is in charge of development loans and JICA is in charge of technical assistance and, to some extent, grants. Both the MOF and JBIC officials had the opportunity to understand the implications and role of the HIPCs debt relief, and thus the PRS and other instruments, and the concept of fungibility. If these opportunities had been taken, they could have also understood the expected function and relevance of GBS. Even though some of the individual MOF/JBIC officials did understand these recent changes, their understanding was not shared throughout the MOFA/JICA. After the enhanced HIPCs debt relief, MOF and JBIC substantially suspended development loans to poor countries, especially those in Africa. Only the MOFA and JICA are responsible for day-to-day operation in the fields of poor African countries. But, especially in the earlier 2000s, they did not share an understanding on the PRS/GBS and fungibility. Japan's weak commitment could be explained by this failure of inter-ministry linkages. Behind this failure, one might be able to find serious vertical sectionalism, which is deeply rooted in the modern history of the Cabinet system of Japan.

In addition, the low profile of Japanese officials in the PRS or GBS related meetings, as mentioned above, is due partly to the weak function of embassies and JICA offices in terms of development policy discussions. Embassy officials in charge of aid are often those temporarily transferred in from ministries other than MOFA and thus are not aid experts at all. Until recently, JICA's attention has been sometimes narrowly focused on its own projects, without extending to the recipients' comprehensive policies. Therefore, dealing with the PRS/GBS was not their responsibility.

Fifth, the weak commitment of Japan may also be linked with the nature of Japanese society after World War II. As explained in Chapter 4, after its devastating defeat, Japan avoided intervening in the domestic affairs of foreign countries. This may be a kind of manifestation of Japan's traditional tendency to distinguish *uchi* (inner society) and *soto* (outer world), and to be hesitant to meddle in the affairs of the *soto*. Yet Japan's hesitant stance in affairs of the *soto* has not been ever continuous in nature. For example, Japan had an aggressive posture towards the Asian continent before the World War II. This current hesitation can be understood as an (over-)reaction to its defeat, which became the psychological basis of post-war Japan. Whether this stance is positive or negative depends on one's viewpoint; this hesitant stance, however, has made the Japanese aid machinery focus narrowly on concrete outputs rather than comprehensive outcomes, including economic development and poverty reduction on the side of recipients.

In the case of African countries, Japan's hesitant position has been reinforced by both practical and psychological remoteness. After World War II democracy and pacifism took root in Japan. In view of this, what has happened in many African countries has been far from being acceptable to Japan. Yet this did not lead to Japan intervening in African countries in a straightforward way, like the Western countries. This point will be discussed in the section on 'Selectivity and new international dependency' (see also Takahashi 2002).

GBS, African states and Japan

The Poverty Reduction Aid Regime vs. endogenous political process in Africa?

A typical aid document which showed the philosophical basis of the Poverty Reduction Aid Regime was *Shaping the 21st Century* (DAC 1996), an epoch-making policy paper published by the Development Assistance Committee of the Organization for Economic Cooperation and Development (OECD-DAC) in 1996. OECD-DAC is the formal club of bilateral ODA donors. The policy paper emphasized ownership and partnership as the key concepts for new thinking about ODA. These two concepts were rather differently perceived by Japan and Western donors.

Japanese officials thought that the concept of ownership was affirmation of its own idea of support for self-help, which was heralded in its 1992 ODA charter, and partnership was literally assistance provided in the manner of respecting self-help efforts. This author takes the view that the idea of self-help support was a product of Japan's euphoria over being at that time the largest bilateral donor and the closest partner of East Asian high-growth states. Behind the concept of self-help support, Japan's hesitation on intervention in domestic affairs of recipient countries was hidden, as discussed in the previous section, 'Explaining Japan's weak commitments'.

Western donors perceived these two concepts very differently. They thought partnership meant deeper involvement in the domestic affairs of recipient countries for the purpose of promoting development, poverty reduction and perhaps even democratization. Ownership, in their vocabulary, meant the recipients' commitment to implement what was acknowledged by partners (i.e. donors). Partnership and ownership needed to be stressed to achieve a breakthrough in view of low aid effectiveness and the negative effect of fungibility in low-income countries, especially those in Africa.

The Poverty Reduction Aid Regime for low-income countries was founded on the Western donors' perception of partnership and ownership. Their efforts to restructure aid modalities included the challenge of realizing a good partnership (or donorship), and to this end they are now equipped with effective instruments of leverage. In other words, what was discussed in the section on 'Fungibility, aid modalities and Japan' is related to the quest for achieving better outcomes mainly on the supply side of aid.

What is perhaps more important are the conditions on the demand side (i.e. the recipient side). Recalling the episode of the Vienna Opera, what actually makes the effect of fungibility negative? The answer is the recipient governments. The World Bank indirectly admitted this point by indicating in *Assessing Aid* (1998) that policies of the recipient governments determine the effectiveness of aid.

One could then ask what determines the quality of the policies of the recipient governments. Western donors, rather simplistically, use vague language about how poor countries should introduce political and administrative systems that are decentralized, transparent, open and accountable. It should be noted, however, that even Western countries have not been able to adopt their own requirements until quite recently. All the more problematic is that there is little reference to endogenous determinants of domestic political economy of recipient countries. The system the West recommends is a desirable goal that all donors hope will materialize throughout Africa in the future. Yet each country goes through its own historical process, which affects its goals.

Booth, a leading advocate of GBS, exceptionally indicated the importance of considering domestic politico-economic mechanisms of recipient countries. Citing the argument of Chabal and Daloz, Booth (2003: 10) emphasized the necessity of understanding the basis of neo-patrimonial mechanisms. Interestingly, Booth's argument attracted the attention of Ishiwaka, the most respected development thinker in Japan.

Booth's claim and Ishikawa's interest have intellectual support. In retrospect, students of African studies have developed an extensive series of explanations about the internal mechanisms of African countries' failures in terms of development, poverty reduction and democratization. Those explanations can be roughly classified into two schools of thought. One is based upon the so-called New Political Economy represented by Rational Choice theorists headed by Bates (1981), and the other school looks at the non-modern characteristics of Africa's political economy. The latter school consists of mainly Europeans such as Hyden, Bayart and Médard (Bayart 1989; Hyden 1983; Médard 1982).

What is interesting is that both schools have tried to explain the phenomena of aid failures through the domestic factors of recipient countries. Bates set forth a well-known theory based on urban-biased policies of rational African governments, which are desperate to survive politically. This urban bias causes broad dissatisfaction among farmers and leads to shortages in food provision, so the governments distribute many development projects to rural populations to win over the latter's support (Bates 1981: 91–5). One could easily presume that if there is really such a distribution of projects by African governments, it could lead to project proliferation.

Hyden, one of the pre-eminent theorists of non-modern African states, claims that African societies are still under pre-capitalist 'economies of affection'. According to him, in Africa micro-projects such as those focusing on basic human needs tend to be increasingly fragmented. For under an economy of affection, where the state is not independent from its society, the state cannot withstand the citizens' demands to extract resources which benefit them directly. It could also be a convincing explanation of proliferation of aid projects (Hyden 1983: 165–7).

Chabal and Daloz (1999) proposed an explanation of Africa's failures to develop and democratize with more serious implications. Their logic is a hybrid: they accept the argument by Médard that contemporary African states are 'neo-patrimonial states' and they place importance on patron–client relationships; at the same time, however, like Bates, they focus on the political elites' strategy to perpetuate their power. Chabal and Daloz set forth the concept of the 'Africanization' of politics, where political elites convert the Western-style of politics into the African style. The gist of their argument is as follows: African elites make full use of the uncertainty and violence caused by the lack of institutions to rule the society. This elite behavior is called the 'instrumentalization of disorder'. They are against institution-building and the establishment of the rule of law, which are both essential for development and democratization. But at the same time they need aid resources to strengthen their power. Therefore, they pretend to fulfil the demands of donors in terms of development and democratization superficially but never actually put them into practice. Chabal and Daloz describe this kind of practice as 'politics of the mirror'. In short, they maintain that donors' agendas are destined to be aborted in African countries where elites rule by the instrumentalization of disorder.

In his popular introductory book, Collier (2007) states that in poor countries there are Villains (greedy elites) and Heroes (reformers) whom the donor community should trust, assist and protect. Needless to say, his juxtaposition is oversimplified, but perhaps useful for the purpose of enlightening lay people. If Chabal and Daloz are more or less justified in arguing that there are endogenous politico-economic mechanisms hindering development and democratization, what the Poverty Reduction Aid Regime should do is not confront the individual Villains but rather address the mechanisms underpinning the African system.

Booth agrees with Chabal and Daloz in that neo-patrimonial political economies have survived the democratization of the 1990s and, in some cases, such regimes even have been strengthened. He also points out that African administrative institutions are fragmented by the personal rule of elites. On the basis of these notions, he supports the donors' stance to shift their priority from project aid to GBS, because the provision of project aid only advantages elites by strengthening their personal rule over their clients or followers (Booth 2003: 9–13). This argument by Booth is persuasive when one recalls project proliferation. With project proliferation, elites can reinforce their personal rule as resource distribution is freed from constraints set by the comprehensive frameworks and stricter control of the budgeting authority. Here, GBS is regarded as an important and effective instrument to rectify anti-developmental rule imposed by African elites.

Selectivity and new international dependency

For GBS and other instruments to work effectively, donors' enthusiasm alone is not a sufficient condition. To recap, what is essentially required is commitment by the administrative machinery led by the budgeting authority and political will to support it. Britain's Department for International Development frankly admitted that GBS is to be provided partly for the purpose of giving the budgeting authority space to manoeuvre politically. It also means the donors clearly recognize that GBS and other assistance are to be associated with deep involvement not only in policies but also in politics inside recipient countries.

However, what would happen if the budgeting authority is not reliable? As early as 1989, Bates (1989) predicted that there would be a possibility to form a reform alliance between economic officials concerned about national crises and international donors. Though one should pay homage to Bates' far-reaching foresight, it is not always easy to find, among high economic bureaucrats, many who are both sincerely concerned about public interests and politically strong enough to override domestic opposition from other elites (or Villains). As Collier (2007) legitimately states, in almost every poor country, donors can find reforming heroes with whom they can ally, but these heroes do not necessarily belong to the budgeting authority or hold the political power to sustain sensible budgeting. Also, one should recall the remark by Chabal and Daloz (1999) that African elites can pretend to be reformers under the 'politics of the mirror'.

If donors cannot find reforming heroes in positions of power whom they can trust, what can they do? In reality, what the donor community as a whole has been doing is not to select recipients with whom donors cannot be satisfied. Donors have developed criteria to help choose the countries with better governance and allocate aid money according to the performance of recipients. This tendency of donors is called selectivity.

Then, what happens to those recipients who have not been selected? While careful empirical examination is needed, the series of state collapses in Africa in the 1990s to 2000s were likely related to donor desertion. Recall that, during the 1990s, ODA became unpopular in donor countries and donors were driven to select better recipients. For the poor African countries that had become dependent upon aid, the withdrawal of aid had devastating impacts on public finance and administration and thereby on neo-patrimonial politico-economic mechanisms. Some of the deserted African countries, especially those where elites plunder their government's assets, lost even more financial resources trying to maintain their security organizations such as the armed forces and police, resulting in the collapse of the state. Soldiers and police officers became bandits or armed robbers in order to sustain themselves, which destroyed the state's hold on the legitimate monopoly of violence.

As a matter of fact, selectivity could impact on providing discipline to recipients with a minimum level of political will for reform. They are likely to make considerable efforts to meet donors' expectations in order to avoid slipping down into the hell of a state collapse. But, behind this disciplining, one should recognize the serious dependency this creates between recipients and donors. Also, one cannot forget the many human disasters that take place in collapsed states.

Collier (2007) critically argued that under the new approach to aid, governments of poor recipient countries have become more accountable to donors than their own citizens. It is certain that in better performing poor countries government officials, including those in the budgeting authority, are busy attending joint policy formulation meetings, monitoring and reporting information about resource allocation and spending, and installing a more transparent and accountable administration system. Collier is right in indicating that they are carrying out these exercises vis-à-vis donors and not their own citizens.

The phenomena mentioned here could be regarded as a new mode of international dependency. Dependency in this case is not structured by the selfish interests of the rulers and the forced obedience of the ruled as during colonial times. It is based, instead, upon donors' wish to see what they hope to be recipients' willing compliance. Their wish is not necessarily an ethical evil but could be an officious kindness if democratic support from and accountability to the recipient countries' citizens are not present.

Also, serious problems caused by selectivity must be addressed. Rejecting poor countries with bad governance effectively means they are deserted, which can lead to state collapses as elaborated above. Acute poverty and human misery, which development aid should in principle treat as a top priority, tend to exist more pervasively in the abandoned countries rather than the better performing recipients. This is a serious dilemma of aid. Beneath the new structure of international dependency and the Poverty Reduction Aid Regime, there have been widespread human disasters in these rejected countries.

In the meantime, selectivity could function effectively when donors exert their aid leverage in a unified manner and agree on what should be requested of recipients. The Poverty Reduction Aid Regime created a framework for this unified approach. Japan, though not too committed to the logic of the regime and wondering whether or not there could be an alternative approach, has tried not to disturb the donors' unified approach. For the most part, challenges to the unified approach seem to come from other actors: the so-called emerging donors such as China, the Arab governments and others.

Japan and the Poverty Reduction Aid Regime

The deep intervention of Western donor agencies in the recipient countries reflects their own dependence on public opinion. Donors are susceptible to their own citizens' perceptions and expectations, and should be responsive and accountable to them. Blair and Short's quest for social justice in developing countries received considerable support from British society. If they had adopted a more reserved stance, it would have invited strong criticism from influential corners of UK society. On the other hand, the civil societies in the West are sometimes intolerant of the political and economic situations in developing countries that do not necessarily fit their value standards. Such intolerance underpins the Western donors' substantial involvement in the recipients' domestic affairs and the West's strict selectivity as explained above. Around 2000, poor recipient states, having become aid-dependent and overwhelmed by their debt burden, had few choices but to accept the donors' demands or to risk state collapse by refusing or ignoring the demands. Here, the Western civil societies' value standards directly confront Africa and make African governments dependent.

Until recently, the Japanese situation was different from the West. Due to large informational asymmetry among the concerned ministries, development failures in poor recipients and subsequent debt cancellation were not questioned nor discussed by opposition parties, mass media or civil society. For instance, in terms of accountability to the taxpayers, the wholesale debt cancellation for HIPCs was so problematic that officials in charge should have been liable for repayment failure. But they have never vindicated themselves in public and thus have never been accused. This aggravated the situation discussed in the section 'Explaining Japan's weak commitments' where the meanings of the PRS/GBS were never shared among relevant ministries/agencies and thus Japan's engagement was considerably delayed. Also, Japanese citizens could likewise be concerned about human right abuses, atrocities in armed conflicts or acute poverty in poor countries in general and those in Africa in particular, if they were well informed. But a very important factor is that aid for poor countries in Africa accounted for no more than 10 percent of Japan's total amount of ODA, and thus did not attract enough attention from legislators or the mass media to bother to investigate and raise the issue against the government.

In the meantime, the adamant stance of Western societies is the basis for generating and sustaining the Poverty Reduction Aid Regime, which is influencing the direction of poor countries' political and economic changes. The West's position has definitely driven African governments toward reforms which will benefit poor people. No one can deny its effectiveness. The said intolerance, however, might be causing inflexibility in donors' thinking which could make them overlook an important aspect of African states.

Bates (1989), while talking about the 'predatoriness' of the African rational state, indicated the weak capability of African governments. In Hyden's works (e.g. 1983), this aspect was more conspicuously manifested through his famous concept of the 'uncaptured peasantry'. Lawson (2003) straightforwardly maintained that the African state was socially rootless. Rootlessness has been a long-lasting and critical issue of studies on African states. This author is of the opinion that under the Poverty Reduction Aid

Regime, the concept of a rootless state has been ignored. This neglect is deeply linked to the situation criticized by Collier (2007), in which African governments have been made accountable not to their own citizens, but to donor agencies.

As previous studies have argued, the rootless African states can barely mobilize (or exploit) resources of people, especially those in rural areas. An important indicator is the virtual non-existence of certain kinds of direct taxes, such as an income tax on ordinary farmers or a land tax. As one could infer from this example, the rootlessness of African states is deeply intertwined with the politico-economic structures of the societies, such as the artificialness of states and the underdevelopment of markets, including that of land. The weak response of states to the needs of societies is a reflection of this rootlessness.

As we have seen, Chabal and Daloz (1999), like others, puts great emphasis on elitist personal rule through patron–client relations (or simply neo-patrimonialism) as a major cause for underdevelopment and delayed democratization in African countries. There is no doubt that personal rule and patron–client relations are themselves serious problems to be dealt with in the future. Under certain circumstances, it might even be detrimental to efficiency and equity in resource allocation. It is, therefore, understandable that in implementing the PRS/GBS in poor African countries, the question of how to contain the influence of neo-patrimonialism should be an important issue (Booth 2003).

Nevertheless, we could not agree with the idea that neo-patrimonialism is the fatal factor depriving any nation of the possibilities of economic development and political democratization. It would be incorrect to maintain that, without eliminating neo-patrimonialism, a nation could not develop or progress. The modern histories of East Asian countries are eloquent counter-examples. The importance of neo-patrimonial relations is characteristic of both Asia and Africa, but such relations are perhaps more continuous and systematized in Asia. Japan had developed factional politics under the parliamentary dominance of the Liberal Democratic Party (LDP) before the 2000s. In Korea, there have been cases of extensive personal connections between politically influential people, notably entourages of successive presidents, and leaders of '*chaebols*'. Not only in the Philippines but also in Indonesia, so-called crony capitalism is said to exist. Finally, it is often argued that it is not law but human relations that rule Chinese society. Here, human relations mean vertical connections between the powerful and the powerless.

It is clear that neo-patrimonialism does not necessarily obstruct development and democratization. One could not say patron–client relations in Japan's LDP factions seriously hindered economic development and social democratization. While it is certain that LDP factionalism impacted negatively on politics and its administrations, it definitely did not hinder substantially the consolidation of democratic institutions and human rights after World War II. South Korea's strong bonds between politicians and business leaders also have not obstructed the country's industrialization, starting in the 1960s, and democratization in the 1980s. Some may be satisfied with attributing everything evil such as underdevelopment and authoritarianism to so-called crony capitalism in several Southeast Asian countries, but they would face difficulties in explaining the region's high economic growth until the 1997 Asian financial crisis. Few can deny that widespread personal human networks coexist historically with periods of high economic growth in China.

If Asia and Africa have neo-patrimonialism in common, then what are the reasons behind their differences in development? An indispensable factor is probably the relationship between the state and society. No one can describe the Japanese, Korean, or Chinese states as rootless. Rather, based on their histories of feudalist and mercantilist-like relations, they have been able to effectively mobilize or simply exploit resources from all of society, and thus one can claim that states in East Asia are relatively deeply rooted in their society. And, at least in Japan, the past system of exploitation of peasants was such that the ruling and the ruled shared interests in terms of expanding the total amount of products. This feudalist system was a foundation for the development of a democratic taxation system today, which African countries lacked at the time of their independence.

Neo-patrimonialism in Asia, while being very diverse, could be said to have at least coexisted with the relatively strong states rooted in their societies, even in the latter half of the 20th century. Sometimes it may have been an integral part of the political mechanisms of Asian countries, including Japan. At the same time, various types of human network, including vertical ones, have functioned in businesses and industrial organizations along with market transactions. The reason why neo-patrimonialism has not fundamentally obstructed East Asian development is that there are effective social deterrents to its influence: comparatively strong state administrations which are not necessarily prone to be eroded by personal relations, and which are perhaps partly underpinned by traditional bureaucratic ethics; competition among private agents in the market which naturally needs expertise and meritocracy in corporate organizations; and a widely based commitment to development, especially in the latter half of the 20th century.

East Asian democratization has been a struggle against the strong and socially rooted states. Roughly speaking, rulers in Asian agriculturally based countries, perhaps since the days of feudalism and mercantilism, have known that unless they incorporated the livelihood and economic activities of the masses, they could not extract resources from them. Moreover, in Chinese or Japanese pre-modern thinking, too much exploitation and extravagant luxury was the worst immoral act of ruling princes, although there were many idiosyncratic cases. This tradition has been somehow transferred to modern politicians and bureaucrats.

The historical significance of East Asian development and democratization (and probably that of Western Europe too) is the redirection of the elites' accountability from the elites themselves to the people as a whole. Elites already knew how to mobilize domestic resources, though now they are obliged to obtain democratic consent for taxation and other resource mobilization. Elites today also, at least legally, have to use those resources for the sake of their people's welfare. Asian elites have certainly felt that there are shared interests with the masses even before democratization. Democratization has provided an institutional basis for this interest-sharing.

Having described East Asian experiences, what can be said about Africa? First, if neo-patrimonialism is not the cause of the elimination of the possibilities of development and democratization, it is not very wise to concentrate donors' attention on eliminating patrimonial human relations. At least, foreign aid alone is not capable of doing it. Therefore, Western donors have been selecting out countries where they regard patrimonial politics as rampant. However, this approach has brought about numerous state failures. Attempts to eliminate neo-patrimonialism are radical and surgical so to say, which might kill the society as a whole. The more sensible approach is a gradual one, which fosters social institutions and other factors to contain and reduce the influence of personal rule and patron–client relations.

However, Africa's historical backgrounds are very different from Asia's. Policies should start by rooting African states securely to their societies, while democratizing politics and building market economic systems. Needless to say, these efforts should not obstruct the process of democratization. Yet, democratization is the process under which people are not only granted rights and entitlements but are also assigned responsibility to bear the costs for public welfare. In concrete terms, people should begin not only to vote but also to pay taxes. A historically unique challenge for Africa is to mobilize the domestic resources required for development and to make progress in democratization at the same time. But this approach may be the only authentic way to establish the states' accountability to the people themselves instead of donors.

Japan, having belonged to the OECD for over 40 years and having been deeply associated with economic development of East Asian countries, has demonstrated the advantages of the gradualist approach. If Japanese civil society is more tolerant of differences between developing countries and itself, it could even be an advocate of the gradualist approach. It would need a more patient and tactful aid approach as well as a profound understanding of the economics and politics of Africa. Japan, however, all the more needs the political will to withstand the painful labors of intermediating between the West and Africa.

Conclusion

The Poverty Reduction Aid regime has been quite successful in mobilizing concerted endeavors by Western donors and promoting efforts by governments of well performing recipients. It is a basis for international commitment for achieving the Millennium Development Goals (MDGs) and recovering the volume of aid given to poor countries in the mid 2000s. This momentum came to a peak when the Blair government in the UK sponsored the Gleneagles Summit, where the G8 leaders committed to increasing the aid amount for Africa by 100 percent by 2010. Japan contributed to the momentum by promising a doubling of aid at the fourth International Conference on African Development (TICAD-IV) in May 2008.

At the same time, the landscape of African aid began to change. After many years of stagnation, natural resource-rich countries in Africa started to grow rapidly in response to booms in international markets. Against the same backdrop, China and other countries have strengthened their relationships to Africa.

Despite increases in the volume of aid by donors, Western donors' selective approach may not be as effective in terms of imposing discipline as hoped. Growing foreign exchange earnings might make recipient countries less dependent on the West. At the moment, China is an emerging donor that has little reason to understand the concept of fungibility. As a donor, China seemingly does not really care about the development and democratization of African countries, and thus has no interest in intervening in domestic affairs. By generously providing monies without any governance conditionalities, China is buying support from some African leaders. In so doing, China is virtually undermining the political and economic value standards that Western donors expect poor African countries to follow. Needless to say, China has little incentive to participate in exercises of the PRS/GBS. Rather, it is aggressively providing aid projects to obtain visibility without any consideration of harmonization among donors.

Moreover, expanding the inflow of financial resources can enable recipient governments to extend priority sectors from basic education and primary healthcare to infrastructure development, which may cause difficulty for the de-projectization of aid and thus in resource integration into national budgets. These circumstances will provide Japan challenges and opportunities. Quite subtle differences between Western and Japanese approaches to aid may become relatively insignificant as a result of the emergence of China as an outsider to the aid regime. Japan's stance in Africa may be complicated as Japan feels pressure from China's growing presence in Africa. However, it would not be wise for Japan to opt to seek its own narrow self-interest through aid, as its neighbor is actually doing, and thus forgo the harmonious framework of the conventional donors. This option would substantially eliminate Japan's difference from China and would destroy the trust of the West in Japan as a fellow donor. More importantly, Japan's assimilation with China could deprive all the stakeholders in African development of opportunities to reconfigure the aid approach.

If Japan can consolidate its intellectual capability and political will, it could transform this challenge into an opportunity. As China's neighbor and close economic partner, Japan can understand China's strength and weakness as an emerging donor. Japan is the only non-Western conventional donor and is most familiar with East Asian development experiences. Related to these issues, Japan understands the exogenous impact of economic development and political democratization through the dismantlement of neo-patrimonialism. This process could be aborted unless it is sustained by efforts generated from inside developing countries. Only the states and the people of developing countries should take the initiative in this process. One should characterize it as essential self-help required for development. Japan's own experiences and philosophy could help connect the West and the non-West in more productive ways.

If a long-lasting partnership framework for African development is to succeed, the Poverty Reduction Aid Regime should incorporate China and other emerging Asian donors, and it should be based upon far more respect for Africa's own efforts. Japan is in the most pivotal position as the country could consolidate all of the important stakeholders under the new partnership framework. With its philosophy of self-help, Japan can understand and believe that African people can decide the way towards development and democratization. African people should control the fungibility of their own budgetary resources. That should be the most important pillar of the new framework.

Appendix

The case of the Vienna Opera can be interpreted by claiming that aid for the power plant project was fully diverted for the reconstruction of the opera building. A more formal interpretation is as follows: denoting total expenditure of a recipient country, including resources from outside the country, as E, the amount of productive investment and extravagant investment in E are denoted as Y and C respectively.[10] Furthermore, the ratio of Y and C to E are denoted by y and c, and the total amount of aid is A.

Assuming that the entire budget is put into productive investment Y and luxurious investment C, and no investment is made to other intermediaries, then we can write:

$$y + c = 1 \qquad (1)$$

In the anecdote of the Opera House, one can consider that the luxurious investment (namely, the additional cost to construct an Opera House = ΔC) increases as the development aid increases (see items (a) or (b) in Appendix Table 7.1). If we assume that the recipient country covers ΔC, utilizing the financial margin produced by the assistance for construction of a power plant (the cost is equivalent to additional financial aid = ΔA) – in other words, ΔC never exceeds ΔA – then we can write it as:

$$1 \geq \frac{\Delta C}{\Delta A} \geq 0 \qquad (2')$$

If development aid is released for a project to construct infrastructure such as an electric power plant, the donor normally expects the net amount of additional financial aid to be distributed into productive investments of country X (Table 7.1(b)). However, the recipient country X could have constructed an electric power plant spending an amount equivalent to ΔA

Table 7.1 Various effects of additional development aid

(a) Before aid release

C_0	Y_0	aid increment Δ

(b) Donor's expected case (increment only in productive expenditure)

C_1	$Y_1 (> Y_0)$

(c) Donor's expected case (increment only in productive expenditure)

$C_1 (= C_0 + \Delta A)$	$Y_1 (= Y_0)$

(d) Increment in both expenditure

$C_1 (> C_0)$	$Y_1 (> Y_0)$

without the development aid. Then, if the entire financial margin produced by the input of ΔA is allocated to cover the cost of the construction of an Opera House, namely, if

$$\frac{\Delta C}{\Delta A} = 1 \qquad (2')$$

it means the deviation of country X from the expectation of the donor and additional input of ΔA increases none of productive investments of country X (Appendix Table 7.1(c)).

In this case, the increment ΔA replaced (substituted for) country X's own budget for the construction of an electronic power plant. The replaced and thus saved amount of the budget equivalent to ΔA is now fungible to other purposes, deviating from the donor's intention. This is the situation which Nurkse's warned of (Table 7.1(d)), where it can be approximated as follows:

$$\frac{\Delta C}{\Delta A} = 0 \qquad (2'')$$

While the desirable situation which Nurkse might have meant is that all the effects given by development aid emerge as increases in productive investments of the recipient country, merely negotiating on a power plant construction project will not achieve this situation automatically. An assistance agreement between a donor as a principal and the recipient as an agent require neither part to take responsibility for controlling additional expenses on luxuries which may follow the project.

If the donor expects the recipient to control public investments on luxuries, then the expected results must be included in the terms of the agreement. Nurkse (1953: 96) proposed to make a comprehensive development plan or public expenditure plan of country X beyond each development project to promote effective growth of productive investment and to control extravagant investments. In actual cases of development assistance, such development policies and public expenditure plans are formulated in an approach from the donor side. Regarding a public expenditure plan which includes donors as stakeholders, contracts can not only determine direct expenditure (namely, the objective of the project) but also indirect effects of the financial aid. As an actual case of these indirect effects, Nurkse indicated that substitutable effects (or fungible effects, using our terminology) of financial resources replace the increments of financial aid.

Nurkse's idea, which puts emphasis on comprehensive development plans, has affected many government planners in charge of national development strategies in developing countries in the aftermath of independence. At the same time, his idea has provided a theoretical background for donor countries to step away from the framework of project assistance to commit themselves to resource allocation in recipient countries. In this sense, the framework of project aid after structural adjustment and poverty reduction originally stems from Nurkse's perception, processed through the discussions of Chenery and Strout (1966).

In planning the distribution of the financial resources of the recipient country, donors need to think about not only ways to increase the absolute amount of productive investment but also its ratio. Defining the period before the reception of aid as 0 period and the period after as the first period, the objective to be achieved can be expressed as follows.

$$y_0 < y_1 \quad \text{or} \quad c_0 > c_1 \qquad (3)$$

Here we assume that the additional aid merely increases ΔA, and ΔC is induced by ΔA. Then, the condition for (3) to be achieved is:

$$c_0 \Delta A > \Delta C \qquad (4)^{11}$$

That is, the proportion of financial resources invested in luxuries that is induced by the additional aid must be suppressed to be smaller than the current amount of expenditure on luxuries (see Table 7.1(d)).

Now, how can one ensure and check that (3) and (4) have been achieved? Two main measures can be proposed. First, the conditions of (3) and (4) need to be included in the agreement between the donor as a principal and the recipient as the agent. Practically, this agreement usually emerges in the form of a comprehensive development aid plan for the public expenditure of the recipient country, as Nurkse has indicated. Second, some measures can be taken to ensure that the recipient government follows the contract.

Notes

1 More precisely, it was the offer of collateral regarding the European Recovery Programme.
2 The World Bank (1998), which raises international attention to the problem of fungibility, also mentioned the fact that the problem was recognized as early as in the 1950s. They cited however only the name of Rosenstein-Rodan, the most preeminent economist in the early days of the World Bank. Both Rosenstein-Rodan and Nurkse were the leading economists at the dawn of development economics, sharing many common discourses such as low-level equilibrium, necessity of general investing policy led by government, etc., as well as recognition of fungibility issues.

3 Today, art activities, including music, which are able to attract many tourists, can be regarded as industries playing an important role in a national economy, especially those of developing countries. They can certainly add economic value and can bring in foreign currencies. Likewise, the Vienna Opera probably should not be regarded as a mere luxury good. In the context of the donor–recipient relationship, however, the Vienna Opera episode can be compared to the construction of a presidential palace that is disproportionately extravagant in terms of the national income or anti-developmental expansion of military expenditure.

4 It should be also mentioned here that the scale of fungibility is sometimes substantially different between aid-in-cash and aid-in-kind. More correctly, the scale of fungibility is defined whether the aid is tied or not. Aid-in-kind is often tied and aid-in-cash is untied. Here, 'tied' means that the contractor or the supplier of aid activity must be the nationality of the donor country. Most Japanese grant aid and technical assistance is still tied to Japanese nationals in this sense. It means that their unit costs are extremely high. This type of aid-in-kind with higher unit costs is fungible with a smaller amount of the recipients' budgetary resources, as it can provide a smaller number of units for the same amount of money. For example, in the case of Japan's aid, the construction costs of an elementary school in a developing country are estimated to be twice to ten times the costs that would be needed if the school is built by a local contractor using local materials. The costs vary from country to country, depending on productivity and the level of prices. While such high costs can be regarded as evidence of high quality, it also implies irrelevant luxuriousness. More precisely, let us assume five school buildings are constructed by Japanese aid totalling US $1 million, and each of the buildings cost five times more than the unit cost of a local contractor. If these five schools had been planned initially to be built by the recipient government itself, then the contribution of Japanese aid is equal to US $0.2 million dollars, not US $1 million, for the recipient government could have constructed the schools by spending only US $0.2 million. That is, Japan's aid has wasted financial aid resources by constructing schools that are too expensive. In this case, the financial space created in the recipient's budget by the fungibility effect is limited to US $0.2 million. The fungibility effect seems limited, but this should not be regarded as advantageous, as this implies in fact the cost-ineffectiveness of Japanese aid.

5 In her memoir, Former Secretary of State Short reviewed the political process for reaching the agreement at the G7 Summit and indicated several terms added as conditions to the HIPCs, such as planning of the Poverty Reduction Strategy Papers (PRSPs), combating corruption, improving public expenditure management, and reinforcing educational and health services (Short 2004: 81–5).

6 In the case of the HIPCs, almost all of the forgiven debts are public debts in the form of official development aid. Thus, most of the creditors are donor countries and organizations.

7 The concept of the international regime is based on the idea of Bratton and Van de Walle (1997) who applied Krasner's concept as a heuristic analytical instrument (1983).

8 Lack of communication between donors might deserve serious exploration, when one considers the lack of interaction between north-western European donors (the so-called Like-Minded Group) and other bilateral donors, including not only Japan and North Americans but smaller Southern European donors. If a lack of contact between these groups is really serious, Japan's isolation cannot

be explained only by the distance between the West and the East.
9 One should note that Japan assisted in the formulation of the National Development Plans in Southeast Asian countries such as Indonesia. Yet, Japan's assistance has been quite limited in the technical dimension.
10 The World Bank (1998) refers to the fact that development aid serves not only to increase the expenditure deviating from the donor's expectation but also to reduce the public income. In this chapter, both of them (increase of luxurious disbursement and decrease of tax revenue) are regarded to have the same effect.
11 To clarify, the equation (4) is listed below:

$c_0 > c_1$ can be expressed as

$$\frac{c_0}{E_0} > \frac{c_1}{E_1} = \frac{\Delta C + C_0}{\Delta A + E_0} \qquad (3')$$

multiplying (3)' by $\Delta A + E_0$, we get

$$\frac{\Delta A + E_0}{E_0} C_0 > \Delta C + C_0 \qquad (3'')$$

By rearranging (3)'', we obtain

$$\frac{C_0}{E_0} \Delta A = c_0 \Delta A > \Delta C \qquad (4)$$

References

Bates, R.H. (1981) *Markets and States in Tropical Africa: The Political Basis of Agricultural Politics*, Berkeley and Los Angeles: University of California Press.
Bates, R.H. (1989) *Beyond the Miracles of the Market*. Cambridge: Cambridge University Press.
Bayart, J.F. (1989) *L'Etat en Afrique: la politique du ventre*, Paris: Fayard.
Booth, D. (2003) 'Introduction and Overview', in D. Booth (ed.) *Fighting Poverty in Africa: Are PRSPs Making a Difference?* London: Overseas Development Institute, 1–55.
Bratton, M. and van de Walle, N. (1997) *Democratic Experiments in Africa*, Cambridge: Cambridge University Press.
Burnside, C. and Dollar, D. (2000) 'Aid, Policies, and Growth', *American Economic Review* 90(4): 847–68.
Chabal, P. and Daloz, J.P. (1999) *Africa Works: Disorder as Political Instrument*, Oxford/Bloomington: James Currey/Indiana University Press.
Chenery, H.B. and Strout, A.M. (1966) 'Foreign Assistance and Economic Development', *American Economic Review* 56(4): 679–733.

Collier, P. (2007) *The Bottom Billion: Why the Poorest Countries Are Failing and What Can Be Done About It*, Oxford: Oxford University Press.

DAC (Development Assistance Committee) (1996) *Shaping the 21st Century*, Paris: DAC.

Department for International Development (DfID) (2004) 'Poverty Reduction Budget Support: A DfID Policy Paper', London: The Stationery Office.

Hyden, G. (1983) *No Shortcuts to Progress: African Development Management in Perspective*, Berkeley and Los Angeles: University of California Press.

Krasner, S. (1983) *International Regimes*, (ed.) Ithaca: Cornell University Press.

Lawson, L. (2003) 'Globalisation and the African State', *Commonwealth & Comparative Politics* 41(3): 37–58.

Médard, J.F. (1982) 'The Underdeveloped State in Tropical Africa: Political Clientelism or Neo-patrimonialism?', in C. Clapham (ed.) *Private Patronage and Public Power: Political Clientelism in the Modern State*, London: Frances Pinter, 162–92.

Nurkse, R. (1953) *Problems of Capital Formation in Underdeveloped Countries*, Oxford: Basil Blackwell.

Short, C. (2004) *An Honourable Deception? New Labour, Iraq and the Misuse of Power*, London: Free Press.

Takahashi, M. (2002) 'NEPAD and Governance in the Twenty-First Century', *Japan Review of International Affairs* 16(4): 263–82.

World Bank (1998) *Assessing Aid: What Works, What Doesn't, and Why*, New York: Oxford University Press.

Index

Abe Shintaro (Minster of Foreign Affairs, Japan) 16
accountability: African aid 138; African society 140; democratization 140; donor community 136; foreign aid 30, 36; General Budgetary Support (GBS) 118, 125–9; Japan 130; recipient countries 53, 132, 136
Adem, S. 26, 29
Africa Union (AU) 18
African aid: aid fatigue 56; amount 105f6.4; bilateral aid 83t5.4; China 141; debt cancellation 78; fungibility 121; increased 15; Japan 131–41; lessons 33–6; proportion 105f6.3; sustainable growth 34; uncaptured peasantry 137
aid 12, 30
aid absorption 120, 122
aid agencies 36–7
aid coordination: aid harmonization 94; donor community 98–9; Japan 108, 112; Like Minded Group (LMG) 100, 104; Nordic Initiative 101; policy dialogue 111; Poverty Reduction Support Credit (PRSC) 99; UN summits 95; United Kingdom (UK) 104
aid dependency 49, 54, 56, 61, 63t4.2, 65
aid fatigue 17, 42, 56, 59, 62
Aid for Improved Development Policies and Programs and Implications for Aid Co-ordination 98

aid harmonization: coordination 94; DAC Working Party on Aid Effectiveness and Donor Practice 107; donor community 33, 99; General Budgetary Supports (GBS) 53; Japan 112n7; Like Minded Group (LMG) 104; Nordic Plus donors 102; overcrowding 102; Paris Declaration 64; policy dialogue 128; Sector Investment Programs (SIPs) 98; Short, Clare (International Development Minister, UK) 102
aid-in-cash 125, 126, 128
aid-in-kind 122–3, 130
aid modality 122–31, 132
aid policy: characteristics 9–10; coordination 55, 93, 112; debt relief 107; Development Assistance Committee (DAC) 98; failure 56–9; governance 37; Japan 40, 54–5, 130; Millennium Development Goals (MDGs) 95; UK and Japan 104–8
aid proliferation 53, 125, 128, 130
aid reform 58, 60, 65, 118, 122
aid reforms 55–62
aid relations 59, 68, 120–2
aid strategy 13–14, 95, 106, 107, 111
aid trends 40, 52–5
Akira, N. 30
alignment 6, 53, 99
allocation 52, 53, 138, 140, 145
Amari Akira (Minister of Economy, Trade and Industry, Japan) 20
ambiguity 4–5, 39, 68

apartheid 18, 21
Armacost, M. (Under Secretary of State, USA) 15
Asahi Shimbun 15
Asian Development Bank (ADB) 49
Asian region 2, 3, 11, 19, 21
assertiveness 25, 28
Assessing Aid 121
attitudes 18–19, 21, 93, 109f6.5
Austria: European Recovery Programme (ERP) 119

Bates, R.H. 133, 135, 137
bilateral aid 14, 16
bilateral relations: aid reform 60; aid relations 68; China and Africa 19; foreign aid 35; history 10; Japan and Africa 9, 22; Japan and China 142; Japan and USA 10, 21, 70n15; partnership 107
Birmingham 1998 G8 Summit 51
Booth, D. 133, 134
bureaucracy 4, 122

Calder, K.E. 9, 47
Cassen, R. 57–8
Chabal, P. 133, 134, 138
Chenery, H.B. 56, 145
Children Summit (1991) 94
China: African aid 8, 141–2; African policy 20; aid from Japan 9; democratization 140; donor community 36; foreign aid 7, 19, 61, 68; foreign policy 1, 3; invaded by Japan 40–1; Japan 27; neo-patrimonial states 138; Poverty Reduction Aid Regime 136; reparations 41
civil society: aid policy 65; debt cancellation 77, 82; famine relief campaign 15–16; foreign aid 22; foreign policy 16; Japan 137, 140; Jubilee 2000 90–1; Third Way 31
Cold War 46, 58, 118
collaboration 62, 108
Collier, P. 134, 135, 136, 138
Cologne 1999: G8 Summit 78
Cologne 1999 G8 Summit 51, 102
Colombo Plan 11, 41
commercial banks 82–3

Commission for Africa 106
commitment 7, 9, 16, 129–31
competition 20, 26, 57–8, 61
completion point 87t5.6
Comprehensive Development Framework (CDF) 98
conflict 89–90, 91
Confucianism 48
consensual leadership 10
consultation 100–1
cooperation 22, 49, 50, 66
coordination: aid policy 55, 112, 128; country development 52–4; donor community 106; foreign aid 93; lack of 57, 102
corruption 101, 127
Country Assistance Programs 62
country development 52–4
country development coordination 52–3
Country Financial Accountability Assessment (CFAA) 127
Country Procurement Assessment (CPA) 127
Court, J. 33, 36
Cox, A. 101
cultural values 31

DAC TAsk Force on Aid Effectiveness and Donor Practice 99
DAC Working Party on Aid Effectiveness and Donor Practice 107
Daily Yomimuri Online 36
Daloz, J.P. 133, 134, 138
debt: issues 77t5.1; management 5–6; policy 90; rescheduling 74, 76
debt cancellation: civil society 82; conflict 89; debt overhang 74–5; donor community 90; external credibility 78; foreign aid policies 6; governance 86, 89; health expenditure 81; Heavily Indebted Poor Countries (HIPCs) 51, 79, 101, 117; HIPC Initiative 124; increased 77; introduced 91; Japan 2, 5, 75; lawsuits 84t5.5; macroeconomic management 85; moral hazard 84; opposed by Japan 76; resources 80; World Bank 85–6
Debt-cancelled 110, 111

Index

debt overhang 5, 71–2, 73–5, 78, 91
debt relief: Department for International Development (DfID, UK) 101; development planning 126; Heavily Indebted Poor Countries (HIPCs) 52, 55; introduced 19; Japan 107, 123–5
decision point 80, 85
democratization: Africa 55–6; East Asia 139–40; foreign aid 16; instrumentalization of disorder 133; neo-patrimonial states 134, 138–9, 142; partnership 132; rootlessness 140
demography 48, 49
Department for International Development (DfID, UK) 52–3, 58, 101, 102, 104, 134
development: Africa 28; agenda 94–8; aid 129; barriers 33; cooperation 50; industrial 11; infrastructure 28, 36; Japan 11; long term 35; policy 18–21; policy coordination 94; policy dialogue 104; self-directed 29–30; strategy 106; Tokyo International Conference on African Development (TICAD) 8
development assistance 54–5, 56–7, 62, 118–22
Development Assistance Committee (DAC): *Aid for Improved Development Policies and Programs and Implications for Aid Co-ordination* 98; aid policy 98; criticisms of Japanese aid 45; High Level Forum (HLF) 99; Like Minded Group (LMG) 103; Millennium Development Goals (MDGs) 34; New Development Strategy 58; *Shaping the 21st Century: The Contribution of Development Co-operation* 95, 131; UN summits 95
development coordination 54, 59, 64
development model 3, 26–9
development planning 120, 126, 127, 144, 145
development policy 111
development strategy 17, 53
developmental strategy 25–6
diplomacy: China 19, 20, 21; diversification 46; Japan 10, 13, 20, 40, 42; natural resources 14; South Africa 18; Tokyo International Conference on African Development (TICAD) 17
Disch, A. 93–4, 100
diversification 4, 12, 13, 42, 46
Dobson, H. 10
domestic affairs 44, 49, 54, 59, 117, 132
donor community: aid coordination 98–9; aid fatigue 56; aid harmonization 33, 99; aid policy 95; assertiveness 28; collaboration 102; competition 57–8; control 121; cooperation 14–16; coordination 106; debt cancellation 90; debt overhang 73–5; domestic affairs 42; General Budgetary Support (GBS) 125; globalization 1; instrumentalization of disorder 134; international dependency 136; International Development Targets (IDTs) 111; intervention 122, 136; Japan 13, 16–18, 36, 67; leadership 25; Like Minded Group (LMG) 52, 102–3; New Public Management 55; policy coordination 94, 108, 110; Poverty Reduction Aid Regime 141; recipient countries 135; relationships 103f6.2; selectivity 141

East Asia: concentration of aid 42–4; demography 49; development model 26–9; distrust of Japan 41; economic development 140; economic growth 34, 61; Japan 67; neo-patrimonial states 138; on-request aid 30; poverty reduction 31–2; rootlessness 139
East Asian Miracle 49
economic: conditions 56; development 26, 28–9, 72, 140; model 3; pressures 1; relations 8; ties 10
economic growth: disparities 62; East Asia 34, 42, 61; Heavily Indebted Poor Countries (HIPCs) 85; Japan 5, 9, 11, 14, 40; long term 26; natural resources 18; post World War II 48–9; poverty reduction 31, 33; state intervention 26–7

Index

economies of affection 133
education 29, 49, 59, 81t5.3, 89t5.8
effectiveness 28, 64, 93, 130
employment 26, 50, 109
Environment and Development (Earth) Summit 1992 94
ethical debts 40–2
Ethiopia 15, 16, 62
European Recovery Programme (ERP) 119
evaluation 54, 65
excessive borrowing 5, 72
experiences 50, 68
exports 11, 27, 29
external borrowing 72, 73, 90
external credibility: Africa 5–6; debt cancellation 74, 75–6, 78, 82, 124; declined 83; Heavily Indebted Poor Countries (HIPCs) 90; Japan 75
Eyinla, B. 16

famine relief campaign 15
feudalism 139
Finance Act (Japan) 75
financial laws 5
financial sources 45
fiscal gaps 44
Fiscal Investment and Loan (FIL) system 45, 69n5
flexibility 53, 99
Food Summit (1996) 94
foreign aid: alignment 6; alternative support 27; ambiguity 4–5; assertiveness 25; bilateral relations 35; bureaucracy 122; development planning 144; developmental strategy 25; disdain 27; effectiveness 93; effects 143t7.1; globalization 1; history 10–21; industrialization 62; Japan and Africa 14, 35; Japanese models 31–3; long term 29; luxuries 145; Millennium Development Goals (MDGs) 18; monitoring 54; on-request 12; pacifism 122; political implications 16; poverty reduction 32; reductions 3; self-help policy 30; strategy 32; technology transfer 37
foreign direct investment (FDI) 20
foreign policy: coordination 6–7; Japan and Africa 1; Japan and East Asia 27; political constraints 36; reactive state 9; third parties 19; trade interests 20; triangular relationships 21–2
Forum on China-Africa Cooperation (FOCAC) 19
Fukuda Yasuo (Prime Minister, Japan) 8
fungibility: African aid 117–18, 142; China 141; defined 119–20; development assistance 118–22; development planning 120; foreign aid 146n4; General Budgetary Support (GBS) 54, 125–9; Japan 122–31; negative effect 53, 122; Poverty Reduction Aid Regime 7; recipient countries 132

G7 Summit, Tokyo 106
G8 Summit: Birmingham 1998 51; Cologne 1999 51, 78; Gleneagles 2005 18, 106, 141; Kananaskis 2002 18
gaiatsu (foreign pressure) 9–10
General Budgetary Support (GBS): accountability 118, 125–9; African aid 131–41; aid harmonization 53; aid modality 111; Country Financial Accountability Assessment (CFAA) 127; Department for International Development (DfID, UK) 134; fungibility 54; intervention 60; Japan 7, 65, 129; Like Minded Group (LMG) 99, 108; policy dialogue 110; Tanzania 64
Germany 11, 51–2
Ghana: case study 108–11; Country Assistance Programs 62; debt-cancelled 111; economic development 28; foreign aid 7; Kimura Toshio (Minister of Foreign Affairs, Japan) 13; Poverty Reduction Strategies (PRS) 109
Gilson, J. 10
Gleneagles 2005 G8 Summit 18, 106, 141
globalization 1, 14, 35, 46, 104
governance: aid policy 37, 106; changes in net donations 88t5.7; debt cancellation 84, 86, 91; debt

Index

overhang 73; Heavily Indebted Poor Countries (HIPCs) 89; Official Development Assistance Charter 107; Poverty Reduction Strategies (PRS) 109; self-help policy 32; Third Way 31; World Bank 92n6
government 28–9, 44, 51
Grant, R. 29
grants 2, 15
Green Revolution 49
growth rate 85f5.1
Gulf War 16, 23n2

Harrold, P. 98
Harsch, E. 35
Hayami, Y. 31, 32
Healey, J. 101
health expenditure 81t5.3, 89t5.8
Heavily Indebted Poor Countries (HIPCs): debt cancellation 51, 101, 117; debt overhang 71–2; debt relief 52, 55; growth rate 85f5.1; poverty reduction 6; Poverty Reduction Strategies (PRS) 98; status 79t5.2
heavy debt 72, 78, 82
High Level Forum (HLF - DAC): *Partnership for Poverty Reduction: From Commitment to Implementation* 99
Hino, H. 30, 35–6
HIPC Initiative: decision point 80; Ghana 110; Japan 108, 124; macroeconomic management 86; poverty reduction 82; World Bank 82
Hiroshima 41
Hook, G.D. 10
Hughes, C. 10
Human Development Index 81t5.3, 82
human rights 16
Human Rights Summit (1993) 94
human security: aid policy 121; China 20; foreign aid 66; Official Development Assistance Charter 19, 51, 107; official development assistance (ODA) 46; poverty reduction 34
Hyden, G. 56–7, 133, 137

identity 3, 4, 26, 27–8, 51

Iimi, A. 30, 35–6
imports 11, 15, 29
increased poverty 72
Indonesia 14, 138
industrialization 28, 31, 39, 48, 62
infrastructure: aid-in-kind 123; development 28, 36; external borrowing 73; foreign aid 62, 143–4; Ministry of Foreign Affairs (MOFA) 36
Inoguchi, T. 27
instrumentalization of disorder 133
International Bank for Reconstruction and Development (IBRD) 82
international circumstances 9
International Conference on Education for All (1990) 94
international dependency 52, 118, 122, 134–6
international development 111
International Development Association (IDA) 82
International Development Targets (IDTs) 6, 95, 98, 104, 111
International Monetary Fund (IMF) 35, 54, 84, 100, 121
international policy 94–8
international relations 13, 121
intervention: China 141; development planning 120; donor community 122, 136; General Budgetary Support (GBS) 60; Japan 131; Japanese aid 59, 67, 118; Public Expenditure Review (PER) 127
investment 28, 74
Ishikawa, S.: foreign aid 25; General Budgetary Support (GBS) 133; policy dialogue 30, 65; reparations 27, 30; self-esteem 67
isolationism 27, 93, 124, 129

Japan Bank for International Cooperation (JBIC) 60, 130
Japan International Cooperation Agency (JICA): African development 33; DAC Working Party on Aid Effectiveness and Donor Practice 107; employment 50; identity 51; Poverty Reduction Aid Regime 128–9; technical aid 130; weakness 131
Japan, the Ambiguous, and Myself 39

Japan, the Beautiful, and Myself 39
Japan Times 34
Japanese aid 109f6.5, 118, 131
Japanese culture 29
Japanese thought 39
Jayasuriya, K. 31
Jiang Zemin, (President, China) 19
Joint Action Plan 93, 102–4
Jubilee 2000 77, 86, 90–1, 101

Kananaskis 2002 G8 Summit 18
Kawabata Yasunari: Japan, the Beautiful, and Myself 39
Kimura Toshio (Minister of Foreign Affairs, Japan) 13, 14
knowledge gap 60, 66
Koizumi, Junichiro (Prime Minister, Japan) 28, 32, 34–5
Korea 40–1, 138

Lawson, L.. 137
lawsuits 84t5.5
leadership 9, 10, 25, 28, 69n9
Learning Network on Program-Based Approaches (LENPA) 99
lessons 33–6
Like Minded Group (LMG): created 93; donor community 52; General Budgetary Support (GBS) 108; Japan 103; origins and influence 100–2; regional influence 104; sector-wide approaches (SWAPs) 99; United Kingdom (UK) 101, 104
Live Aid 15–16
loans: financial sources 45; foreign aid 2, 4; infrastructure development 28; Japan 123; Ministry of Finance (MOF, Japan) 130; official development assistance (ODA) 11–12, 45; repayment 30

macroeconomic management 53, 84, 86, 90, 109
Mandela, President Nelson (South Africa) 18
market growth 26
Maswood, S.J. 10
Médard, J.F. 133
Medium-Term Expenditure Framework (MTEF) 127

Meiji period 26, 29, 39, 48, 76
Millennium Development Goals (MDGs): Development Assistance Committee (DAC) 34; foreign aid 6, 18; New Development Strategy 58; poverty reduction 33; Poverty Reduction Aid Regime 141; United Nations 94–5; United Nations Goals 96t6.1, 97t6.1
Ministry of Agriculture, Forestry and Fisheries (MAFF, Japan) 49
Ministry of Finance (MOF, Japan) 9, 60, 130
Ministry of Foreign Affairs (MOFA, Japan): foreign aid 11; infrastructure 36; Japan International Cooperation Agency (JICA) 50; Official Development Assistance Charter 108; poverty reduction 32, 34; public opinion 51; scandals 19; sustainable growth 35; technical aid 130; Tokyo International Conference on African Development (TICAD) 36; United Nations (UN) General Assembly 14
Ministry of International Trade and Industry (MITI, Japan) 9, 11, 45, 49
Miyashita, A. 9–10
monitoring 54, 65
moral hazard 6, 51, 82, 83, 84, 124
motivations 25, 55
Mozambique 15, 17, 101
Multi-Donor Budget Support (MDBS) 110

Nafziger, E.W. 29
Nagasaki 41
National Security Council (NSC, USA) 15
nationalism 12, 21, 41
natural resources: Africa 2, 141; competition 20; diplomacy 14, 19; economic growth 18; Japan 13
neo-patrimonial states 133, 134, 138, 142
New Development Strategy 58
new initiatives 62–6
New Money Approach 5, 75–8, 90
New Partnership for Africa's Development (NEPAD) 18
New Political Economy 133

New Public Management 55, 64
Nigeria 13, 16, 21
non-governmental organizations (NGOs) 22
Nordic Council 100–1
Nordic Initiative 101
Nordic Plus donors 102–4, 112n6
Nurkse, R. 119–20, 126, 144, 145

Oe Kenzaburo: Japan, the Ambiguous, and Myself 39
Official Development Assistance Charter: future prospects 66–7; global issues 107; introduced 21, 47; Japan 2, 16; on-request aid 30; poverty reduction 31; revised 19, 51
official development assistance (ODA) 129; aid dependency 49; allocation 52; Asian economic model 28; Asian region 11–12; background 40–2; changes in net donations 47f4.2; distribution 42, 43f4.1a, 43f4.1b; formulation 40; history 2–3; Japan 8, 46, 117; Japanese policy 31; medium term 32; mercantilism 45–6; policies 25; reduced 50; reformed 19; reparations 41; resource transfers 82; size of donations 47; trade interests 15
Ogata, S. 33
Ogata Sadako (President, JICA) 50–1
Ohno, I. 28, 32
oil crisis 13–14, 46, 48
Okita, S. 27
on-request aid 12, 13, 30, 59–60, 107
Organisation for Economic Co-operation and Development (OECD) 39, 48, 131, 140
Organization of Petroleum Exporting Countries (OPEC) 13
Owada, H. 106, 107
ownership: aid strategy 107; foreign aid 2, 6, 28–9, 31; General Budgetary Support (GBS) 127, 128; New Development Strategy 58; on-request aid 30; post-Washington Consensus (PWC) 32; recipient countries 94, 98; self-help policy 36, 65; *Shaping the 21st Century: The Contribution of Development Co-operation* 131–2; sustainable growth 34

pacifism: foreign aid 122; human security 66; Japan 3, 4, 31; Japanese aid 131; official development assistance (ODA) 42
Paris Club 5–6, 75, 76
Paris Declaration 64
Paris Framework 99, 100f6.1
partnership: aid coordination 98; aid rules 102; aid strategy 95, 107; bilateral relations 107; foreign aid 28; Like Minded Group (LMG) 99; New Development Strategy 58; *Shaping the 21st Century: The Contribution of Development Co-operation* 131–2
Partnership for Poverty Reduction: From Commitment to Implementation 99
peace-building 19, 22, 50, 66
perception 58, 62, 64, 131–2
Philippines 16, 138
philosophy 40, 50–2
policy coordination 108–11
policy dialogue: foreign aid 65; General Budgetary Support (GBS) 110; Japan 129; Like Minded Group (LMG) 108; Millennium Development Goals (MDGs) 95; self-help policy 30; United Kingdom (UK) 104, 128
political: commitment 16–18, 36; stability 86; structure 9; support 17, 20; vulnerability 73
Population Summit (1994) 94
post-Washington Consensus (PWC) 31
poverty reduction: aid coordination 106; aid trends 40; debt cancellation 6, 77–8, 80; economic growth 31, 33, 72; heavy debt 73; HIPC Initiative 82; macroeconomic management 84; meritocracy 49; Millennium Development Goals (MDGs) 33; policy dialogue 128; post-Washington Consensus (PWC) 32; resources 91; social development 34
Poverty Reduction Aid Regime: African aid 131–4; China 142; donor community 141; donor pressure 61; Japan 52, 128, 136–41; Japan and Africa 7; rootlessness 137–8

Index

Poverty Reduction Strategies (PRS): aid strategy 111; Cologne 1999 124; development planning 127; development strategies 53; Ghana 109; Heavily Indebted Poor Countries (HIPCs) 98; Japan 123–5
Poverty Reduction Strategy Paper (PRSP) 99, 109, 146n5
Poverty Reduction Support Credit (PRSC) 64, 99, 125
power balance 65, 121
Preston, P.W. 29
private sector development 30, 34
production 26, 33
program-based approaches (PBAs) 99
Progress Assessment Framework (PAF) 110
project proliferation 58, 134
Public Expenditure Review (PER) 127
public opinion 51, 136–7

reactive state: debt cancellation 52; foreign policy 59; Japan 9, 16, 21, 22; official development assistance (ODA) 47
recipient countries: accountability 136; aid absorption 122; aid failure 133; aid-in-kind 123; aid management 102; aid strategy 111; domestic affairs 42, 117; donor community 135; economic conditions 56; ethical debts 40–2; foreign aid 12, 57t4.1; fungibility 121, 132; General Budgetary Support (GBS) 125, 134–5; integrity 127; international dependency 122; intervention 136; macroeconomic management 53; ownership 29, 98; policy coordination 108, 110; policy dialogue 128; resources 142; self-reliance 67; stakeholders 52; support 61; transaction costs 93; weakness 59
reform 3, 4, 19, 52–5, 137
refugee protection 50
reorganization 50
reparations 11, 27, 30, 41, 42, 45
resentment 13–14, 17
resources: aid-in-kind 123; allocation 53, 138, 140, 145; debt cancellation 80; demand 61; poverty reduction 91; transfer 82
riots 13–14, 46
rootlessness 137, 139, 140
Rosser, A. 31
Rwanda 17

safe water access 80, 81t5.3, 89t5.8
sanctions 16, 18, 21
scandals 19, 51
Sector Investment Programs (SIPs) 59, 98
sector-wide approaches (SWAPs) 64, 99
selectivity 134–6, 140, 141
Self-Defense Forces (SDF) 17, 27
Self-Help 48
self-help policy: ambiguity 4–5; explained 30; foreign aid 1–2, 28, 47–8, 67; Japan 3, 5; Japanese aid 65; Official Development Assistance Charter 51, 107; official development assistance (ODA) 46–50; on-request aid 13; ownership 28–9, 36, 132; post-Washington Consensus (PWC) 32
Senegal 13, 62
Shaping the 21st Century: The Contribution of Development Co-operation 95; Development Assistance Committee (DAC) 131
Short, Clare (International Development Minister, UK): aid harmonization 102; debt relief 52; Department for International Development (DfID, UK) 101; fungibility 124; General Budgetary Support (GBS) 125; Poverty Reduction Strategy Paper (PRSP) 146n5; public opinion 136–7
Smiles, Samuel: *Self-Help* 48
Sonoda Naoshi (Minister of Foreign Affairs, Japan) 13
South Africa 14, 17, 18, 21
South Korea 61
state authority 9–10
state collapse 135, 136
state intervention 26, 29, 31
strategy 32, 33
Strout, A.M. 56, 145

Index 157

Structural Adjustment Programs (SAP) 56, 121
sustainable growth 34, 35, 106

Tanaka Kakuei (Prime Minister, Japan) 14
Tanzania 13, 57, 62, 64, 101, 129
taxation 138, 139, 140
technology transfer 12, 29, 37, 60–1
third parties 8–9, 22
Third Way 31
Tokyo International Conference on African Development (TICAD): African attitudes 18; aid strategy 106; confidence 49; created 5; development strategy 17; Japan 2, 25, 50; self-help policy 33, 34; TICAD-IV 8, 22, 42, 52, 61, 141; UN politics 20
Toronto Terms 74
trade 20, 28, 85
trade interests 2, 8, 15, 17, 18, 19–20
transaction costs 53, 57, 126
transparency 53, 127, 132
triangular relationships 21–2

United Kingdom (UK): aid coordination 112; attitudes to aid 109f6.5; Department for International Development (DfID, UK) 101; exports 11; foreign aid policies 6; General Budgetary Support (GBS) 125; HIPC Initiative 124; Japan 104–8; policy dialogue 128; Short, Clare (International Development Minister, UK) 52
United Nations Development Program (UNDP) 98
United Nations Security Council 17, 20–1, 50
United Nations Social Summit (1995) 94
United Nations (UN) 17, 25, 94

United Nations (UN) General Assembly 2, 12, 14, 15
United Nations Women's Summit (1995) 94
United States of America (USA): aid reduction 58; bilateral aid 16; bilateral relations 21; donor community 13; economy 14–15; hegemony 9; official development assistance (ODA) 46

vertical sectionalism 4, 44–5, 60
Vestal, J. 26
Vienna Opera House 119, 142–5

Washington Consensus 3, 25, 31, 32
World Bank: aid coordination 98; aid to Japan 12; *Assessing Aid* 121; bilateral aid 83t5.4; debt cancellation 85–6; development coordination 54; *East Asian Miracle* 49; HIPC Initiative 82; lawsuits 84; Nordic Council 100; policy dialogue 128; Poverty Reduction Aid Regime 52; Poverty Reduction Strategy Paper (PRSP) 98; Poverty Reduction Support Credit (PRSC) 125; Sector Investment Programs (SIPs) 59, 98; Structural Adjustment Programs (SAP) 121; Tokyo International Conference on African Development (TICAD) 25
World War II 2, 39, 119, 131

Yamauchi. M. 34
Yasutami, S. 30
Yasutomo, D.T. 10
yen 46–7
Yom Kippur War 11, 13

Zaire 13, 17
Zambia 16